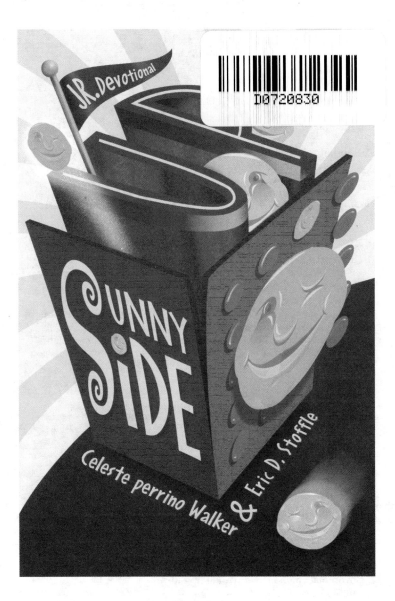

JR.Devotional

SUNNY SiDE

Celeste perrino Walker & Eric D. Stoffle

REVIEW AND HERALD® PUBLISHING ASSOCIATION
HAGERSTOWN, MD 21740

Scriptures credited to EB are quoted from *The Everyday Bible, New Century Version,* copyright © 1987, 1988 by Word Publishing, Dallas, Texas 75039. Used by permission.

Texts credited to NIV are from the *Holy Bible, New International Version.* Copyright © 1973, 1978, 1984, International Bible Society. Used by permission of Zondervan Bible Publishers.

Texts credited to NKJV are from the New King James Version. Copyright © 1979, 1980, 1982, Thomas Nelson, Inc., Publishers.

Bible texts credited to TEV are from the *Good News Bible*—Old Testament: Copyright © American Bible Society 1976; New Testament: Copyright © American Bible Society 1966, 1971, 1976.

Verses marked TLB are taken from *The Living Bible,* copyright © 1971 by Tyndale House Publishers, Wheaton, Ill. Used by permission.

This book was
Edited by Jeannette R. Johnson
Designed and illustrated by Willie S. Duke
Desktop technician: Shirley M. Bolivar
Typeset: 9.5/10.5 Veljovic

01 00 99 98 97   5 4 3 2 1

PRINTED IN U.S.A.

R&H Cataloging Service
Walker, Celeste perrino, 1965-
    Sunny side up, by Celeste perrino Walker and Eric D. Stoffle.

    1. Teenagers—Prayer—books and devotions—English.
2. Devotional calendars—Juvenile literature.   I. Title.
II. Stoffle, Eric Delayne, 1963-

242.6

ISBN 0-8280-1140-0

Dedication

This book is lovingly dedicated
to my sister,

Faith DuBois,

who has always believed in me,

no questions asked,

and her little "junior,"

Zebulon DuBois.

—*Celeste perrino Walker*

For all the times you pop in
while I'm writing,

wanting me to do things with you . . .

Corey,

I'm proud to be your dad

and glad you want me to be

your friend.

—*Eric D. Stoffle*

Introduction

I will be joyful in God my Savior. Habakkuk 3:18, NIV.

When you think of Jesus, do you ever imagine Him laughing? Or smiling, even? It can be easy to picture Jesus as a stern person, someone keeping an eagle eye on us from way up in heaven, someone who is more apt to be serious or frown in our direction when we are doing something wrong.

This may surprise you, but Jesus has a sense of humor.

Think about it. He'd have to. He made the platypus, the giraffe, the octopus, and the kangaroo. He's the one who gave us ticklish spots. He's the one who created all our laughs, from the belly-whumping, nose-snorting, hee-hawing howl to the most reserved and prim little giggle. And He put in each of us the ability to enjoy a good joke or funny circumstance.

Face it: Jesus laughs. Yes, He does!

And He wants you to laugh and to enjoy life and the things He has made—from the beautiful to the hysterical. But don't keep it all to yourself. Share it! Because you know what? Not everyone sees life the way you do.

As Christians we know that there is something better waiting for us. Some people can't see that, because they don't know Jesus and have never heard the good news. So don't be stingy. Share the joy, share the gospel, share Jesus . . . with everyone you meet, with people you may never meet, with best friends, with enemies, and with relatives.

This devotional book will give you some ideas about how you can do this, and it contains stories that will inspire you, but it can't help you if you just read it and stop there. Do something. Get involved. Put some of the ideas into practice.

Maybe they aren't all things you feel comfortable doing. That's OK. Find the ones that work for you and use those. Most important, show the world a true picture of Jesus, a loving Jesus full of joy. Get out there and face the world, one day at a time, sunny side up!

In Christ,
Celeste and Eric

No Guts, No Glory?

Love your enemies, do good to them. Luke 6:35, NIV.

atter up!
Branch Rickey needed a baseball player. Not just any player. He needed a great player. Branch Rickey was the president of the Brooklyn Dodgers, and he wanted to bring the first African-American ballplayer to the major leagues. He knew just the player.

But if he was going to break down racial prejudice, Branch Rickey first had to know if Jackie Robinson was the right choice, not only as a great player, but even more important, as a great example. So Rickey hurled insult after insult at Jackie as a test. He said the fans and players would be much worse. "Can you handle it, Jackie?"

"Mr. Rickey, do you want a ballplayer who's afraid to fight back?" Jackie asked.

Branch Rickey replied, "I want a player with guts enough *not* to fight."

Jackie promised there would be no problems. He was signed to the Montreal Royals, the Brooklyn Dodgers' top minor league team. Many times he might have been justified in fighting back after hearing insults from players, as well as baseball fans, but he was determined not to let it bother him. Instead, he proved he could play ball better than anyone else. A year later, in 1947, he was moved to the Dodgers.

During his first year with the Dodgers, Jackie was voted rookie of the year. In 1955 Jackie helped the Dodgers win their first World Series championship. They also won six National League titles during the 10 seasons Jackie played for them. Because Jackie Robinson had the courage not to fight back, he made even more positive changes against racial injustice.

Where does your courage lie?

- Why is it harder to be nice to people who aren't nice to us? How does Jesus treat people who don't like Him?

- Smile at someone you know who doesn't really seem to like you very much. Don't say anything; just smile. It just might be catching.

Sink or Sing

Be joyful always; pray continually. 1 Thessalonians 5:16, 17, NIV.

*C*harlie was cold, shivering, and alone. His canoe was upside down, and he was floating, tired and helpless, in the frigid waters of Lake Ontario. He knew that by morning he would be dead. No one could survive immersion in such cold waters for long. Worse still, a heavy fog had rolled in. Even if anyone realized he was missing, how would they be able to find him? Soon he didn't even know where shore was.

Charlie's spirits sank. He was doomed. As his body temperature slowly ebbed away, all he could do was pray for God to help him. Certainly hypothermia would eventually kill him.

But after telling God about his problem, Charlie began to feel better. He continued to pray. Soon his lips parted and the first verse of his favorite hymn rolled across the water into the dense fog. Words he never thought he would remember suddenly came easily, and Charlie sang verse after verse of hymns he had learned while growing up. Soon he was singing as loudly as he could. Even when he thought he might die, Charlie sang joyfully.

Suddenly from out of the dense fog boomed another voice. At first Charlie thought that he was delirious and that what he had heard was just his own voice somehow haunting him. But the voice boomed again.

"Hello! Don't stop! Keep singing, and we'll find you!"

🙂 **Think about the songs you sing in church and with your family. Have you ever felt worse when you were singing than when you weren't singing? Why does singing make us feel better?**

🙂 **Plan a sing-along witnessing program with your Sabbath school class for a senior citizens' home or a nursing home in your area.**

The Girl Nobody Wanted

Be joyful in hope, patient in affliction, faithful in prayer. Romans 12:12, NIV.

At 17 Charlotte Anne Lopez was Miss Teen U.S.A. But if Charlotte had a claim to fame, it wasn't her glittering crown or her instant, dizzying rise to popularity. It was her positive personality and her cheerful attitude about life.

Charlotte was only 3 years old when social workers placed her, her sister Diana, and brother Duane in foster homes. The girls were separated from Duane and moved together from family to family. They grew up in the foster care system, living in many different homes, but never being adopted. Charlotte later called it being "lost in the system."

"After a while I came to terms with it and decided that I had to love myself and cherish the life I had," she says.

Charlotte decided to be joyful in all things, even the foster care system. "I really believe in God, and I always believed He would prepare some kind of opportunity for me to get into the spotlight so I could talk about foster care."

Instead of focusing on what she didn't have, Charlotte decided to do what she could to help other kids caught in the same situation as she was. She concentrated on her strengths and decided to try out for the pageant.

"The whole point of going out for the pageant wasn't only to fulfill a fantasy," Charlotte explains, "but to stand up for foster kids and represent them."

During her reign as Miss Teen U.S.A, the girl nobody wanted to adopt helped people reevaluate the foster care system and gave encouragement to everyone she spoke to. Why? Because she had the courage to look on the bright side.

And Charlotte? Well, after 15 years in the foster care system she was adopted.

"Don't look at your obstacles as impossible; look at them as a challenge."
—Charlotte Anne Lopez, Miss Teen U.S.A., 1993.

The next time something goes wrong, and you feel like complaining—don't! Instead, be joyful! Try to see the positive side and laugh about it.

9

Karibu: A Parable

Love one another. As I have loved you, so you must love one another. By this all men will know that you are my disciples, if you love one another.
John 13:34, 35, NIV.

Karibu is my dog. And he's a great dog. Well, let me qualify that. He's lazy; slobbers great, big, long, shoestrings of goo; eats like a horse; smells like the bottom of the garbage pail from rolling in nasty stuff in the woods; and basically sheds hair all over the house.

But Karibu loves me. Yessiree, he sure loves me! When I get home from school, who puts his muddy paws all over the front of my clean white shirt? Karibu! Who stuffs his grimy nose into my hand so I'll pat his head? Karibu! Who wags his tail so hard he slaps my legs and gives me black-and-blue marks? Karibu!

I know, he sure has some funny ways of showing me that he loves me, huh? But you know what? I wouldn't trade Karibu for all the money in the world, because he loves me and he shows it.

Karibu isn't embarrassed about loving me. He doesn't try to hide it, and he doesn't try to love me the way someone else tells him he should. He just loves me in his own, slobbery way. That's the important thing.

And that's how God wants us to love Him. No-holds-barred, all-the-stops-out, full-blast, no-yield, turbocharged love. That kind of love shows up like a blinking neon sign. Or a handful of gooey drool. He'll give us that kind of love for other people too. Friends and enemies alike. Just ask Him.

- **Unscramble the words for an important message: gthli a refi orf dog dna oyu lilw eb oto tho rfo naats ot nd-hale.**

- **Call a friend and say you appreciate them. Be specific.**

(Answer: Light a fire for God and you will be too hot for Satan to handle.)

Good Habits Aren't Hard

Blessed is the man who finds wisdom, the man who gains understanding.
Proverbs 3:13, NIV.

Ever wonder why bad study habits are easier to form than good study habits? Because bad habits are loafers. They're lazy. You don't have to feed them; they just help themselves. In fact, bad habits don't have jobs. They just hang around and make you look bad.

Good habits are different. They take a lot of training, because if they're going to work for you, you want them to do a good job. Now is a good time to start learning how to kick out the bad habits and create good habits that will make learning much easier and a lot more fun.

Here are some tips to start you off:

1. Study at a certain time each day. By doing this, your body and mind get used to this good habit and automatically gear up for learning.

2. Study in the same place every time you crack a textbook. Find a place that's quiet and well lit, with lots of room to spread out your books. Use it every time you study. Putting this good habit to use will inform your body and your mind to get ready, get set, and learn!

3. Does homework ever make you feel sleepy? Do you find your thoughts beginning to wander? Then it's time to sit up and study actively. The gym isn't the only place active students hang out. If you start thinking about friends or sports or even just forget what you're doing, say "Stop!" Then concentrate again until learning becomes a habit.

Don't become discouraged. Soon studying will be easier and more fun.

☺ **How will forming good habits make you a better student? How can forming good habits make learning fun?**

☺ **If you have some bad study habits, why not start changing them today? Ask your parents to help you set up a place to study, with everything you need to make it easy and fun.**

11

Right, Just, and Fair

Then you will understand what is right and just and fair—every good path.
For wisdom will enter your heart, and knowledge will be pleasant to your
soul. Proverbs 2:9, 10, NIV.

L ook at this!" Elizabeth sputtered. She held up an article from the Pittsburgh *Dispatch* for her mother to see. The article was entitled "What Girls Are Good For," and it opposed women's rights. "I'm going to write a reply," Elizabeth stated.

Elizabeth had decided early in her life that she enjoyed writing, and wanted to become a writer. Even though women didn't have the right to vote at that time, and there were few job opportunities outside the home, she believed she could do anything she wanted to do.

After George Madden received the rebuke to his article, he was so impressed with the writing of the anonymous reply that he inquired about the identity of the author, hoping to hire such a good writer for his newspaper. But after learning the author was a woman, he decided Elizabeth should write under a pen name. From then on, Elizabeth wrote as Nellie Bly.

Nellie Bly became the byline of many articles exposing social injustices found in factories, hospitals, slums, and orphanages in the late 1800s. Pittsburgh businessmen reacted furiously after seeing their unfair business practices exposed, and Elizabeth was pressured into leaving Pittsburgh.

But she did not give up. Instead she went to a bigger market— New York City—and wrote for the *World*, where she continued exposing unfair labor practices and encouraging women's rights, sometimes by going undercover in dangerous situations. No one knew Nellie Bly's true identity, but because of Elizabeth Cochrane's stories, many employers, mental institutions, and other public services made improvements in how they operated.

💬 **Elizabeth Cochrane (1867-1922) used her talents to improve people's lives. Do you use your talents wisely? How can you make the world a better place by your actions?**

💬 **Observe a good deed in your town and write about it in a letter to the editor of your local newspaper.**

That Other Cheek

But I tell you, Do not resist an evil person. If someone strikes you on the right cheek, turn to him the other also. Matthew 5:39, NIV.

Have you ever felt as though you were cruising along, minding your own business, when suddenly, *blam!* out of the blue you're the brunt of someone's joke? Your "friends" are snickering at you, having a great laugh at your expense. You can feel the blush creep up your face. The moment is critical. What do you do?

Blow up?

Snap at them?

Die of embarrassment?

Ken Davis, a Christian comedian, has some advice for handling "meanies." "When they laugh at you, laugh *with* them. It takes all the sting out of their efforts to make you feel bad. Being able to laugh at yourself is a sign of confidence and strength. Mean kids avoid those with confidence and strength."

It's not always easy to laugh at ourselves, especially when the joke hits a little too close to home. Try laughing at yourself sometimes. Practice not taking yourself too seriously, and laughing at yourself will get easier. In the process, you will also be giving "meanies" a good picture of God and His love for them.

"But God demonstrates his own love for us in this: While we were still sinners, Christ died for us" (Romans 5:8, NIV). "I love this text," Ken says, "because it reminds me of how much God cares for me. I like people who are nice to me. God liked me before I was ever nice to Him. That inspires me to love other people in the same way."

☺ **What did Jesus do when people were mean to Him? How did He treat those same people later on? Do you think Jesus ever laughed at Himself?**

☺ **Instead of taking it personally the next time someone tries to get a laugh at your expense, laugh with them and see what happens.**

13

Angels of Mercy

Be kind and compassionate one to another. Ephesians 4:32, NIV.

Joshua hadn't had water in so long he couldn't even sweat anymore. He rubbed his face and squinted. There was nothing at all to give him hope. The Salt Desert lay hot and empty before him. His sisters could hardly move their feet. Even the oxen were staggering.

Suddenly someone toward the front of the wagon train yelled, "Look! An oasis! There are trees and grass. There must be a spring over by that rock!"

The cry of relief swept down the line to Joshua's ears. Mom and Dad got smiles on their faces. He noticed his sisters began to walk a little faster, and they were smiling too. Suddenly Joshua didn't feel as tired either.

But the green oasis was not trees or grass at all. There wasn't even any water. It was just a rock out in the desert. And by the time the wagon train found out that it was just a strange mirage, no one was strong enough to go any farther. Like everyone else, Joshua and his family collapsed on the hot, powdery dirt and waited to die of thirst.

But way out in the middle of the Salt Desert, there were some mysterious, kind strangers who would not let the pioneers die. History doesn't record who these people were, just that every day they drove wagons from Pilot Peak across miles of hot, dry desert to bring water to dying travelers and their animals.

Who would live out in the middle of the desert and haul water for people they didn't even know? Do you believe these mysterious good Samaritans could have been angels? How grateful would you have been for water to drink if you were dying of thirst?

When it is a hot summer day and you hear your neighbors working in their yards, mix up a cool pitcher of juice and offer them some. Notice the smiles and thanks you receive.

The Secret Gift

But when you give to the needy, do not let your left hand know what your right hand is doing, so that your giving may be in secret. Then your Father, who sees what is done in secret, will reward you. Matthew 6:3, 4, NIV.

Samantha Reese hugged the row of lockers as if the cold metal could somehow prevent her from falling flat on her face. She licked her lips and tried to get her knees to co-operate and go in the same direction at the same time. A loud whooshing in her ears beat in time to the frantic thudding of her heart as it banged away in her chest. The small piece of paper in her hand was damp from the moisture on her palm.

"Come on, Sam, get a grip!" she whispered to herself. She tried not to think about what would happen if someone were to catch her at that precise moment, glued to the lockers and talking to herself. There would be a lot of explaining to do, that was for sure.

She edged down the row of lockers, looking for the number written on the slip of paper in her hand. In her other hand she held a box of brand-new computer disks, wrapped up in bright paper, with a card that said *Your Secret Pal.* Finally she found the locker she was looking for. Glancing around furtively, she opened it and quickly put her offering inside.

Trying to look nonchalant, she hurried around the corner and off to her next class. Wouldn't Baxter Burney be surprised? He'd be even more surprised if he knew who the disks were from, because Baxter didn't like Sam very much. And Sam wasn't exactly fond of Baxter.

What do you think Sam accomplished by giving a gift to someone who didn't really like her, and not even saying who the gift was from?

Is there someone you don't really get along with? Why not make yourself that person's secret pal for one year? Now and then, send them cheerful cards and leave little gifts where they will find them.

Rescuing Hero, Part 1

Love your neighbor as yourself. Leviticus 19:18, NIV.

Seven children—sisters, brothers, and cousins—were playing in an apartment building in Baton Rouge, Louisiana. All the children were younger than 5. The youngest, 2 years old, had a book of matches he had found and was playing with them on the bed.

Suddenly the bedspread caught fire. The other children screamed and ran. The 2-year-old boy, afraid he was in trouble, ran to another room and jumped on the bed, covering his head with the blanket.

In another part of the building, 11-year-old Jason Dent had just settled down to watch television. Suddenly he heard screams. Following the sounds of the screams, Jason and his sister Catina ran to the staircase. Six children raced down the stairs from an upstairs apartment building and ran past them.

"What's happening? What is it?" Catina demanded.

Jason looked up the stairs, his heart thudding wildly against his chest. One of the windows was unusually bright, and the acrid smell of smoke drifting down the stairs stung the back of his throat. "Fire! I think it's a fire!" Jason shouted.

Although the children had all fled to the safety of the street, screams were still coming from the apartment.

One of the kids is still up there, Jason thought. Without thinking of his own safety, he plunged up the staircase. A voice he believed to be God's whispered in his ear, leading him to the room where the 2-year-old boy sat sobbing and screaming on the bed, his head half covered with the blankets.

"God, please help me get through this," Jason prayed. Through the open master bedroom door he saw the flames that had already consumed the bedspread lick hungrily at the curtains.

How do you think Jason loved his neighbor as himself? What would you have done in his place?

If you do not know what to do in case of a fire, ask Mom or Dad to tell you.

Rescuing Hero, Part 2

"Because he loves me," says the Lord, "I will rescue him; I will protect him, for he acknowledges my name. He will call upon me, and I will answer him; I will be with him in trouble, I will deliver him and honor him." Psalm 91:14, 15, NIV.

Come on, we've got to get out of here!" Jason told the little boy. He grabbed the child and ran for the door.

As he passed the master bedroom he heard the windows cracking. Fear shot through him. Gripping the child tighter, he raced down the stairs. He entered his family's apartment and tried to set the boy down, but the child clung to him, terrified, and kept screaming, "I want my mommy; I want my mommy!"

"It's going to be OK," Jason told the boy. "Your mother's coming."

The child slowly released his grip on Jason and slipped to the floor, where he looked around him with a sooty, tear-stained face.

"I called the fire department," Catina said.

Then Jason realized that the danger wasn't over. Their apartment could catch fire too! "Let's get out of the house until the fire department gets here," Jason urged.

Within minutes the fire trucks and the police arrived. Firefighters raced into the building, dragging fire hoses behind them. The flashing lights on their trucks sent shafts of red light bouncing around the neighboring apartment buildings. A police officer pulled Jason aside and questioned him about the fire.

"You did a good job, son. I'm real proud of you," the police officer told him.

"It wasn't hard," Jason said. "I would do it again if I had to."

🙂 Chances are that you have never rescued someone from a burning building. But have you done anything else that is considered heroic? You know, even small things done in the spirit of sacrifice are considered heroic.

🙂 The next time your mother, father, or teacher asks you to do something you don't especially like, be a real hero and do it cheerfully, without complaining.

Tried and Tested

The teaching of the wise is a fountain of life, turning a man from the snares of death. Proverbs 13:14, NIV.

Do you have a spelling, math, history, or geography test this week? *Oops!* You forgot, didn't you? Or maybe you didn't forget your test, but you wish you could. It won't go away just because you forget it. There are two things you can always count on—your fingers, and tests!

OK, so you may never learn to love tests, but it would be fun to learn how to get good test scores, wouldn't it? The most important way to do well on a test is to study, and study some more. Everyone knows that, but not very many students do it. But there are a few ways to make studying more interesting.

A good way to study for tests is to ask yourself questions about what you've learned. Which makes sense, because that's what tests do. For instance, if you are studying that John Adams was the second president of the United States, make a question out of it. Ask yourself, "Who was the second president of the United States?" Making up questions will make it easier to think of the answers when you take a test.

Do you take tests with multiple choice answers? Next time, cover the choices and try answering the question in your head before you look at the possible answers. This idea might keep you from getting confused by all the multiple choice answers.

Remember, everything we do—even taking tests—we do for Jesus. And we want our love for Him to show in all that we do. So do your very best!

🙂 **Do you enjoy learning? Do you enjoy getting good grades on tests? Why is it important to get good grades in school?**

🙂 **When you are studying today, see how many questions you can ask yourself. Then grade yourself:**

20-30: You're on your way to being the next president!
10-20: Keep up the good work!
5-10: Practice makes perfect!
0-5: You are asleep!

The Good Stuff

Command them to do good, to be rich in good deeds, and to be generous and willing to share. 1 Timothy 6:18, NIV.

O fficer Ralph Shelby rolled his police cruiser into the school parking lot, surprising Allen Tracey, who had been spray-painting graffiti on the school building. Officer Shelby was acting on a call that someone was involved in some suspicious activity on the school grounds, and he was nervous. Just two weeks before, a police officer had been shot and wounded while checking on a disturbance.

Shelby knew that any time a police officer got out of their cruiser, they were putting themselves at risk. He crossed to the school building and began a perimeter search of the area. Nothing happened, though he could sense that someone was nearby.

Suddenly a shadow broke from behind the trash dumpster and sprinted across the school grounds. Officer Shelby began the chase and soon discovered he was chasing a young man who could run very fast. He was impressed with the young man's speed and endurance.

But Officer Ralph Shelby liked to run too. He had been running since he was a teenager. He entered marathon races whenever he could. But even more than running, Officer Shelby enjoyed working with troubled kids.

Two days later Officer Shelby stopped by Allen Tracey's house dressed in sweats. "You run well enough to be a track star," he told Allen. "Would you like to go running with me this afternoon?"

Allen's mouth dropped open. He didn't know what to say. No one had ever said he was good at anything except getting into trouble.

Suddenly Allen smiled big. "Sure," he said.

- Is it important to recognize the talents of other people? Think about it: Do you like people to notice the things you do well?

- What are your friends good at? What about people you don't know very well? Today, recognize the talents your friends and classmates have. Tell them you appreciate their talents.

If You've Got It, Share It

Here is a boy with five small barley loaves and two small fish, but how far will they go among so many? John 6:9, NIV.

Junior couldn't believe his mother let him go alone. What a break! He could almost smell the excitement in the air as he stood with thousands of others and listened to the Teacher. His stomach rumbled a warning as noon approached, and he glanced thankfully at the basket of food his mother had packed for him that morning.

As he looked around, he couldn't help noticing that no one else seemed to have thought ahead and brought food. That worried him a little. He was a growing boy, and the gnawing feeling in the pit of his stomach informed him that the five barley loaves and two small fish would just about quiet it until he walked home for supper.

That's why he nearly jumped out of his sandals when a man tapped him on the shoulder and asked what was in his basket. "Uh, some bread and a couple fish," he stammered, feeling his face flush. He recognized the man immediately as one of the Teacher's disciples.

"Would you share it with us?" the man asked.

Junior looked at the basket with longing eyes, then at the crowd of hungry people. He gulped. How could he be stingy with the little he had when the need was so great? "Yes, of course," he told the disciple, handing him the basket.

He watched as the disciple handed the basket to Jesus, who gave thanks and began handing out bread and fish to everyone. As much as they wanted.

How do you think Junior felt when he saw Jesus multiply his lunch to feed 5,000 people? What would you do if someone asked you to share your lunch with them?

This week, make it a point to share something with someone. (And don't allow yourself to wonder when you're going to get it back.)

Many Hands

And Jesus grew in wisdom and stature, and in favor with God and men.
Luke 2:52, NIV.

Tommy glared at the piles of shingles, tar paper, roofing nails, and flashing that was laid out neatly on the front lawn. Dad would have to pick today to reroof the house. Why today, of all days? His friends were playing a game of baseball in the schoolyard. This project was going to take all day. By the time they finished, there would be no time left to play ball.

Dad rubbed his hands together as he surveyed the setup with satisfaction. "Looks like we're ready to get started, son," he said with a smile. "I'm so glad you're helping me today. Let's get going so we'll be ready to take a break when Mom has lunch fixed. What do you say?"

Tommy wanted to say "See ya later," but he decided that silence was the better part of wisdom. Heaving a big sigh, he held the ladder while Dad climbed onto the roof, carrying the supplies they would need. Then Dad steadied the ladder from the top while Tommy climbed up.

Tommy wasn't that crazy about heights, but it wasn't the height that made him catch his breath when he reached the top. It was the sight of all his friends and their fathers trooping down the road toward their house, dressed in work clothes. They were going to help!

"Many hands make light work!" one of the men said, giving Tommy a smile. "If we all pitch in, we'll still have time for a ball-game after lunch."

🙂 Jesus learned to be a carpenter like His earthly father. He helped Joseph in his shop. Do you think He also helped people build their homes and furniture whenever He could? Do you think Jesus liked to work with His hands?

🙂 Does anyone in your family need help with a project? Suggest to your mom or dad that your whole family could help.

21

Sweet Things

How sweet are your words to my taste, sweeter than honey to my mouth.
Psalm 119:103, NIV.

Shonna maneuvered around her brother as he measured out the flour with a fussy kind of precision. Leave it to Terry to make sure every ingredient was exactly right. She shifted from one foot to the other impatiently.

"Get on with it already!" she groaned. "The cookies aren't going to explode if there's a few too many oats in them, you know."

Terry didn't even raise an eyebrow in her direction as he shook a little more oatmeal from the measuring cup back into the container. "You can't rush perfection," he said smugly.

Shonna rolled her eyes. "They're just *cookies,* Terry."

Dad poked his head in the kitchen and sniffed appreciatively. "How's it coming?" he asked.

"Trust me, Dad; you've never seen cookies like these, and you might *never* see them if Terry doesn't hurry up."

"Ta-dah!" Terry chirruped triumphantly. "Done."

Shonna peered over his shoulder as he scooped out the chocolaty, gooey mixture and dropped it by spoonfuls onto a cookie sheet. Soon they would harden, and then they could put them into the bags they had decorated with Bible verses. They planned to pass them out that afternoon when they visited the shut-ins with the Sunshine Band.

🙂 **How do you think the people felt when Shonna and Terry delivered their cookies?**

🙂 **Make a batch of the cookies to share from the recipe below. Place the cookies in brown paper lunch bags you have decorated with Bible verses.**

No-Bake Cookies
Place the following ingredients in a pot on the stove:

2 cups sugar	¼ cup margarine
4 tablespoons cocoa	1 teaspoon vanilla
½ cup milk	

Bring to a boil, stirring constantly. Boil for one minute. Remove from heat. Add:

3 cups oats	½ cup peanut butter

Drop by spoonfuls onto wax paper or aluminum foil. Let set until cool, and then watch 'em disappear!

An Honest Heart

A truthful witness gives honest testimony, but a false witness tells lies.
Proverbs 12:17, NIV.

Samantha Reese tried not to notice the smirk that Baxter Burney had plastered all over his face. She was determined to be nice to Baxter today, no matter what he did. She concentrated on the computer screen in front of her. Just then the entire screen dissolved into a moving pattern of black and white dots, and the word *Gotcha!* flashed across the screen.

Sam pushed herself back from her desk to call for the teacher. She turned just in time to see Baxter show David Fielding the copy of a computer disk. On the disk she could clearly see the word "Gotcha."

"Yes, Samantha, what is it?" Mrs. Elderly asked, as she came up behind Sam, scowling at the screen. "Why, this is the third terminal to contract this virus! Do you have any idea where it came from, Samantha?"

Sam swallowed hard. Out of the corner of her eye she could see Baxter watching her closely, a scowl on his face. If she told Mrs. Elderly that Baxter might have planted the virus, she would get him in trouble. If she was wrong, she would look very stupid. But she had to tell the truth.

"No, Mrs. Elderly, I don't know where the virus came from," Sam said firmly. "Baxter has a disk with 'Gotcha' on it, but I don't know what's on it."

As Mrs. Elderly approached Baxter for the disk, Sam sat back in her chair with a sigh of relief. She'd told the truth, and she hadn't blamed Baxter. If he wasn't guilty, then he had nothing to worry about.

- Have you ever been asked to give an account of something that happened? How accurate was your testimony? Did you make accusations or add a lot of extra things to spice it up?

- The next time you are a witness to an event and asked to recount it, make sure you are honest and stick to the facts.

Taking the Wrong Flight

Whether you turn to the right or to the left, your ears will hear a voice behind you, saying, "This is the way; walk in it." Isaiah 30:21, NIV.

Ted Mackey braced himself in the twin engine commuter plane. Panic gripped his heart so hard he broke out in a cold sweat. And he wasn't even in the air yet! The plane was just taxiing out to the end of the runway.

This can't be happening, he thought. *I can't be on the wrong airplane.* But when he checked his ticket for the fifth time, it was very obvious that he was on the wrong flight.

While he had waited in the airport—and even as he had walked out on the tarmac and climbed into the airplane—he had known exactly where he was going. He was looking forward to going home. He was happy. He had been away on a long business trip and was tired.

But when the flight attendant said, "You are on Flight 432 bound for Boise, Idaho," he soon discovered that he wasn't going home at all. He was flying to a strange place full of unfamiliar people. Worst of all, he wouldn't be spending the evening with his family.

Jesus wants us to be in heaven with Him. He wants us to be on the right flight.

Ted Mackey got a second chance. The pilot informed the tower he was turning around to let a passenger off. He even asked the tower to keep the flight Ted was supposed to be on from taking off for a few minutes.

Have you ever flown in a passenger airplane? Do your parents triple-check their tickets to make sure they are getting on the right flight? Are you happy Jesus wants us to be with Him in heaven? Will going to heaven be like going home?

Jesus wants us to be in heaven with Him. Share Ted's story with a friend. Ask them if they want to go home with Jesus.

A Clear Mind and a Healthy Body

To these four young men God gave knowledge and understanding of all kinds of literature and learning. And Daniel could understand visions and dreams of all kinds. Daniel 1:17, NIV.

Remember the story of Daniel and his friends? They refused to eat the king's food and drink his wine, and asked for healthy food instead. Did you know that bogging down your mind with unhealthy food makes it hard to learn? One of the best ways to help your mind learn is to eat healthfully. Here are some suggestions that everyone agrees on:

Eat a variety of healthful, natural foods.

Avoid foods with a lot of fat.

Always eat a good mixture of vegetables, fruits, and grains.

Slow down on the sugars and speed up your mind. You might have noticed that when you eat lots of sugar, you soon feel really tired and unable to concentrate. Sugar gives you an energy boost at first, but then it brings your energy level way down.

Even though our bodies need salt, too much isn't good for us.

If you want a snack, choose something like carrot sticks dipped in salsa or air-popped popcorn. Or try filling the middles of apples with peanut butter. Too much snacking isn't good, though. Remember, your stomach works hard digesting food. It needs to rest sometimes too.

It used to be that everyone drank water because that's all there was. Now liquid refreshment is available in every conceivable flavor, and in colors not even found in nature. The original beverage, water, is *still* the best thing to drink.

When you eat natural, healthful food, you will help your mind to be clear and eager to learn new things.

- **Why do you think that humankind hasn't been able to make improvements on the food God provided for us to eat?**

- **Read Daniel 1. Try eating healthful foods and see if it helps you concentrate.**

25

What Part of No Don't You Understand?

Do you not know that your body is a temple of the Holy Spirit, who is in you, whom you have received from God? You are not your own; you were bought at a price. Therefore honor God with your body.
1 Corinthians 6:19, 20, NIV.

When my brother Philip and I were junior age, there was an empty lot between our house and Tom's house where we built a track to race our bikes. Tom was about our age, so we raced a lot together and had a lot of fun. But as we grew older, Tom started hanging around with friends from his school, and Philip and I did more things with friends from our school. Eventually we all moved away.

It was quite a shock one night when Philip looked up from behind the counter where he works as a deputy sheriff to see Tom being brought into jail. Tom was to be booked for drug possession, and my brother was the one who would be doing the booking. I guess it was an awkward moment for both of them.

In the news you hear a lot about drug smuggling, drug dealing, drug possession, drug abuse, and drug pushing. In your own school you probably know who does drugs and who doesn't. Kids start using drugs for lots of reasons—boredom, peer pressure, curiosity. Can you think of any good reason to do drugs?

Neither can I.

God says our bodies are temples of the Holy Spirit. I want to keep my temple clean for Him. The best answer you can give someone who offers you drugs is "No." Just say no, and walk away.

How do you feel about drugs and alcohol? Could you say no to drugs if one of your friends tried to persuade you to use them? How would you react? How would you feel? Do you choose your friends wisely?

Pass out copies of *Listen* magazine to your friends. You never know who you will help.

A Good Friend in Prince, Part 1

The horse is made ready for the day of battle, but victory rests with the Lord. Proverbs 21:31, NIV.

Chester Evans was only a boy when he bought a strawberry roan colt he named Prince. From the start Chester and Prince were inseparable. They grew up together, and Prince would try to follow Chester everywhere Chester would let him go.

In 1878 Chester and Prince were called on to make a wild ride to Fort Monument to warn of Indian trouble at Cheyenne Creek. Not willing to let Chester and Prince get away, 15 Cheyenne Indians gave chase.

Prince ran as fast as he could for several miles, but soon the Indians were close enough to start shooting arrows. One sank into Prince's neck. Chester yanked it out right away. Then he had to ride with his finger plugging the hole. Another arrow got Chester in the leg, but he pulled that one out, too. Prince took another one in the rump before they finally made it to the fort. But Chester and Prince survived together.

Two years later Chester and Prince got caught in a prairie fire. When the fire began creating its own wind, it caused the flames to travel faster than Prince could run. For a while it looked as though Chester and Prince would both be consumed by the flames.

Suddenly they came to a buffalo wallow, where Chester might have had a chance to at least save himself. But there was no way to save Prince, too, so he stayed in the saddle and kept riding. Together they barely made it to a fire break before the flames caught up with them.

What would you have done if, like Chester, you had a chance to save yourself but not your horse? How do you think God helped Chester, even if he may not have realized it?

Is there a humane society near where you live? Why don't you volunteer there this week to groom and walk the animals?

A Good Friend in Prince, Part 2

A friend loves at all times. Proverbs 17:17, NIV.

*C*hester and Prince continued to stick together. They had done a lot of ranch work and had ridden some cattle drives together. But on January 7, 1887, Chester was called on once again to make a ride. This time he was sent to get the doctor in Wa Keeney, Kansas, to come and deliver his aunt's baby.

Chester and Prince made the ride to town all right, but on the way back that night they got caught in a blizzard. Soon neither Chester nor Prince knew where they were or where they were headed.

They fought the blizzard all night and all the next day, still unsure where they were. Several times Chester got off and walked to keep warm and to help Prince break through the mounting snow drifts. During the second night Chester could hardly keep going. When he sat down in the snow to rest, Prince would nudge him with his nose, or paw at him, to make him get up and keep moving. It wasn't until late that second morning that they stumbled upon a ranch and were saved.

When Chester married and started a family, he bought a small pasture for Prince and built a shed for him. As Chester's children grew up, they learned how to ride on Prince. Prince was a part of the family. Then one day, when Prince was 38 years old, he had an accident. Chester stayed with Prince all day and all night, just as they had always stuck together. But the next morning Prince died.

Chester said of Prince, "He had been my constant companion and my friend during his whole life. No man could have had a more congenial companion or truer friend."

🙂 **How were Chester and Prince good friends? Do you consider your pets friends? Why do you think Jesus made animals?**

🙂 **Do you know a shut-in who has a dog or cat? Offer to groom his or her pet and take it for a walk.**

Jumping for Joy

Whoever welcomes one of these little children in my name welcomes me; and whoever welcomes me does not welcome me but the one who sent me. Mark 9:37, NIV.

After two months of summer, Christy Johnson decided she wanted to do something nice for the kids in her neighborhood. She talked to her best friend, Renee, about an idea she had come up with, and they both agreed it would be a lot of fun.

Three weeks earlier Christy's mom and dad had bought a trampoline for the family. They had all had a lot of fun jumping on it, but Christy had gotten better than anyone else. She spent hours jumping and doing forward and backward somersaults. She could even do more amazing gymnastics on the trampoline than her older sister. And she had noticed that some of the younger kids in her neighborhood seemed to be watching when she was playing on the trampoline.

Christy and Renee drew up posters announcing a special free trampoline show in the neighborhood, complete with cookies and juice. Then they took their posters around their neighborhood.

When it was time for the show, eight neighborhood children and several parents came to watch. Christy and Renee performed all their gymnastics at least twice because the children were really enjoying the show. Every time they finished a jump, everyone clapped.

After the show Christy helped a few of the younger kids learn how to jump safely. When little Jimmy smiled big and Samantha started laughing, Christy felt happy, too.

"You know what, Renee?" Christy said before her friend went home. "This was the most fun we've had all summer."

🙂 **Have you ever made a child smile or laugh? It probably made you feel good too.**

🙂 **Try this: Put on an exhibition of your favorite sport for the neighborhood. Afterward, put on a clinic and teach anyone who wants to learn your sport some of the techniques you have learned.**

Jesus Loves a Good Romance

The Lord helps them and delivers them; he delivers them from the wicked and saves them, because they take refuge in him. Psalm 37:40, NIV.

Do you like a good romance? I do. And I think Jesus does too. Kathy was trapped. She wanted to leave the place she was living in so she could live as she believed a Christian should. One day she and eight other women decided to escape. A great religious revolt was sweeping through the country, leading many people to change their beliefs, and Kathy was one of those who wanted to change. They needed help to escape, however, so they asked a man named Martin to help them.

Although it could mean his death to help Kathy and her friends, Martin decided to help anyway. He arranged for a merchant to hide them in empty barrels in his wagon after he had delivered his supplies and take them far away. Kathy and her friends escaped safely.

All of them but Kathy soon found husbands. When asked who she would marry, Kathy replied that she would marry only one of two men. One of those men was Martin, the very man who had arranged for her escape.

Martin and Kathy were finally married in June of 1525. Kathy became a devoted wife to Martin. They raised six children together. Kathy also took in several nieces and nephews to raise and provided meals and lodging for many homeless people. She was a source of constant spiritual strength to her family and friends. Kathy was definitely the right hand of one of the greatest patriarchs in history, Martin Luther.

- Why do you think Martin risked his life to help Kathy and her friends? Do you think there is anything worth risking your life for? What is it?

- Take a risk. Write an encouraging Bible verse on a piece of paper and slip it into someone's locker at random.

New but Not Blue

I the Lord do not change. Malachi 3:6, NIV.

*Z*ebulon Dalton squared his shoulders and walked purposefully into the computer class. Every head turned to follow his progress as he concentrated hard on not tripping over his own sneakers or doing something else mondo embarrassing. He finally launched himself into his chair. Safe!

A snicker from the girl at the terminal next to him caused him to stiffen. Dancing blue eyes were watching him frankly out of a face he would have said was pretty, if the girl's eye hadn't sported the biggest shiner he had ever seen.

"You made it!" she said, chucking him on the shoulder. Hard.

Zebulon rubbed it ruefully.

"Don't be nervous. We've all been tested for rabies."

"What happened to your eye?" he asked, ignoring her comment.

She shrugged. "Ran into a linebacker yesterday in football practice."

Zeb nearly choked. "You play *football*?"

One cocky eyebrow shot up in surprise. "Don't tell me you've never heard of football! What school did you transfer from? Mars?"

Zeb shook his head incredulously. "*Girls* don't play football."

"Well, they do here," the girl said, smiling. "Do you play?"

Zeb sat up a little taller. "I'm a pretty fair quarterback."

The girl slapped him on the shoulder again, making him flinch. "Great! You're hired. We just lost ours. Coach will be really glad to see you. Meet you at practice tonight."

"Yeah." Zeb stared at her, hardly able to believe the conversation he'd just participated in. "I'm Zeb," he added lamely. "What's your name?"

The girl smiled broadly. "Sam. Sam Reese."

🙂 **When someone new comes to your school or your church, how do you treat him or her? Can you think of any interesting ways to welcome new people that says you are glad they are a part of your life?**

🙂 **The next time you have a chance to meet someone new, make an effort to include him or her in the activities of you and your friends.**

31

Marvelous Monday!

Let the wise listen and add to their learning, and let the discerning get guidance. Proverbs 1:5, NIV.

Do you like school?

Today is Monday. Are you eager to begin school today, or do you wish it were Friday afternoon again? Maybe you wish it were still Christmas break. Are you worried about a test? Is your homework finished? *Oh, no! Homework?*

God gave us great minds to use. Did you know that if we use our brains to do interesting, exciting things they can actually *grow!* Scientists have found that if we mentally exercise our brains by doing things like learning math (if that's hard for us) or learning to play an instrument, it may cause our brain cells, called neurons, to branch wildly.

Arnold Scheibel, director of UCLA's Brain Research Institute, tells us to think of the brain as a computer with a bigger memory board. "You can do more things more quickly."

God wants us to be as energetic with our minds as we are when we play basketball or volleyball or any other sport. If you enjoy learning something interesting, you may find that you remembered it well without even trying. But when you *had* to learn something you didn't think was interesting, you may have had to study it again and again until you remembered it.

There are many great study methods to help you get good grades in school. All you have to do is try them and find the ones that work best for you. Are you willing to try? Remember that learning can be fun. Think of it as sports for the brain.

🙂 **Does it make you happy to learn something new and interesting? Do you think Adam and Eve asked Jesus a lot of questions about the new world they were living in? Do you think Jesus enjoyed teaching them about all the interesting things He had made?**

🙂 **Try this: Just for today be curious about everything, even the boring stuff. Ask your teachers a lot of questions. You might be surprised by how much you remember.**

Gimme a Lift

Out of the depths I cry to you, O Lord; O Lord, hear my voice. Let your ears be attentive to my cry for mercy. Psalm 130:1, 2, NIV.

I know I've had some bad times when I felt as if nothing would ever go right again. You have probably felt the same way. It's not easy being joyful when bad things happen.

In the valley where I live, Shane will always be an inspiration. When he was 11 years old, his mother ran a red light and collided with another car. The accident killed Shane's two brothers and his mother and left his own body badly broken.

Shane spent the next several months in the hospital encased in a body cast. When the cast on his right leg was eventually removed, Shane continued to have problems. His leg was still very weak. While playing basketball one day, Shane broke his leg again.

Later, doctors told him that his right leg had stopped growing and in a few years his right leg would be two inches shorter than his left leg. Lengthening his right leg would mean surgery and long months of rehabilitation. But after praying about it, Shane chose to go through the long, difficult process.

So the doctors broke Shane's leg again and screwed four eight-inch pins into the bone—two above the break and two below. Three times a day for five months Shane had to twist a knob on his cast that pushed the bones farther apart.

Five years after the accident Shane is a senior in high school and now runs cross-country and competes in track meets. He is looking forward to earning an athletic scholarship for college. Whenever I need some inspiration, I can think about Shane.

- **What is your favorite inspirational story? Have you had some bad times, or do you know someone who has? How did it make you feel?**

- **The next time you hear of a tragedy in your town, send an inspiring card to the person involved.**

A Good Neighbor

I was thirsty and you gave me something to drink. Matthew 25:35, NIV.

"Dillon!" Sam yelled, pounding on the door of Dillon's hide-away (or the old boathouse, depending on who you were talking to). "Can we come in?" She tugged on Zeb's shirt-sleeve and motioned for him to help her push in the door.

Dillon, hunched over an impressive computer system, barely bothered to acknowledge their presence.

Sam jerked a head in his direction. "When he's around Albert, it's like he's just lost in cyberspace."

Zeb looked around. "Who's Albert?"

Sam chuckled. "The computer. Dillon named it after Albert Einstein. What are you doing, Dillon?"

Dillon muttered something unintelligible. "But I'm stuck," he finished.

"Well, that's simple," Sam said. "Just do this." Reaching around him she punched a few keys.

Dillon leaned back in his chair. "I hate it when you do that," he said, taking his glasses off and giving them a polish. He looked at Zeb, focusing on him for the first time. "Hi."

"Who's that?" Zeb asked, pointing out the window.

Next door, a man was pushing an ancient lawn mower. He glistened all over, as if he'd been at the tedious chore half the day.

"That's Mr. Barnes," Dillon answered, after a cursory glance out the window. "Why?"

"He looks hot and tired," Zeb observed. "Do you have anything to drink around here? I'd like to offer him something to drink."

Dillon sized Zeb up with one long, careful look. "That's a good idea." He disappeared out the door and reappeared moments later with a pitcher of lemonade and a glass. Together the three of them made their way across the lawn to make Mr. Barnes's day.

- No matter where you live, you have neighbors. They may be far away—or only a wall-width away. What do you know about your neighbors? How do you help them?

- If you don't know your neighbors, get to know them. Make it a point to smile and say hello the next time you see them.

34

Filled With Joy

Our mouths were filled with laughter, our tongues with songs of joy. Then it was said among the nations, "The Lord has done great things for them." The Lord has done great things for us, and we are filled with joy. Psalm 126:2, 3, NIV.

When was the last time you were so joyful that people asked what was making you so happy? Has it *ever* happened?

Carole was just like everyone else she knew. She had her share of problems. Sometimes it felt as though she'd somehow gotten someone else's share too. But when she compared her life to others, she could see how much God had blessed her.

One day Carole was walking home with a new friend. A car drove by and got hung up at a red light. The driver had his radio turned up so loud that the girls could hear it from the sidewalk where they were walking. Immediately Carole began walking in rhythm to the music and humming along.

"What is it with you?" her new friend asked. "I see you around town, and you're always like this, so happy and carefree. What have you got that I don't have?"

Surprised, Carole thought for a minute. What *did* she have that made life cheerful and happy for her, even though it was often hard? It wasn't material possessions, because she didn't have many. It wasn't free time, because she was too busy to enjoy that.

"I-I guess it's a positive outlook," she stammered. "Every day I take time to appreciate how much Jesus has done for me. And I know that nothing will happen that He and I can't handle together, so I don't worry much about the future. Instead I try to enjoy the present."

🙂 **Why do you think the nations assumed that the Lord had done great things for the children of Israel? What do you think people think when *you* are happy?**

🙂 **Decide that just for today you are going to be happy and positive and smile at everyone you meet, whether you know them or not.**

Kindness Clown

But I said, "I have labored to no purpose; I have spent my strength
in vain and for nothing. Yet what is due me is in the Lord's hand,
and my reward is with my God." Isaiah 49:4, NIV.

Is it hard to be nice? Well, sometimes maybe it is. But don't give up and say it's not worth it. Take Cory McDonald, alias Mr. Twister, for instance.

Mr. Twister is a clown—a clown with a big heart, who was nice to people even though they may never know it. In his hometown, whenever Mr. Twister saw a city parking meter whose time was about to expire, he dropped more money in just to be nice. It kept the driver of the vehicle from getting a parking ticket, and it made Mr. Twister feel good to help.

But sometimes being nice isn't so easy. The city had a law forbidding anyone from putting money in other people's parking meters without their permission. And sure enough, Mr. Twister got caught and was fined.

We aren't always rewarded for the nice things we do here on earth, but we can be sure that our heavenly Father sees everything we do and is preparing a reward for us. And when you stop and think about it, which is more important? Earthly praise? Or knowing that we are doing something that will make Jesus happy?

🙂 **Can you think of some times Jesus got in trouble for being nice? Did it stop Him from helping people? If you were told to stop being nice to someone, would you do it?**

🙂 **Do your neighbors need help with their lawns? Check it out. Maybe while they are gone you can surprise them. Check out other kind things you can do to show that you enjoy helping people, and try to do them without letting them find out about it.**

George's Mistake

He who heeds discipline shows the way to life, but whoever ignores correction leads others astray. Proverbs 10:17, NIV.

George Washington's first battle, which was the beginning of the French and Indian War, was not a stunning success. In fact, he surrendered to the French in July of 1754. He limped away from the battlefield at Great Meadows after losing nearly half his command in a miserable defeat.

Earlier Washington had surprised and attacked a small French detachment, and in retribution the French sent a much larger force against his troops. Washington probably shouldn't have attacked the small French detachment in the first place if he was not prepared to fight the 900 French who would attack him later.

Even so, George Washington would later become commander-in-chief of the Continental Army during the American Revolution and lead the fight for America's independence. Without such a leader independence might not have been possible. In 1789 Washington was elected president of the United States. He was wise and capable in his presidency, and his sound leadership helped America's new government get off to a good start.

George Washington was 22 years old when he lost the battle at Great Meadows. I suppose he could have quit after that. But it is more important that every failure Washington experienced made him a little wiser the next time. God is happy to see us learn from our mistakes. Even if we feel that we have failed so miserably there is no way He could forgive us, He is always happy to see us try again. God even lends us a hand when we ask for His help.

If you have made a mistake, take this chance to learn from it and become wiser.

- 😊 **What are some mistakes you have learned from? When are some times when you have felt like giving up? Why didn't you?**

- 😊 **The next time you make a mistake, think of it as an opportunity to learn, and make a wiser decision in the future.**

Small Talk

Do not let any unwholesome talk come out of your mouths, but only what is helpful for building others up according to their needs, that it may benefit those who listen. Ephesians 4:29, NIV.

Wow! No, *Yawn!* For 15½ hours Senator Huey Long of Louisiana spoke to the Senate. He started a little after noon on June 2, 1935, and didn't sit down until 4:00 the next morning. Senator Long's long-winded speech became the longest speech on record.

Why did the senator talk so long? Because he wanted to obstruct the passage of a bill, he used a strategy called filibustering.

What did Senator Long talk about? Nothing important.

Did anyone listen? Probably not for very long.

Was Senator Long's speech exciting? No. Sometimes he spouted off cooking recipes, just to take up more time.

After Senator Long finally finished his speech, it cost $5,000 to print it for the *Congressional Record.* I don't imagine anyone was very happy about wasting 15½ hours of time and spending that much money, do you?

- Have you ever been around anyone who talked and talked, but never said anything important? Was that person boring? Did he or she give you any interesting or helpful information?

- When you talk to people, think about what you are saying. Are you saying something that will make a positive difference in their lives, or are you just filibustering?

I Want to Learn

By the word of the Lord were the heavens made, their starry host by the breath of his mouth. Psalm 33:6, NIV.

W e've already said that learning energizes our brain cells and makes our minds fit, just as physical exercise makes our bodies fit. But what if going to school and sitting in class just doesn't sound like fun? And what about homework? *Ugh!*

If you can't seem to get in gear to do your homework, there are a few ideas you might try to get going and get it done:

✔ Instead of putting off an assignment until the last minute, try doing it as soon as possible. This will help keep your homework from stacking up. It also creates a more relaxed learning environment, and when you are relaxed, learning is much easier and more fun.

✔ Who are the best students in your class? Who has their homework finished on time all the time? Who is always ready for tests? Ask how they do it. They might have some good ideas that will help you.

Think of these different ideas to help you study as tools. Tools are devices that make a job easier, just as a hammer and saw makes a carpenter's job easier. Of course, not all study tools help everyone in the same way, because each person is different. You will have to find study tools that work best for you.

God gave us a wonderful world in which to live and study. He doesn't want us to drag our feet and grumble when it comes to learning. He wants us to love to learn.

😊 **What are some ways you can think of right now that will make studying fun and enjoyable?**

😊 **Now that you have thought of some ways to make studying easier for you, write them down. Call them study tools. Ask someone in your class who you think does well in school to share some of his or her study tools.**

Acts of Kindness

Honor your father and mother, so that you may live long in the land the Lord your God is giving you. Exodus 20:12, NIV.

I watched Mom pull out of the driveway to go run an errand. She would be gone for quite a while. I turned to my brother Philip. "What do you want to do? We have the house all to ourselves."

Philip shrugged. "I don't know. What do you want to do?"

We gave the matter some careful consideration. After all, it wasn't every day we had the house to ourselves. Watching TV didn't sound very interesting. Neither did playing with the model train. Suddenly we were struck with an exciting idea.

My brother and I vacuumed every carpet. We made every bed. We washed every dish. We dusted. We even cleaned the bathrooms. And we worked *fast,* because we weren't sure when Mom was going to come home, and we wanted to be completely finished when she walked through the door.

We did finish before Mom got home. That day stands out because Mom was so happy to see all the housework done and because we showed her how much we loved her. Out of all the things my brother and I could have done that day, I'm glad we chose to make Mom happy.

This happened many years ago. I can't remember the other times when my brother and I stayed home by ourselves. They might have been important to me at the time, but now they have no significance. I do remember that day, however, because of the kindness we showed our mother. I doubt that I would still remember that day if we had just watched television.

Do you remember the times you were helpful to your family without being asked? How did it make them feel? Did it make you happy to make someone else happy?

Schedule a time this week to surprise your mother and father with an act of kindness.

Hidden Treasure

If you look for it [wisdom] as for silver and search for it as hidden treasure, then you will understand the fear of the Lord and find the knowledge of God. Proverbs 2:4, 5, NIV.

W hat are we doing at the laundromat?" Dillon whined. "I've got homework to do for computer lab and a quiz to study for."

Samantha gave him an exasperated look. "Dillon, you've studied for that quiz every day for the past week. Pretty soon Mrs. Allen is going to ask you to *teach* the class. And I'm going to do that computer lab homework *with* you when we get back," she promised. "Right now we've got something more important to do."

Whistling tunelessly, she wandered around, absorbed in watching the clothes tumble dry. Dillon followed her around like a lost puppy, staying tight to her heels. The place was surprisingly deserted. Why would people go off and leave their clothes?

"What is it you're looking for that's so important?" he asked.

"Nothing in particular. Just a good place to leave these." Sam pulled out a stack of tracts that said "Jesus Loves You" on the front.

"How about the chairs?" Dillon suggested.

"Good idea," Sam agreed. She handed Dillon a bunch of tracts and began to lay one down on each seat.

"Whatever made you think of doing this?"

Sam continued distributing tracts as she answered him. "Well, I thought I'd like to pass out tracts, but I'm too chicken to do it, and most people probably wouldn't take them. But I remember how bored I used to be when my mom dragged me to the laundromat. I would have read anything. Maybe people will be more inclined to look at them here."

- Have you ever thought of the laundromat as a witnessing field? What other places do you often go that could be considered a good place to witness?

- The next time you are going somewhere, bring along a handful of tracts or some handwritten cards with an encouraging Bible verse on them and spread them around. What a nice surprise someone will have!

41

From Tragedy to Triumph

Although the Lord gives you the bread of adversity and the water of affliction, your teachers will be hidden no more; with your own eyes you will see them. Isaiah 30:20, NIV.

When was the last time you felt down in the dumps or sorry for yourself? When we're in the middle of a big ol' pity party, we can't see any good that may come from our situation.

On May 27, 1995, actor Christopher Reeve tumbled over the head of his horse and broke his neck. The fall paralyzed him from the shoulders down. Suddenly the man who was best known for his role as Superman was near death. He might never walk again or be able to move his arms.

At first living may not have seemed worth it. He was a long way from his once-active lifestyle. What would be the point in going on? How could life possibly be worth living now?

Yet Reeve was determined not to let his tragic accident overcome him. Five months later he made his first public appearance at a benefit dinner. Maneuvering his electric wheelchair by blowing through a tube, Reeve presented an award to fellow actor and comedian Robin Williams, who had come to give him encouragement a few days after the accident.

Reeve then related how he had summoned up the courage to attend the benefit: "I once overheard my English teacher tell another student, 'The only excuse you could have for skipping school is a quadruple amputation, and even then you could come in a basket.' So I thought I'd better show up."

- Have you ever wondered how someone who has had a terrible personal tragedy can be happy? How would you feel if you couldn't walk or move your arms?

- Keep a lookout for people who need encouragement. When you see someone, make a special point to be an inspiration to him or her. You might just be the spark that helps someone else see that life can be worth living. Remember, be joyful because Jesus is in you.

42

Paradise Lost, Paradise Found

I am going there to prepare a place for you. John 14:2, NIV.

I don't know about you, but I wouldn't mind living on a small Caribbean island all by myself. I think I could get used to deep blue sky, waving palm trees, and white beaches. All I would have to do is lie on the beach and listen to the waves gently lapping the shore. It's a nice dream, isn't it? But who could ever afford to have an island all to themselves?

But there *is* such an island. It's called Necker Island, and it's owned by Richard Branson. Branson doesn't have much time to spend on his island, however, because he is busy running his business empire. So he lets anyone rent it who wants a vacation in paradise.

But even vacationing on someone else's island will be only a dream for most of us. Spending just one day on Necker Island costs $15,000, and that doesn't include airfare. I don't know about you, but that's a lot more money than I've got to spend on a one-day vacation.

I've got a better idea! Let's plan the greatest vacation of all! It won't cost even a dime, because the price has already been paid. The flight there is free. The in-flight entertainment will be some great singing, and I can guarantee a most spectacular view.

Best of all, Jesus wants us to be with Him on this vacation. He is eager to try our favorite sport and play our favorite games. I imagine He wants to talk with us and laugh with us, and hike our favorite trails with us.

Final vacation destination? Heaven!

Why does Jesus want us in heaven with Him? What do you imagine heaven will be like?

Write an invitation to a friend to go with you to heaven. Describe what you think heaven will be like, and be sure to let your imagination get wild. I think we'll get to do things we never even imagined existed, don't you?

43

What Kind of Stuff Are You Made Of?

So in everything, do to others what you would have them do to you. Matthew 7:12, NIV.

The year was 1934, and a young guy from California was going to school at Duke University law school in North Carolina. At that time race relations were very bad. The entire campus was filled with an atmosphere of prejudice. There was a total of only one Black student on the entire campus—and he was ignored by everyone.

By everyone, that is, except for one student. That one young man from California believed that every person should be treated alike. And he acted like it, even though it wasn't easy. During lunch the two of them would sit together in the cafeteria. His friends stared at them and made wisecracks. In spite of that, he made a decision to stand up for equality, and even though it wasn't easy, and often was unpleasant, he stuck by that decision. That young man's name was Richard Nixon. He later became president of the United States.

We all have certain values and principles that we stand for. Sometimes it takes a crisis to help us realize just how much we value certain things. When Richard's friends were making fun of him, he could have said, "Aw, what's the difference? Maybe they're right. Maybe I'm making too big a deal out of this." But, he didn't. He stood up for what he believed in.

We don't know if his friends respected him in the end. But that isn't as important as the fact that Richard could respect himself.

Have you ever been in a position similar to the one Richard Nixon was in? How did you act? Do you wish you had acted differently? Explain, in your own words, what the following statement means: If you can't stand up for what you believe in, then sit down.

Ask the least popular kid in school to do something with you. Remember to smile when you ask.

The Mysterious Tree: A Parable

But he was pierced for our transgressions, he was crushed for our iniquities; the punishment that brought us peace was upon him, and by his wounds we are healed. Isaiah 53:5, NIV.

A man who had been shipwrecked at sea washed onto the shore of a white, sandy beach on a beautiful tropical island. As he sat on the beach considering his good fortune, a boy dressed in simple clothes emerged from the trees.

"Welcome to our island," the boy said.

"Thank you. I'm very grateful to be alive," the man replied.

"As a guest of our island you may go anywhere you wish and eat any fruit that pleases you." Then the boy turned and pointed to a particular tree. "But you must not eat the fruit of that tree."

While this sounded reasonable to the man, he was curious. "Why can't I eat of that tree?"

The boy took the man to the fence surrounding the tree and pointed to a notice written in blood. "Our chief warned us by his own blood not to eat this fruit," the boy said.

This satisfied the man for a while, but then he began to think that the chief might be trying to scare the islanders into not eating the fruit so he could keep it all to himself. *Maybe the fruit is the source of the chief's power,* the man thought.

Convinced that his theory was correct, he ignored the notice and ate the fruit. Instantly his body felt as if it were on fire. He yelled out in great pain, and the boy came running to see what had happened.

"Tell me about the fruit," the man begged. "Why didn't it affect your chief?"

"The forbidden tree grew mysteriously on our island," the boy explained. "Our kind chief would not let anyone touch its fruit for fear that it might be poisonous. But the fruit was very beautiful, and everyone wished to try it. One day the chief said he would test the fruit for us. I am sad to say that our chief died, just as you will. His last wish was that we use his blood to warn others of the danger."

😊 **Who do you think the people in the parable represent?**

😊 **Write your own parable about sin and how Jesus died for us.**

Boring!

Look to the Lord and his strength; seek his face always. Psalm 105:4, NIV.

Baxter Burney rubbed his eyes and yawned.

Knock! Knock! Samantha Reese poked her head inside the door. "What are you doing?"

"Studying," Baxter said sourly. "Why?"

"Want to go skating?"

"Sure, but I'm studying for our geography test tomorrow. I've been here so long I just can't think straight anymore."

Sam jumped onto the bed with just a little more energy than was necessary and Baxter scowled at her. "Look, Baxter, you've got more time tonight to study. Why don't you take a break and let your brain cells cool off for a little while?" Sam suggested. "Then when you study later on you'll be fresher."

Baxter hopped out of his chair. "That's a great idea. Let's go!"

Did you plan a fun activity last week with your family or friends? Did having fun help you forget all about schoolwork for a while?

What? No one has ever told you that *fun* is a great study tool? Learning isn't supposed to get you down. If it does, then you probably aren't learning as easily as you could if you gave your mind a chance to relax.

Minds that have been filled with facts and ideas for long periods of time need a chance to rest and relax so they can digest all that information. Even while you believe you are not giving a thought to schoolwork, your subconscious is working at sorting out all that valuable information you have stored in your mind. Scheduling time for fun may help you remember what you studied.

God gave us wonderful minds to use. Let's keep them healthy and happy and ready to learn.

🙂 **Have you ever gotten up and done something else when you were studying a difficult assignment because you couldn't figure it out? What happened when you came back to it? Did you discover a solution?**

🙂 **The next time homework is bogging you down, get up and take a walk. The solution might be waiting for you when you get back.**

I Don't Want to Go!

My Father, if it is not possible for this cup to be taken away unless I drink it, may your will be done. Matthew 26:42, NIV.

The story goes that a mother was having a hard time convincing her son to go to school.

"No one likes me at school," the son said. "The teachers don't like me, and the kids don't. The superintendent wants to transfer me, the bus drivers hate me, the school board wants me to drop out, and the janitors have it in for me. I don't want to go."

"But you've got to go," the mother insisted. "You're healthy. You've a lot to learn. You have something to offer others. You're a leader. Besides, you're 40 years old, and you're the principal. You've got to go to school!"

Of course, that turned out to be a funny story in the end. But we all have days when we would rather not go to school or work. There can be lots of reasons for this. How many can you think of?

Jesus also did some things He wasn't exactly happy about doing. Remember the night He was in Gethsemane? The Bible says He was "sorrowful and troubled." He even told His disciples, "My soul is overwhelmed with sorrow to the point of death." Now, I'm guessing that you've never been that sad about going to school!

Jesus prayed for His Father to help Him be strong and accept God's will for Him. And we can do that too! God helped Jesus, and we know that He will help us also.

 **What do you usually do when you just don't feel like doing something you know you have to, or should, do? Does the way you act let other people know that you rely on Jesus for your strength?**

There's power in prayer. The next time you are faced with something you don't feel like doing, ask God to help you do it cheerfully so that you will bring joy to God, other people, and even yourself.

A Peculiar People

But ye are a chosen generation, a royal priesthood, an holy nation, a peculiar people; that ye should shew forth the praises of him who hath called you out of darkness into his marvellous light. 1 Peter 2:9.

Have you ever found yourself trying to bluff when people ask what you believe or why you act different? Well, let's face it, no one wants to be different, so we resort to diversionary tactics.

In that way we're like the octopus. When an octopus is threatened, it tries to bluff its way out of trouble. First, it might try bristling its skin to scare away its enemy. If that doesn't work, it puffs up and raises its tentacles. And if all else fails, the octopus shoots clouds of purplish-black ink from its ink sac as a smoke screen to fool its enemy while it makes a quick getaway.

Sometimes we just want to fade into the background where no one will notice us, so we try to act like everyone else. The octopus does the same thing. The color of an octopus changes continually to that of its environment so that it remains inconspicuous to its enemies, another way the octopus protects itself.

But it's hard to blend in when you're "peculiar." Did you ever wonder what peculiar means? Probably something different than you think. After all, you don't have to be a Christian to be peculiar. There are lots of peculiar people in the world today. Being peculiar means that we belong to God. We're set apart. We're special. So don't be afraid to tell others why you are special.

🙂 **What do you say or do when a stranger asks if you are a Christian? What kinds of questions do people usually ask you? How do you answer them?**

🙂 **This week share your faith with someone who isn't a Christian—maybe a non-Christian friend at school. Be prepared to answer questions about what you believe and why. Also, be positive! Sharing your faith is exciting!**

Love, Zlata

May the God who gives endurance and encouragement give you a spirit of unity among yourselves as you follow Christ Jesus, so that with one heart and mouth you may glorify the God and Father of our Lord Jesus Christ. Romans 15:5, NIV.

When Bosnia became independent from Yugoslavia in 1992, war broke out. Serbia remained part of Yugoslavia, and the Serbs who were in Bosnia and opposed the country's independence began fighting. As the storm of war broke out all around her, Zlata Filipovic started recording her everyday life in the pages of her diary.

Like others in the city of Sarajevo, Zlata and her family were forced to live like prisoners in their own home. At times they sought refuge from bombs and mortar shells in their cellar. As Zlata watched from her window, the city was destroyed. Some of her friends from school and her neighbors were killed.

She wrote everything in her diary, which she named "Mimmy," and she signed each entry, "Love, Zlata." One of her teachers read her diary and sent it to a publisher. It soon became a book, *Zlata's Diary: A Child's Life in Sarajevo,* and was a best-seller.

Zlata and her family escaped with the help of the French government. She now lives in Paris and is going to school, but she worries about friends and family who were left behind. Her diary let others know what it was like in Sarajevo. Zlata hopes that by letting others know, they will help the people who are still there.

- Can you think of a time when you have spoken out about some injustice that was happening? What happened when you did? If you saw something happen that was not fair, what would you do?

- Not everyone who writes a diary will have it published, but that's no reason not to start one! Any notebook will do. Date each entry and record things that happen, as well as your hopes, dreams, and even your prayers.

49

The Late Thank-You

He comforts us every time we have trouble, so that we can comfort others when they have trouble. We can comfort them with the same comfort that God gives us. . . . Our hope for you is strong. We know that you share in our sufferings. So we know that you also share in the comfort we receive.
2 Corinthians 1:4-7, EB.

By the time Diane Hanson had walked the three blocks to the bookstore from the school where she taught, she felt as if she'd traveled three miles. The sharp, biting wind and blowing snow only deepened her depression about life.

Paul, Diane's husband, had been killed in a traffic accident on New Year's Eve by a drunk driver. The tragedy seemed to snatch the life out of Diane as well. The bookstore had become a favorite hideaway during the past few months since Paul's death. She browsed for a while before purchasing an old textbook that she took home and set aside until after supper.

As Diane scanned the pages of the book before going to bed, a small card tumbled out of the book and onto the floor. The card had been written by a child 15 years before:

Dear Mrs. Porter,

Thank you for being my teacher. I think you are the greatest teacher. I know you are sad your son had to die from cancer. I was afraid you couldn't be happy anymore, but Mom says praying to Jesus makes people feel better. Every night, when I say my prayers, I ask Jesus to help you be happy again.
Sincerely,
Jeff

Diane folded the note with a little smile and slid to her knees beside the bed. "Dear Jesus . . ." she began.

😊 **Do you know someone who has experienced a tragedy in their life? How did it make you feel? What did you want to do for them? What *did* you do for them?**

😊 **Write an encouragement or thank-you note to one of your teachers this week. And make sure it gets delivered!**

The Ultimate Valentine

For God loved the world so much that he gave his only Son. God gave his Son so that whoever believes in him may not be lost, but have eternal life. John 3:16, EB.

What we call Valentine's Day today is generally thought to have been based on a tradition that started in about the 1400s and doesn't actually have anything to do with two martyred Saint Valentines of the third century. For many years young people living in France and England would get together on Saint Valentine's Eve. All of their names were put into a box, and each person became the "valentine" of the one whose name they drew from a valentine box.

But the spirit of Valentine's Day actually began many, many years before that. A long time ago—before Adam and Eve sinned in the Garden, before the earth was created, even before Lucifer rebelled, taking a third of heaven's host with him—God and His Son had Their own valentine box. And Jesus drew each of our names out of it. Then He planned the most perfect, most wonderful, most awesome valentine of all time.

You see, God had a plan for salvation before there was even a need for it. That's because He knew that Lucifer would rebel and that Adam and Eve would sin. So He and Jesus designed the ultimate valentine for us. He planned how He would show us His love for us by saving us from eternal death so that we could live forever with Him.

Can you think of a better Valentine's gift than that?

- How can you relate the story of God's love for us to others on this special holiday about love? How can you show Jesus how much you love and appreciate Him today?

- With your family and/or friends, decorate a shoebox in red and white. Put everyone's name in the box, and let each one draw a name out. Then, sometime on Valentine's Day, do something to show that person how much you love them.

51

Coping With Grace, Part 1

Words from a wise man's mouth are gracious, but a fool is consumed by his own lips. Ecclesiastes 10:12, NIV.

I live in Vermont. It's a great state, and I'm not just saying that because I live here. We make some of the best maple syrup; we have great apples, lots of skiing, the Green Mountains, the Long Trail; and we're the home of Ben and Jerry's famous ice cream. (Need I say more?) Some people even say that there are more cows in Vermont than there are people.

I don't know about cows, but there are definitely more White people than there are Black people in Vermont. You see, Vermont is called the "whitest state in the country" because very few people of other nationalities live here. That's something that George Cook, the only Black soccer, basketball, and lacrosse referee in Vermont, is reminded of every day at his job, because he faces prejudice from fans, coaches, and even some players.

One day George stood with his hands clasped behind his back while he was slapped over and over by a White player and called racist names.

"I knew that everyone would remember how the referee reacted, not the provocation," says George. "I took the path of nonviolence for my fellow officials, as well as for my fellow African-Americans. I hope [my 16-year-old son, who was in the stands] learned something about how to deal with hate and not to lash out."

Prejudice has its roots in ignorance. People are sometimes afraid of things they don't understand, and they lash out because of their fear. By cutting others down, they are trying to bring themselves up to make themselves look more powerful than the object of their fear. But that's not what happens. Prejudice only pushes people apart and builds a wall we can't climb over.

Why do you think that God created everyone equal? How do you personally treat people of other races?

Get to know people of other races whenever you get a chance. Each of us is unique, created by God to enrich each other's lives.

Coping With Grace, Part 2

Then Peter began to speak: "I now realize how true it is that God does not show favoritism but accepts men from every nation who fear him and do what is right." Acts 10:34, 35, NIV.

Do you realize that you might be prejudiced?

"Not me!" you say. "I've got lots of friends who are of different races and skin colors. I'm not prejudiced."

But what about other people who are different from you? Do you love everyone the same? Fat kids? Thin kids? Slow kids? Super-smart kids? Rich kids? Poor kids? Smelly kids? Dirty kids? Have you ever found yourself making excuses for not being friends with someone because you didn't like the way he or she looked or talked or walked or whatever?

Guess what—that's prejudice! Some kids have to deal with it every day. Maybe they're the last one picked every time for any athletic game, or everybody calls them names, or no one wants to sit with them at lunch. You may have felt the sting of prejudice yourself a time or two. How do you deal with something like that?

George Cook, who is a Black referee, says, "Basically, you have to learn to have a sense of humor and to kill them kindly with a smile. They're looking for a reaction." George knows what he's talking about, because he has to deal with prejudice almost every day, on and off the playing field. He says that things are not getting better in terms of race relations.

And they won't get better until you—yes, *you!*—do something about it. Don't wait for things to get better. Help make them that way yourself.

In God's eyes we are all equal. Isn't it about time we started treating each other that way?

- **If you were the object of prejudice, how would you act? What would you do if a friend of yours was the object of prejudice? How about if it was someone you didn't know?**

- **If you observe prejudice in your school or town, ask your parents, pastor, or teacher what you can do to fight it.**

Johnny's Attitude

Provide purses for yourselves that will not wear out, a treasure in heaven that will not be exhausted, where no thief comes near and no moth destroys. For where your treasure is there your heart will be also. Luke 12:33, 34, NIV.

At 25, Johnny showed up in the Ohio River valley with his Bible and began reading to the settlers wherever he went. This began Johnny's unique ministry. For the next 50 years he traveled throughout the frontier with his Bible, reading and preaching to those who would listen.

Johnny not only befriended the pioneers, he was respected among the Indians as well. During his travels he planted herbs and was skilled at making poultices to heal wounds. The Indians considered him to be a healer.

Johnny was a unique individual. Born in 1774, he was often quiet and unassuming in deed and action; he let his lifestyle speak for him. You might envision him as a man who had a sunny-side-up approach to life because of his generous spirit.

You see, not only did Johnny read the Bible to the early pioneers, plant herbs, treat wounds, and befriend the Indians, but he also went about planting apple trees. You might know Johnny better as Johnny Chapman, or Johnny Appleseed.

Johnny Appleseed must have cared a lot about people to spend his life providing for their physical and spiritual needs. He certainly did not become wealthy planting apple trees and preaching to settlers. If the settlers paid him money for his apple seedlings, Johnny gave the money to the poor, bought religious books, or fed broken-down horses. Mostly he was paid in cast-off clothing or cornmeal. Nevertheless, Johnny Appleseed gained another kind of wealth, the kind that can't be stolen.

☺ **How was Johnny Appleseed wealthy? What does it mean to have a generous spirit? Who are some people you know who have generous spirits?**

☺ **Your neighbors might not appreciate it if you planted apple trees in their front yards, but you might buy some flower seeds and make them some special planters this spring.**

Pressed Down and Running Over

Give, and you will receive. You will be given much. It will be poured into your hands—more than you can hold. You will be given so much that it will spill into your lap. The way you give to others is the way God will give to you. Luke 6:38, EB.

O h, no, no, no!" Baxter Burney groaned from his console in the computer room at Lake Union High School. Samantha Reese, the only other person in the room, turned to look at him. She and Baxter had stayed late to work on some extra-credit assignments.

"What's the problem?" Sam asked.

"There's not enough room left on this disk to save my work," Baxter explained. "And I don't have another disk."

Sam glanced from Baxter to the one remaining disk in her box and then back to Baxter again. "Well . . ." she began. If she gave Baxter her last disk, she'd have to buy another box out of her allowance. Sam decided to try something her Sabbath school teacher once told her: "Just ask yourself what Jesus would do." That was easy. Jesus would give Baxter the disk!

"Here, you can have this one," she said generously.

"Thanks, Sam," Baxter smiled. It was something he didn't do that often, and it made Sam feel warm inside.

Later that night when Mr. Pines picked her up to baby-sit for him, he met her at the door of her house carrying a big box. "Samantha, could you use a bunch of disks for your computer?"

Sam's eyes widened. "I sure could. And so could my friends."

"I sold my computer," Mr. Pines explained, "so I don't need them anymore."

Sam looked at the gift in her arms. And to think that just that morning she'd given away her last disk. God was so thoughtful. "And so are you, Mr. Pines," she added aloud. "Thank you so much."

 **When you give something to someone, what kind of attitude do you have? Would you rather not give it? What kind of attitude do you think you should have?**

Give something away. What it is doesn't matter so much as your attitude when you give it.

Trailblazer

Your word is a lamp to my feet and a light for my path. Psalm 119:105, NIV.

It was in St. Louis, Missouri, that Jedediah Smith, at the age of 23, approached General Ashley for a position on his expedition up the Missouri River. Right away General Ashley liked the brown-haired, blue-eyed young man, and after they talked, Ashley saw a lot of promise in young Jedediah.

In 1822 Jedediah left St. Louis on his adventure as a hunter for the expedition. A year later Jedediah had proved himself a capable leader, and Ashley gave him his own command. Jedediah blazed many trails in the untamed wilderness. He is credited with discovering South Pass, the main route by which thousands would later travel west. He went on to lead the first overland journey to California and blaze the first trail from southern California to Fort Vancouver on the Columbia River.

Yet Jedediah was often confronted with bitter disappointments and failures among his many successes. He once survived an attack by Mohave Indians, who killed half his men. Later, while leading another party, all but one of his men were killed by the Kelawatset Indians.

Though at times Jedediah must have been close to complete despair, he never lost faith in God. He held firm his religious convictions even among rough men. His actions proved to many that he was a man of God, for he did not swear or chew tobacco, and he always treated people with respect and dignity. It is said that wherever he went, Jedediah Smith carried a Bible in his saddlebags and read it faithfully.

- **How do you think Jedediah felt spending much of his time in the wilderness with people who were not Christians? Do you think that Jedediah's Christianity helped him become a good leader?**

- **Do you carry a Bible to school? Why or why not? This week why don't you bring God's Word with you to school. But don't just bring it, read it there too!**

Mystery, Anyone?

Whatever your hand finds to do, do it with all your might.
Ecclesiastes 9:10, NIV.

The police department in Uppsala, Sweden, has some pretty short detectives. Well, short *and* young. One hundred twenty kids, ranging in age from 10 to 17, belong to a detective club organized by Officer Goran Harde of the police department in Uppsala.

Officer Harde started the club eight years ago because he wanted to teach kids the basics of police detective work. He also hoped to get kids involved in their community. What he *didn't* realize was that the club members would actually start solving real crimes.

They've done things like tracing and returning stolen bicycles, recovering lost valuables, finding missing persons, and even helping track robbery getaway cars. Once an elderly woman disappeared from a nursing home and no one could find her. Officer Harde requested that the school let his detectives out, and within half an hour they found the woman sitting in a cafe not far away.

No one, least of all Officer Harde, expected the kids to do so well that they would start solving real crimes and doing actual detective work, but the kids were interested in what they were doing, and so they did it well.

How much do you like the things you do? Is school enjoyable? Do you think it's fun to do chores around the house? Do you like after-school activities? God wants us to give 100 percent, no matter what we're doing, whether we like it or not. Whatever we do, we are to do it as if God was supervising the task.

The next time you do something, whether it's waiting for the bus or helping a neighbor do some yard work, do it as if God will inspect the results, and see if it changes the way you do things.

- Have you ever considered being a detective? Why or why not? Why do you think the kids in the story wanted to be detectives?

- Ask your parents to help you find out whether or not there is any kind of program like the one in today's story in your town. If not, why not suggest one?

Poisonous Words

The poison of vipers is on their lips. Their mouths are full of cursing and bitterness. Romans 3:13, 14, NIV.

Sea snakes sound terrifying enough to give me nightmares! After learning their eating habits I would certainly not care to meet these sea creatures face-to-face. A sea snake searches for fish among the coral; then it attacks its prey with fangs and pumps it full of paralyzing venom. The sea snake then swallows its food whole. *Shudder!*

A stinging catfish sports deadly venom-filled spines to remind bigger fish that it is not a healthy snack. A stonefish's triangular body is filled with venomous spines that can give off a poison that can kill a human being.

The sea snake, stinging catfish, and stonefish are either poisonous as a means to protect themselves or to help them catch food. Their poison serves a purpose for survival.

Reef fishes do not start out poisonous. They tend to become toxic, however, if they eat another toxic fish. A small toxic plant will bloom, and a small fish will be tantalized into eating it. Soon another fish will eat the fish that ate the toxic plant.

These reef fishes might or might not be safe to eat. It depends on what they've been eating. Their poison doesn't seem to serve a useful purpose, either. The only reason they are poisonous is that they have been eating poison.

It's sort of that way with us, too. Swearing, pornography, and drugs are a few of the poisons out there. If we fill our minds with these poisons, we begin to speak and act in such a way that we also begin to poison the minds of those around us. We become like the poisonous reef fish, whose poison serves no useful purpose. It only poisons those who come in contact with us.

- **Name some other poisons you see every day. How do these poisons eventually affect those you associate with? Is it possible to be a poisonous example to someone else without realizing it?**

- **Choose to speak only kind, encouraging words today.**

Perpetua's Faith

Anyone who does not take his cross and follow me is not worthy of me. Whoever finds his life will lose it, and whoever loses his life for my sake will find it. Matthew 10:38, 39, NIV.

Hilarian, who was the procurator (governor) of Carthage, questioned Perpetua, "Art thou a Christian?"

Vibia Perpetua, a young woman in her 20s, stood boldly before Hilarian. Five faithful Christian friends stood with her. "I am," Perpetua answered. "I cannot forsake my faith for freedom."

Every one of her friends agreed with her. None would forsake their faith for freedom.

Early in the second century Roman emperor Septimius Severus feared that Christianity would become too powerful a force to control. He issued a decree forbidding anyone to teach Christianity or to bring converts to the Christian faith—on pain of death.

Perpetua had learned from the deacon Saturus about this new religion called Christianity. Her maidservent, Felicitas, was also converted, as were three men whose names were Revocatus, Secundulus, and Saturninus.

As these Christians stood before the procurator, they never resigned their faith, even in the face of certain death. A few days later they were led to the arena to be executed. Perpetua continued to praise God, and sang songs in His name. As she and her friends passed by the procurator, they said, "You may judge us, but God will judge you."

Saturus, the teacher, and the three other Christian men were led to the arena first to be mauled by a leopard, a bear, and a wild boar. Perpetua and Felicitas were thrown into the arena and attacked by a savage steer. Later, after she had suffered wounds from the beast, Perpetua was beheaded by a gladiator's sword. Perpetua died a martyr's death in A.D. 203.

🙂 **What is a martyr? How is it possible to have the same type of faith that Perpetua had? How was Perpetua able to praise God even unto death?**

🙂 **Choose to share your faith today with someone who may not know Jesus as you know Him.**

59

Making Time

There is a time for everything, and a season for every activity under heaven. Ecclesiastes 3:1, NIV.

Right now you probably have about 100 hours before sundown next Friday evening. Sounds like a lot of time. But don't forget that almost 40 of those hours are already planned for sleep. So you've really got around 60 hours. Still a lot of time. But most of that will be taken up with school, and then there are mealtimes and homework and time spent getting ready for the day. How much time do you figure is left?

You might have noticed that your parents keep a schedule to remind them of appointments. They keep a schedule so they can plan time for the important things that have to be done. Scheduling also helps your parents see where their time is going so they can be more productive.

Using time wisely is one of the best things you can learn to do. It's like learning to spend your allowance carefully. Now that you have started setting aside a special time to do your homework, write down that time in your own schedule to help you remember. This idea will help you stick to your study times.

Besides keeping a schedule for your homework, set aside a special time to study your Sabbath school lesson, too. You might choose a quiet time just before you begin studying your homework to study your Sabbath school lesson. When you pray, ask God to help you as you study.

Do your parents plan a schedule for the week? How will a schedule help you do your homework and study your Sabbath school lesson?

Help your parents write their schedule for the week. Maybe you could suggest doing some fun activities together later this week. Be sure and set aside time for worship every day, too, to help you keep in touch with God.

60

"Gawking Fee"

The second most important command is this: "Love your neighbor as you love yourself." Mark 12:31, EB.

In Plano, Texas, after her neighbor's house had burned, 13-year-old Seychelle Van Poole began to notice something really weird happening right outside on the street. People who were driving by would slow down, and even come to a complete stop, to stare at the fire-damaged house. The gawking drivers were causing a major traffic jam right out front. Seychelle began to get upset.

Suddenly an idea occurred to her, and she decided to do something about it. She hurriedly rounded up several of her friends. Huddling together, the kids rehearsed a speech they had come up with. Then it was time to put their plan to work.

Surrounding the sightseers' cars stopped in front of the fire-damaged house, the kids began requesting a "gawking fee." They explained that the donated money would go to help the family whose home had burned. Nearly 150 people donated anywhere from a quarter to $40 apiece for the burned-out family. When they counted up the money at the end of the day, the kids discovered they had collected $610.25 to help Seychelle's neighbors!

Loving our neighbors is so important that Jesus calls it the second most important commandment. I'd say that Seychelle loved her neighbors very much, wouldn't you?

- **What do you think Seychelle felt like when she saw people driving by to stare at her neighbors' burned house? How do you think she felt when she was able to raise money for the burned-out family? Can you picture Jesus helping collect money for the burned-out family?**

- **You may not think you have very many opportunities to help someone the way the kids did in the story, but there are plenty of things you can do. As spring arrives, you and your friends might choose to clean up yards for people who can't get outside. You could also choose a worthy cause, and then sign up sponsors who will donate money to that cause for every hour you work.**

Colder Than Thou, Part 1

Do not judge, and you will not be judged. Do not condemn, and you will not be condemned. Forgive, and you will be forgiven. Luke 6:37, NIV.

It was Maya's first winter in the frozen land of Iceberg, an island just off the coast of the great continent Frigid, a little north of the North Pole. She was going to visit her aunt Lucia and her uncle Alvin for the Christmas holidays.

"Be sure to pack your sweater," her mother advised. "It will be colder than the inside of a snowman in Iceberg."

"Pack two sweaters," her father added. "It will be colder than frostbite in Iceberg."

Maya, who thought her parents were being paranoid (as teenagers sometimes do), nevertheless packed two of her heaviest sweaters. Not because her parents suggested it, she reasoned, but because she had knitted them herself and wanted to show Aunt Lucia.

Each day while she was visiting her aunt and uncle, Maya walked two miles down to the shore to bring Uncle Alvin his lunch. She didn't mind the walk at all, because although it was terribly cold in Iceberg, the sky was bluer than blue and the snow sparkled as if someone had thrown diamonds on it. Of course, Maya was very thankful that she had packed two sweaters, and she wore them both on her way down to the shore. They kept her toasty warm.

One thing bothered her, though. A rather scruffy little boy named Orin, who sat by the wharf dangling a fishing line through a hole he'd chopped in the ice, glared at Maya whenever she passed by. After a week of this, Maya could not take it anymore. One day she marched over to him and demanded, "Why don't you like me?"

🙂 **Can you think of a time when you've had the impression that someone didn't like you, even though they didn't say a word? What did you do about it?**

🙂 **The next time you catch someone glaring at you . . . smile! It's doesn't cost anything, but the look on his or her face might just be priceless!**

Colder Than Thou, Part 2

If you have two shirts, share with the person who does not have one. If you have food, share that too. Luke 3:11, EB.

The little boy chewed sullenly on his lower lip. "It ain't that I don't like you, exactly," he growled, "it's just that I don't think it's very fair, is all."

Maya rolled her eyes in exasperation. "You think *what* isn't fair?"

Orin stared pointedly at Maya's sweaters. "Every day you walk by me wearing *two* beautiful, thick sweaters. And every day I sit here dressed in only this thin shirt." The boy fingered the threadbare material of his shirt and looked up at her with accusing eyes. "Do you think that's fair?"

That morning at the breakfast table Uncle Alvin had read from a very large, worn, old Bible. One of the verses he'd read *had something to do with this exact situation!* Maya remembered it perfectly.

Peeling off her top sweater, she handed it to the astonished Orin. He reached out with fingers blue from the cold and eagerly pulled the still-warm sweater over his head, wrapping his thin arms around himself in a tight bear hug to capture all the warmth he could. He looked up with a shy smile. But Maya wasn't through. She rummaged around in Uncle Alvin's lunch basket and gave Orin half of everything.

As she walked on, she realized that she was a little colder on the outside than usual, but she was a lot warmer on the inside than she ever had been before. Wouldn't Uncle Alvin be surprised when he found out where half his lunch had gone! Maya knew she would have fun describing the look of pure joy on Orin's face as he had eaten it.

- Do you have lots of possessions? Do you know anyone who doesn't have as much as you? How would you feel about sharing what you have with them?

- Go through your room, looking for things that you don't use anymore. Ask your mom or dad to help you find some children who might like them. If they are dirty, be sure to clean them up before you donate them.

Our Strength

I have learned the secret of being content in any and every situation, whether well fed or hungry, whether living in plenty or in want. I can do everything through him who gives me strength. Philippians 4:12, 13, NIV.

Can you imagine having to take care of your whole family? Because this world is full of sin, some kids have a hard life. Seven-year-old Karen is responsible for taking care of her father, who has a mild mental impairment, and her 4-year-old brother, Junior. Many times they are thrown out of their apartment when their father has a fight with the landlord. Each time they move, Karen must find a new route to school that is safe.

Every day she meets her father at the bus stop on his way home from work. Jumping up, she has him carry her home so that she can wrap her arms around his neck and protect him from the mean kids who call him names and throw rocks at him.

At school Karen is smart and loves to learn. She takes care of her classmates, helping them when they have trouble. Karen's life is hard, but through it all she remains strong. She wants to go to a "safe, clean place" where she can help sad people, because "I learned what to do in the bad places."

God knows that our lives won't always be easy. In fact, some people live very hard lives, and terrible things happen to them. But through everything God is with us, helping us, if we want Him to. And He doesn't just help us get through life; He can help us to be joyful, no matter what our circumstances are. Do you know why? Because we have His assurance that someday we will be with Him forever, and this life will be just a dim memory.

- **Maybe your life isn't as hard as Karen's is. But there will always be days when things don't go right, because the world is full of sin. How do you react when bad things happen?**

- **The next time something bad happens, claim today's verse. You *can* do everything through Jesus, who gives you strength.**

Me? Obey *Them?*

Do not be wise in your own eyes; fear the Lord and shun evil. This will bring health to your body and nourishment to your bones. Proverbs 3:7, 8, NIV.

*T*hey don't know what they're talking about, Allen thought to himself as he hopped on his motorcycle. He didn't bother to put on his helmet. His parents were always harping at him about that. "Wear a helmet, Allen," he could hear his mother say. "Drive safely."

Well, Allen was sick of driving safely and wearing a helmet and doing what his parents said. Obedience? What a drag! He didn't have a license and shouldn't have been riding on the road, but he was only going two miles to Robert's house. It made him feel kinda grown up, disobeying his parents like this. He felt the surge of power as he revved the throttle and the bike spun out of the driveway.

Meanwhile, Robert had just watched his parents pull out of the driveway to go to dinner, and decided to go for a joyride in the family's other car. He had just found his favorite radio station. Cranking it up, he totally forgot about the intersection as he took his eyes off the road for a second.

As Allen braked his motorcycle at the intersection, he failed to see the silver Mazda Robert was driving speeding toward him. He let the clutch out and began to turn left. The crash was the last thing that Allen heard.

Allen died long before the paramedics arrived. The car Robert was driving rolled into the ditch, leaving him shaken but alive. Robert will live the rest of his life with that haunting memory.

- When do you enjoy obeying your parents? When is it not so fun? Why do you think God feels it is important for us to obey them?

- The next time Mom or Dad asks you to do something that you don't particularly like, smile and do it cheerfully. (Hint: Watch their expression!)

Kindness Rises Above Chaos

For this is the will of God, that by doing good you may put to
silence the ignorance of foolish men. 1 Peter 2:15, NKJV.

Sadly, Chung Lee's Watts Market on 103rd Street lay in
charred ruins after the Los Angeles riots of 1992. Lee, a
Korean-American merchant, had always been a positive
and generous part of the community, but now, out of hate and
anger, someone had burned his business to the ground.

Lee had spent a lot of time and energy trying to improve race
relations between Korean-Americans and African-Americans in
his community. Anyone who needed help received it from Chung
Lee, because he loved people, no matter what race they were. In
fact, he often made sure the children of drug users had enough to
eat and provided a safe environment for them to come to.

Although his Watts Market had been destroyed, Chung Lee's
efforts at projecting a positive influence did not go unnoticed by
the people in his community. To show how much they cared
about Chung Lee and his family, those who knew him banded together to clean up the rubble and haul it away without Lee's
knowing it.

Chung Lee had no idea his neighbors and friends would do
such a thing. He had hired a contractor to clean up the mess, believing that the project would cost him about $6,000. But when
the contractor went out to look at the store, he discovered that
the job had already been done.

When Chung Lee found out that his store had been cleaned
up, he was touched. He had learned that the kindness he had
shown to others did make a difference. It had brought everyone
closer together.

- Why did people in Chung Lee's community clean up his
store for him? Do you think Chung Lee was kind to everyone because he expected to get something for his
kindness in return?

- True kindness is not selfish. When you choose to be
kind, think about why you are doing it.

66

Never Give up

We have different gifts, according to the grace given us. Romans 12:6, NIV.

I never really liked the schoolwork part of going to school. Sometimes it was just plain hard. My worst subject was math. I hated math. While other students seemed to do well, I continually struggled. I began to think I wasn't as smart as my friends. Have you ever felt that way? Or maybe sometimes you feel you aren't good at anything. It's easy to feel that way. Unfortunately, it's just as easy to give up instead of persisting to learn.

Who knows what you will accomplish unless you keep trying? If you learned to talk before you were 4 years old, you learned sooner than one of the greatest thinkers the world has ever known. If you learned to read before you were 7 years old, then you beat this same great thinker again. You probably even learned to walk before this very same genius did, for he was slow at that, too.

In fact, young Albert Einstein was probably thought to be rather dense as a child, maybe even unteachable. Not until he was 26 years old and had discovered his theory of relativity did the world really become aware of Einstein's genius.

We all are different, so some studies will be easier for some of us than they are for others. Math will be easier for most of you than it is for me. Still, I will keep struggling to learn math, because someday I want to be able to do it well. But I am happy our minds all work in different ways. It makes life more interesting.

How much do you know about Albert Einstein? Why do you think each one of us has special, unique abilities?

List some of your special abilities. Next, list the special abilities your friends have. After you have completed a list for two of your friends, tell them what you think their special abilities are.

Cecilia's Love for Ormand, Part 1

I was sick and you looked after me. Matthew 25:36, NIV.

T he king of a certain country was a strict but fair ruler, and his people lived happily under his authority. But one year a horrible famine came over the land. It continued for several miserable years.

The terrible famine drove people to steal bread from their neighbors and kinfolks, and so the king was forced to issue a decree that anyone caught stealing food would be put to death. It saddened him mightily to be forced to issue such a decree.

Ormand, the son of a peasant farmer, had fallen in love during this time. Ormand noticed neither the famine nor the king's decree, for he lived only for the mysterious maiden who had stolen his heart.

Each evening Cecilia walked the path from the woods to the house of Ormand's father, and for hours she and Ormand conversed and looked upon each other with great affection. One evening Ormand pledged his undying love for Cecilia and asked for her hand in marriage. Cecilia hesitated in her acceptance of Ormand's offer. Certainly she loved Ormand with all her heart, but she wanted to be positive of Ormand's affection toward her.

The next day Ormand fell seriously ill. Because his family had only a few morsels of food each day, he lacked the proper nourishment to recover from his illness. Cecilia faithfully visited Ormand every evening, and often she brought him extra bread for strength.

One evening Cecilia did not come to visit. Nor did she come the next evening. Ormand knew not where she lived, only that she had always walked the path from the woods to see him.

How did Ormand know that Cecilia loved him? Where might the extra bread have come from?

Do you know someone who is sick right now? Do you feel better faster when someone takes care of you when you are sick? Plan ways to help your mother or father feel better when they are sick.

Ormand's Love for Cecilia, Part 2

Greater love has no one than this, that he lay down his life for his friends.
John 15:13, NIV.

Ormand went in search of Cecilia, and after many days found her in the king's dungeon. "Oh, my love, what has happened?"

Cecilia's reply was tearful. "It is for the bread that I brought you. It was not mine to give, and I must be punished by death tomorrow on the king's gallows."

"You did not take it for yourself! You took it to save my life, and I ate of it for my own strength," Ormand said, and left to plead with the prison captain for Cecilia's life.

"There will be no pardon," Ormand was told. "However, you could write a letter to His Majesty whereby you may offer to take the young woman's place at the gallows tomorrow."

Ormand immediately took pen and paper and labored over his letter. "Oh, my good king," he wrote. "Out of my love for Cecilia, I beg that I may take her place at the gallows tomorrow eve. I will gladly bear her punishment so that she may freely live in your kingdom."

The king's heart was immediately touched. He accepted Ormand's request, and on the eve of the next day, Ormand was led to the gallows in Cecilia's place.

When Cecilia saw that Ormand's love was so great that he willingly took her place, she wept with joy. For certainly now there could be no doubt that Ormand loved her as much as she loved him. The king also saw that Ormand's love was great for his daughter. This was the king's test to see who should marry his daughter and inherit the kingdom.

Great was Ormand's joy when he was set free from the gallows to marry his beloved and take his place in the kingdom.

 If you had been Ormand, what would you have done? In this story, how is Ormand like Jesus? How is the king like God? How are we like Cecilia?

Pretend that Jesus is writing a letter to God on your behalf, explaining why He wants to die in your place. What would He say?

Brush Up on Your . . . Moliere?

I can do all things through Christ because he gives me strength.
Philippians 4:13, EB.

You've probably heard of Shakespeare, right? (Hint: "Romeo, Romeo! wherefore art thou Romeo?") But have you ever heard of Moliere? What Shakespeare is to English literature, Moliere is to French literature.

Moliere (his stage name) was born as Jean-Baptiste Poquelin in Paris. His father was a prosperous furniture maker who held the office of upholsterer to the king. However, Jean-Baptiste didn't want to be a furniture maker or to take up the practice of law, for which he had been educated. Instead he took the name Moliere and became a strolling player.

Moliere learned a lot about human nature and used this knowledge in his plays that laughed at the fashions of the day and at the vanity, greed, and selfishness in people. His last play, *The Imaginary Invalid,* was about a man named Argan, whose doctor had convinced him that he was sick, at death's door even, when in fact he was perfectly well. Do you know why the doctor did that? Because the sicker he told Argan he was, the more money Argan spent paying the doctor to take care of him.

That's funny, isn't it? That someone could make us believe something that isn't true? That could never happen to you, right?

Have you ever thought there was no way you could really go to heaven, that you could never be "good enough," that God could never forgive you for something, or that God couldn't possibly love you the way the Bible says He does? Satan, like the doctor in the play, tries to convince us of things that aren't true because it will benefit *him* if we believe them. Like Argan, we can become "sick" if we believe Satan's lies.

🙂 **Have you believed any of Satan's lies? What should you do when negative thoughts come into your head?**

🙂 **On index cards write some positive verses about how God helps us. Today's verse is a good one to start with. Carry the cards with you, or use them as bookmarks in your schoolbooks, and read them throughout the day.**

Love Your Enemies

But I tell you who hear me: Love your enemies, do good to those who hate you, bless those who curse you, pray for those who mistreat you. Luke 6:27, NIV.

What do you want him on our team for?" Zeb hissed to Samantha as she motioned for Baxter Burney to join them. "He hates us. He especially hates you. He'll probably play badly just so our team loses."

Sam turned to face Zeb. "Would Jesus let him play on our team?" she asked.

Zeb squirmed under her frank gaze. A red flush crept up his neck. "Well, I don't know. Would Jesus play basketball?" he countered defensively, shooting Baxter a dirty look.

Sam rolled her eyes at him. "Why not? Jesus wasn't fun-impaired. I think Jesus liked to play games. Especially sports."

"That's beyond the point, anyway," Zeb said obstinately. "Why did you pick him? You had a billion other choices."

"I chose Baxter because he's a good player," Sam said evenly. "It doesn't matter if he doesn't like me, and if I treat him the way you want me to, he never will like me."

Baxter shuffled nervously, and Sam realized that he knew they were talking about him. "Hey, Bax," she said with a smile. "Ready to play basketball?"

He shrugged. "I don't know why you had to pick me. I wanted to be on the other team. Are you afraid they'd beat you if I was on their team?" he taunted.

Sam smiled. "No, but you're such a good player that I wanted you on our team. Now we're unbeatable, right? OK, guys, huddle. This is what we're going to do."

- 😊 **Why do you think that Samantha continued to be nice to Zeb and to Baxter even when they were giving her a hard time? How would you have responded? How would Jesus have responded?**

- 😊 **Responding in anger when someone is mean to you is easy. The next time someone says something not too nice to you, say something nice to them instead of returning their insult.**

Ice Cream Makes Me Smile

He will yet fill your mouth with laughter and your lips with shouts of joy. Job 8:21, NIV.

I'm just wild about ice cream. It is totally my favorite dessert. And believe it or not, ice cream is not a new food that came into existence when refrigerators were invented. Some sweet tooth invented it a long, long time ago.

But whoever had the recipe at first apparently lost it during the Dark Ages, when a lot of other important knowledge was lost. Then in 1295, Europeans got their first taste of ice cream when Marco Polo brought recipes for water ices back to Italy from his travels in China.

Ice cream made its appearance in the New World in the early 1700s, and began to be manufactured in America in 1851. Then one fateful day at the St. Louis World's Fair in 1904, an ice-cream vendor ran out of dishes in which to serve his ice cream. So what did he do? He ran next door to the wafflemaker's concession stand and "borrowed" a thin waffle to fashion a cone-shaped dish from. Suddenly everyone had to try their ice cream in a cone.

Ice cream makes me smile. It makes my friends smile too, and I'm sure it makes you smile. I wonder if Jesus likes a big bowl of ice cream just as much as you and I do?

When we think about Jesus, we should respect His knowledge, His power, His fairness, and most of all, His love. But Jesus also wants us to remember that He is a God of joy, happiness, and humor. After all, God Himself created our funny bones. Laughter is a gift from God when it is used to spread joy to others.

Imagine a fun day with Jesus. What would you do? Would you stop at your favorite ice-cream shop and order your favorite ice cream?

Invite a friend to go to an ice-cream shop with you. Watch and see how many smiles people have when they share ice cream.

Turtle Time!

When birds are sold, two small birds cost only a penny. But not even one of the little birds can die without your Father's knowing it. Matthew 10:29, EB.

My friend Rick and two of his friends decided to go to the corner store to get their lunch one day, so they piled into his pickup truck and took off. Then Rick saw something in the middle of the road.

Uh-oh, he thought, *dead dog.* But as he got closer, he could see that it wasn't a dog. It wasn't even fuzzy. And it was *moving.* Just barely. "It's a—"

"Turtle!" one of the other guys cried. "Man, did you see that thing? It's huge!"

Rick pulled over, and all three guys jumped out of the car. The turtle was in no rush, and they crowded around to look at it.

"We can't just leave it here," one of the guys said. "He'll get run over for sure."

"Come on, let's move it off the road," Rick urged.

Somehow the three of them managed to wrestle the turtle to the side of the road and down the bank to a nearby stream. Although that turtle was the first one they had ever rescued, it wasn't the last. For the rest of the time they worked in that area, every time they saw a turtle who needed to be rescued, they would yell, "Turtle time!" and pull off the road and help it.

Have you ever stopped to help a turtle to the side of the road? I have to admit that I do it too. In a way, those turtles remind me of myself when I don't know I'm in the way of something dangerous. Sometimes we need other people to help us get from one place to another before we get "run over" by life. God sends these people to us—we know them as friends, parents, and pastors.

- Who rescues you when you're stranded? Are there people in your life that you rescue? How does it make you feel to help someone?

- The next time you see a turtle crossing the road, stop, if you can, and help it get across.

73

Creating a Memory Bank

I remember your ancient laws, O Lord, and I find comfort in them. Psalm 119:52, NIV.

Have you tried to remember something and couldn't? We think of that as memory loss, but most of the time memory recall is the culprit. Memory recall is your ability to remember something that you learned.

Everything we hear, see, do, touch, smell, taste, and say can be stored in our memory. Isn't that great? So why is it that sometimes you can't find the keys to unlock your memory?

First you have to put something in your memory, so that it will be there when you want to take it out. One way we store information is by doing something over and over. For instance, when we first learn a computer program, it is hard to remember how to use all the commands, especially as complicated as computer programs have become. But the more we practice, the easier it is to use the program.

Many people think that there is some magical formula to having a good memory. There is a magical formula, but it takes work. We need to understand how our minds function and then, using that information, help ourselves use our memory better.

When we think or do something over and over it wears a path in our memory called a neural trace. After a while we will automatically know our way around the computer program, because the neural traces in our brains have become so well worn.

But at the same time we have to be careful what kinds of neural traces we create. It is just as easy to create bad neural traces as good ones. We need to remember that God created our memories to help us, and when we put bad information into our memories, we are dishonoring God and treating His gift with disrespect.

What types of things have worn neural traces in your memory? How can we use our memories to learn more of the Bible?

Find a favorite Bible text and repeat it as many times as it takes to make a well-worn path (neural trace) in your memory.

74

What Goes Around, Part 1

To your service for God, add kindness for your brothers and sisters in Christ; and to this kindness, add love. 2 Peter 1:7, EB.

J ay Raemont was not a very popular kid in high school. In fact, many of his classmates noticed him only because they liked to pick on him. One day Jay chose to cut through the "smoking lounge" as he was leaving school. Suddenly he was surrounded by "burnouts" who were only too happy to have someone to pick on. Jay thought he was dead.

Then something happened that not only surprised Jay, but probably surprised the guys who had started picking on him, too. One of the prettiest and most popular girls in the school appeared out of nowhere and grabbed Jay's arm.

"What took you so long?" Cindy MacDonald asked. "I've been here since 2:30." Then she took Jay's hand and they walked toward the parking lot.

Before reaching the parking lot, Cindy let go of Jay's hand, explained that she had cheerleading practice, and walked away before Jay thought of thanking her. Jay remembered that Cindy never really knew who he was and that he had never thanked her.

Years later, as Jay was reading the newspaper, he saw a story about a 22-month-old boy who had been born with a condition in which the small bowel does not function properly. The boy's only source of nourishment was through a tube that pumped predigested food into his stomach. Without it, however, the boy could not survive. The boy's only hope was an experimental operation to transplant the small bowel.

The story was written by an emergency room nurse, and the boy she had written about was her nephew. Jay immediately recognized the nurse's name—Cindy MacDonald!

🙂 **What do you think about what Cindy MacDonald did when she saw that Jay was in trouble? Do you go out of your way to help classmates in your school who are not very popular?**

🙂 **Today, look for ways you can be kind to others. What is the smallest kindness you can do for someone else?**

75

What Goes Around, Part 2

*If all these things [kindnesses] are in you and are growing,
they will help you never to be useless. 2 Peter 1:8, ICB.*

Jay Raemont recognized Cindy's name immediately. He remembered the time she had helped him out when he was one of the least popular kids in school. And he remembered that he had never taken the opportunity to thank her. He wanted to change that.

After learning that the insurance company would not pay for an experimental transplant operation and follow-up care for Cindy's nephew (which would cost the family $800,000), Jay decided he would do what he could to help raise the money they needed.

When Cindy heard that Jay was pitching in, she was touched. She remembered going to school with Jay, but she couldn't recall that time she had taken his hand and walked with him out of the room when he was in trouble. For Cindy, being kind had become natural. When she saw that Jay was in trouble, she acted right away. In what had been a tough situation, Cindy had shown Jay the respect and kindness everyone deserves without worrying about how people would see her or if she would be picked on herself.

Often even the small kindnesses we can show people every day will be remembered by them many years later. It might be that even a small kindness we do today will make a positive change in someone's life in the future. Unfortunately, some of the mean, hurtful things we do to others get remembered too. Good or bad, our actions are remembered long afterward. Choose to be kind today.

🙂 **Most of the nice things we can do for other people don't take a lot of planning or time. Why are even the small things so important? Can you make a list of 10 small kindnesses you can do this week?**

🙂 **Now that you know how easy it is, make a habit of being kind.**

Missing the Signs

Everyone who hears these words of mine and does not put them into practice is like a foolish man who built his house on sand. Matthew 7:26, NIV.

The first night my wife, son, and I spent in our own brand-new home came after a long day of moving furniture and cleaning.

Late that night I made one final trip to my parents' garage for a few more things. It was close to midnight before I started back home, and I was tired. Then for no particular reason, I took a different route home. The danger was that I was too tired to think clearly, and I had put myself on autopilot . . .

It's easy to put ourselves on autopilot. Sometimes we go through life oblivious to the dangers of sin. Maybe we have made friends with people who are a bad influence, and we ignore the effect they have on us. Or maybe we have become so used to sinning that we are not alert to the distance it puts between us and God. When we put distance between ourselves and God, it makes it harder for Him to save us, in spite of how much He wants to.

I was so tired that night that it took me a long time to recognize the stop sign. But when *STOP!* finally registered in my brain, it was far too late to keep from going right on through the intersection. And to my horror, I was on a collision course with another car! I didn't just tap my brakes, I stood on them! All four tires locked up, and I skidded sideways through the intersection, missing the other car by inches. After I crossed the intersection, I pulled over and prayed. Remembering that incident always helps me desire to stay close to God.

When were some times that you forgot about God? What are some things that make us forget about praying and studying?

Whenever God seems far away, take a few minutes and talk to Him. Talk to Him like a friend. He wants to hear from you.

77

Bennett's Fantastic Claim

Be self-controlled and alert. Your enemy the devil prowls around like a roaring lion looking for someone to devour. 1 Peter 5:8, NIV.

What if I said I could make you stay home tomorrow? No way? Don't be so sure!

New York *Herald* publisher James Gordon Bennett once claimed that he could make the people of New York do anything he wanted them to do. How could Bennett make such a claim? How could he possibly make every person in New York do what he wanted?

Bennett boasted to his friends that the next morning he would make every New York citizen stay home. Sure enough, not a soul moved on the streets of New York the very next morning. James Bennett had successfully carried out his claim.

The devil makes a similar claim on each one of us every day. He says, "I can get Lisa or Todd or Missy to do whatever I want them to do." Then the devil tries to make good on his claim by causing suffering or spreading lies.

How did James Gordon Bennett convince everyone to stay home? He had the *Herald* run stunning headlines the next morning claiming that dangerous animals had escaped the zoo and were roaming the streets of New York. "Terrible Scenes of Mutilation" and "A Shocking Carnival of Death" screamed the headlines. New York's citizens believed that wild animals were terrorizing the whole city because of what they read in the paper.

So what did they do? Stayed at home, off the streets.

😊 **Why was it so easy for the citizens of New York to believe such a lie? Would you have believed such a lie?**

😊 **Make a poster with the picture of a lion on it, with a red circle around the lion and a slash through the middle (a "no lion" sign). Write the words of 1 Peter 5:8 and 9 on the top. At the bottom of the poster put the words of John 16:33 to remind you that although the devil is real and always working to deceive us, Jesus has already fought him and won.**

Whaling Wall

And God said, "Let the water teem with living creatures, and let birds fly above the earth across the expanse of the sky." So God created the great creatures of the sea and every living and moving thing with which the water teems. Genesis 1:20, 21, NIV.

Wyland is an artist with a mission. It's a whale of a mission. He wants to paint murals of life-size marine mammals in 100 cities. Recently he reached the halfway mark by painting a wall in Atlanta, Georgia. It took 3,000 gallons of paint to cover the side of a downtown parking garage. The wall is seven stories tall and measures 450 feet across. Wyland worked six days, 12 hours each day, to finish it.

Unlike many artists who begin a mural by drawing the picture in a grid and then painting each square in the grid, Wyland paints everything in his mind's eye.

When Wyland was 14, he became interested in studying whales after seeing gray whales migrating off the coast of southern California. He frequently consults with scientists to be sure that his paintings are accurate. His other work includes sculptures and smaller paintings. And why does he do it?

Wyland hopes that his murals will help preserve the earth's oceans and their inhabitants. "If people see the beauty in nature," he says, "they'll work to preserve it."

Since God created the animals many years ago, some have become extinct, some have become dangerously close to extinction, and many are still threatened today. God gave us these precious creatures in trust. If we lose them through our carelessness, future generations will never enjoy their beauty as we do. Each of us is responsible for helping to preserve them.

- What are some things you can do to make people aware of the environmental problems facing the earth's creatures today? Why do you think it is our responsibility to help to preserve all of God's creatures?

- Choose one area of nature that interests you and see what you can find out about it. Who is working to preserve it, and how can you help? Then just do it.

Friends With Fools

Whoever spends time with wise people will become wise. But whoever makes friends with fools will suffer. Proverbs 13:20, EB.

I 'll see you tomorrow!" Sam waved to her new friend.

Dillon glanced suspiciously in Shannon's direction. "Isn't that Shannon you were waving at?" he asked.

"Yeah, so?" Sam said, trying not to look him in the eye.

"You really think that's a good idea making friends with her? I hear she drinks beer and is kinda wild."

Sam rolled her eyes and made a face at Dillon. "Oh, big deal. So what if she does? It's not like she could make *me* drink it. Anyway, she's nice and I'm going to a party at her house this weekend."

"Well . . . Be careful, OK?" Dillon said, but Sam didn't answer.

Monday morning when Sam got on the bus, she hoped she wouldn't have to sit with Dillon, but he had saved her a seat. Unhappily she sank into it.

"Hey!" Dillon said cheerfully. "How was the party?"

Sam sighed. "It was awful," she said. "You were right. I should have been more careful about making friends with Shannon. I went to her house, and she wasn't the only one drinking beer. Everyone was. Her parents weren't home, and her brother had bought it."

"You didn't—drink—any, did you?" Dillon asked hesitantly.

"No," Sam replied. "But I almost did. Everyone was making fun of me and calling me a baby. I ended up phoning my parents to come get me, and Shannon got in big trouble. Now she hates me."

Dillon cleared his throat. "You did the right thing," he told her. "Someone could have gotten hurt."

"Someone did," Sam said quietly. "Me."

🙂 **How do you think your friends influence you? Do you ever experience negative peer pressure (pressure to do bad things)? Or positive peer pressure (pressure to do good things)? Is all peer pressure bad?**

🙂 **Peer pressure can be good when we use it to help our friends do good things. This week, encourage one of your friends to help you do something good.**

Oh, No, I Forgot Again!

Remember this, and do not forget it! Isaiah 46:8, EB.

ou know the depressed feeling you have when you can't remember answers to test questions? Compare that to the contented feeling you have when you have aced a test because you knew all the answers. What makes the difference is reviewing, again and again, what you want to remember well. The next time you study for a test, try to review the material ahead of time. It may take some planning, but remember that by getting to work early on your studies you will feel more relaxed and ready to learn. It is a much better plan than cramming for a test.

Most of us cannot remember half of what we have just read. After 24 hours we will not be able to recall 80 percent of what we read. Wow! What happened to all that information? Well, it's lost somewhere in our minds, because we let that information get away without reviewing it regularly to let it wear a path (neural trace) through our memory. We lost track of the information. That is why review is so important. And that is why cramming just before a test doesn't work.

Cramming at the last minute crowds all those thoughts into short-term memory. But as soon as the crisis is over, the information scatters, leaving no trace of where it went.

Have you ever been interrupted shortly after you have tried to remember something, only to discover that your thoughts instantly disappeared? The same thing happens when you cram for a test. All that information may slowly fade away, or it may seem to vanish all at once.

🙂 **How is cramming for a test wasting your time? Whom do you answer to for how you spend your time? If Jesus had to study for a test, how do you think He'd do it?**

🙂 **Now that you have a good idea about what you have to do to remember what you have studied, plan to study well in advance of your next test. Remember to review what you have read often. See how well you do.**

Humble Servant, Great Princess, Part 1

Therefore by Him let us continually offer the sacrifice of praise to God, that is, the fruit of our lips, giving thanks to his name. Hebrews 13:15, NKJV.

I f there was ever a person who graced this earth by her Christian life, it was Elizabeth of Hungary. Her life is a consummate love story of grace, dignity, and passion.

Elizabeth was born in the year 1207 into a deeply religious family. When she was 4 years old, she was betrothed to Louis IV of Thuringia. The two often played together as children and obviously loved each other very much, for they called each other "brother" and "sister" throughout the rest of their lives. As Louis grew into manhood, he determined to live up his motto, "Piety, Chastity, Justice." When Louis and Elizabeth were married, they agreed that they would be just rulers.

Their love continued to grow. Elizabeth often rode with her husband throughout his land whenever she could. And when she could not, she was always eager to greet him on his return. Their life together was one of Christian love, happiness, and deep affection for each other.

Inspired by Francis of Assisi and Clare of Assisi, Elizabeth resolved to nurse the sick and care for the elderly by making sure they had food and lodging. Louis was proud of his wife for taking on such responsibilities for the least fortunate people in his territory and resolved to support her.

During this time, Crusaders returning from the East had brought with them the dreaded disease leprosy. While most people feared lepers and kept their distance, Elizabeth, remembering that Jesus had associated with lepers and healed them, cared for them in her home. When Louis heard of this, he was deeply moved. When Elizabeth asked to build a home for lepers halfway up the steep climb to Wartburg Caste, Louis agreed, and the home was constructed.

🌝 **If you were a prince or princess, how would you rule your people?**

🌝 **Do you know anyone in a nursing home? Visit them. Or you can "adopt" a grandmother or grandfather to visit.**

82

Humble Servant, Great Princess, Part 2

Do not forget to do good and to share, for with such sacrifices God is well pleased. Hebrews 13:16, NKJV.

Louis was proud that his wife so dearly loved even the poor and unfortunate people in his land. His was a kind heart, also, and he did whatever he could to help relieve the suffering of his people.

In 1226 a terrible famine swept the land. Louis was in Italy with most of his soldiers at the time, so the burden of dealing with the catastrophe fell to Elizabeth. Because of the lack of food, disease and crime erupted throughout the land. Elizabeth thought there might be an uprising if she did not do something to alleviate the suffering. As the hungry came to the castle, Elizabeth opened up her own food stores and ordered the bakers to bake bread night and day. She then distributed bread and soup among the people.

Elizabeth ordered grain storehouses across the land to be opened. Soup kitchens were started and churches opened to lodge the homeless. But Elizabeth did not stop there. She took money from the treasury and gave it to the poor. She even sold her most precious jewels. But with Elizabeth's efforts came the first rumblings against her. Louis's treasurers began accusing Elizabeth of wasting money.

When Louis heard about the trouble the famine was causing and the pressure it was putting on his wife, he left Italy and returned home to help her. He was pleased when he arrived to see the effort Elizabeth had put forth to help the poor and hungry.

Elizabeth and Louis spent some of the happiest months of their lives together in the summer of 1227. However, at the same time Germany was preparing to send men on a Crusade, and Louis was to lead the Central German Contingent. As he told Elizabeth goodbye, she begged him not to go. An awful fear had come over her that she might never see him again.

🙂 **Did Elizabeth do the right thing when the famine came? What would you have done in Elizabeth's place?**

🙂 **With your parents, volunteer at a soup kitchen.**

83

Humble Servant, Great Princess, Part 3

Jesus said to him, "If you want to be perfect, go, sell what you have and give to the poor, and you will have treasure in heaven; and come, follow me." Matthew 19:21, NKJV.

When Louis left, Elizabeth was several months pregnant. Louis entrusted his brother, Henry Raspe, to care for his wife and children in his absence. Unfortunately, those who had disagreed with Elizabeth's generosity during the famine began to complain to Henry about her.

Meanwhile, Elizabeth's worst fear, that she would never again see her husband, came true. Louis became ill and died in Italy at nearly the same time she gave birth to their fourth child, Gertrude. Elizabeth was truly devastated, for she had lost the love of her life. Barely a year later Henry assumed power and, prompted by the rumblings about Elizabeth, cast her out of the castle.

As Elizabeth left, she forgave those who were causing her to suffer. Of all the people she had helped with money and food, none would open a door for her or show her mercy. Henry had forbidden anyone to give her assistance. The next day Elizabeth's children were brought to her, and she sold her remaining jewels for food to sustain them.

Elizabeth would later meet the returning Thuringian Crusaders, who carried with them her husband's body. She was overcome with sorrow, but she had trusted the Lord to be with her. The Crusaders then convinced Henry Raspe to restore Elizabeth to her rightful place and her son to his place to succeed his father. Sadly, Henry soon broke his promise to the Crusaders.

Elizabeth spent the remaining few years of her life once again caring for the elderly and poor. She spent much of her time treating those who suffered the worst diseases. When she wasn't helping others, she spun wool for a living. Elizabeth of Hungary died of exhaustion when she was only 24.

In what ways did Elizabeth model Jesus for the people who knew her? In what ways do you model Jesus for the people who know you?

Do something nice for someone without getting caught.

MARCH

The Bank Teller and the Robber

And we know that in all things God works for the good of those who love him, who have been called according to his purpose. Romans 8:28, NIV.

A friend of mine, Janine, was a new teller at a large bank in Utah. On a particular day of the month all the maids came in to have their paychecks cashed. With the lobby full, Janine eyed the crowd nervously. She'd just watched tapes about security procedures and what to do in the event of a robbery. A robber could easily blend in with this type of crowd.

As she counted out money for a customer, Janine glanced up and saw that the next customer in line had a scarf over her mouth. When she walked up to the counter, she passed Janine a note.

Fearfully Janine took the folded piece of paper. She couldn't believe it! A holdup on her very first day! All of a sudden she couldn't remember anything she'd seen on the videotape. She wondered if she should push the alarm button next to her cash drawer, then she noticed that the teller next to her had seen the woman and was preparing to hit the alarm.

So she slowly unfolded the note and read, *I have just had surgery on my mouth and can't talk. Will you please cash my check? Thank you.*

Things aren't always as they seem, are they? Have you ever judged someone before you knew the whole story? It's pretty easy to do, because we look at the outward appearances and judge from that. Aren't you glad that God looks on the inside and judges the true motives?

🙂 **If things are not always as they seem, how can you tell how they really are? What would you do if a stranger approached you and asked for a quarter to make a phone call? How can you be sure that is what he will use the quarter for? Does it matter?**

🙂 **Find a scripture that tells us how to test things for truth.**

85

Fear No More

*I sought the Lord, and he answered me; he delivered me
from all my fears. Psalm 34:4, NIV.*

Have you ever been afraid of something? You probably
have. There are two kinds of fears that we can have: normal fear and abnormal fear. A normal fear would be, say,
being afraid that you'll flunk a test because you haven't studied.
If you don't study, you could flunk, so your fear is justified.

An abnormal (not normal) fear would be being afraid to go
outside at night because monsters might attack you. Since there
is no such thing as monsters, your fear of being attacked by them
is not real.

If we let them, our fears can control our lives. One thing to
keep in mind is that most of the things we fear won't ever really
happen. But sometimes our fears are so strong they can actually
make us sick, whether they are real or not. You can let go of your
fears by practicing a type of prayer called "affirmation." Instead
of asking God to help you overcome your fear, say, "Thank You,
Lord, for taking away my fear."

An elder who was in the hospital found fear gripping him.
"But," he said, "I was told that many people were praying for me.
So I began to affirm that these prayers were taking effect and
that the Lord was hearing my own prayers. And I had a wonderful experience, for as I affirmed this, all of a sudden every
vestige of fear seemed to leave me. I was at peace and rested,
and felt absolutely confident."

We should walk unafraid, because, after all, God is on our side,
and there is no one more powerful than God. But walking unafraid isn't always easy; we need to build up our faith consciously.

- **When should you pray an affirming prayer? What is
  the difference between a prayer of asking and a prayer
  of affirmation?**

- **Make a list of the things you are afraid of. Now separate
  them into two categories—normal and abnormal. Next,
  pray an affirming prayer and watch your fear disappear.**

Fear or Faith?

So do not fear, for I am with you; do not be dismayed, for I am your God. I will strengthen you and help you; I will uphold you with my righteous right hand. Isaiah 41:10, NIV.

There is a story about a man who used to work late at night, and then walk home. One beautiful moonlit night he decided to go through the cemetery rather than walk around it. He did this for several nights until the moon didn't come out anymore. Still, he thought he knew the path well enough by this time to travel it in the dark.

But one night as he walked the path, his feet went out from under him and he found himself sliding to the bottom of a freshly dug grave. He tried his hardest to get out, but he was too short and the grave was too deep. He decided that the best thing to do was wait until the gravediggers returned in the morning.

Before long another man came wandering down the path and slid into the grave at the other end. The first man watched him for several minutes as he tried to climb out. Finally he spoke up: "Boy, you'll never get out that way."

But the second man did—like a shot!

Let me ask you something. If the second man had the ability to get out of the hole all along, why couldn't he get out when he first tried? He couldn't get out because he didn't have enough faith in his ability. When we have faith in God, He will help us to live up to our potential. We can do things we never dreamed we were able to do if we will trust in Him.

- Could both men in the story have gotten out of the hole had they really tried? Why do you think so? What made the difference?

- Fear can motivate us, but usually not in a positive way. Faith is a much greater force than fear. And if you have faith, it can set you free from fear forever.

Me? Get Help?

Ask and it will be given to you; seek and you will find; knock and the door will be opened to you. For everyone who asks receives; he who seeks finds; and to him who knocks, the door will be opened. Matthew 7:7, 8, NIV.

But I don't understand it!" I wailed. Two trains, each traveling at different speeds, coming from different places. When would they meet? I didn't *care.* I just wished they'd get off the tracks and leave me in peace.

"I think you should ask your teacher for some help," my mother suggested.

I blinked up at her to see if she'd lost her mind. Didn't she know that only the stupid kids asked the teacher for help? And I certainly wasn't stupid. I just didn't have a clue when it came to math. Ask me an English question. Or science. Or history. Anything but math.

The next day I thought again about what my mother had said. I did not want to fail math. I sneaked up to my teacher's desk. "Um, Miss White? Could I—that is—would you—I mean, I don't understand what we're doing. Could you help me?"

Miss White smiled up at me. "I'm meeting with some other kids this afternoon to go over the same thing. Why don't you join us?"

Oh, great. The only thing better than private humiliation was to have some company. "Sure," I mumbled.

When I went to the place where Miss White said we were going to study, I found my friend Pam and a couple other kids I didn't know. "Hey, Pam, what are you doing here?" I asked.

"I'm here to study with Miss White," she said.

"You are?" I couldn't believe it! Pam wasn't stupid either.

"Yeah, I don't understand this train stuff," she giggled.

"Me either," I agreed with relief, suddenly glad I'd asked for help. "Guess we'll learn together."

😊 **Do you think asking for help means that you're stupid? Is it normal to be better at some subjects than others?**

😊 **The next time you don't understand something, ask for help. The only dumb questions are the ones you never ask.**

I Won't Be a Thief! Part 1

You shall not steal. Exodus 20:15, NIV.

anza Mukaley had a problem. A big problem. His mother had died awhile back, and then his father passed away too. Suddenly no one in the village wanted anything to do with him. The woman who had been his next-door neighbor for his whole life—13 years—glared at him without compassion.

"Go to the market," she said loudly, as if she was afraid that he had suddenly become deaf. "That's where you belong now."

Banza drew his thin body up as tall as he could and sputtered with indignation, "But—but I don't want to become a thief!"

Everyone knew that when you went to the market you became a thief. The old woman began to close her door. "There is nothing I can do. I cannot feed you any longer. Your appetite is so large I believe you could eat every morsel of food in Zaire."

The door closed in his face, and Banza was left staring at the dust at his feet. What could he do? He was just a young boy, all alone. A sharp pain in his stomach reminded him that it had been a long time since his last meal, and it might be even longer until his next one.

Suddenly he had an idea. Maybe the governor would help him. What did he have to lose? He began to walk on the dusty road out of town toward Lubumbashi, where the governor lived. Eventually he became aware of a sound behind him. A farmer in a rickety cart, pulled by what had to be the oldest ox in Africa, was coming along the road behind him.

"Can I have a ride?" Banza asked.

The farmer responded with a curt nod, and Banza jumped in with a little running hop and settled down to enjoy his ride.

- **What would you have done if you had been Banza? Is stealing always a sin?**

- **Save up all your change for a month—or a year. Then bring it to the bank for a money order to send to the Adventist Development and Relief Agency (ADRA) to help other kids like Banza.**

89

I Won't Be a Thief! Part 2

Whoever accepts a little child in my name accepts me. Matthew 18:5, EB.

When Banza arrived in Lubumbashi, he looked around, trying to figure out where to go. Finally he asked someone and was directed to the governor's office. He told his story to the woman sitting behind the desk. She smiled kindly at him and told him that he would have to stay with the guards at the governor's palace while she tried to find a place for him.

"I will try to get in touch with ADRA," the lady continued. "There may be a place for you at an ADRA orphanage at Bulaya as soon as it is opened."

The days passed, and it seemed to Banza as if he might be stuck in the guardhouse forever. Then one day the woman brought him a note and told him to whom he should deliver it.

Banza did as he was told. He brought the note to a man who opened it and read aloud: "The carrier of this note is the orphan of whose case you are aware. As agreed, we're sending him to you so you can forward him to Bulaya." The man folded the note and smiled at Banza. "So you're the boy who is going to live on the farm."

Banza nodded, wondering if that was good or not.

"You'll like it there," the man assured him.

Banza could hardly wait to see what this "farm" was. That night he tossed and turned. He was so excited he hardly slept at all. Questions raced through his head. What if he couldn't find anyone to be friends with? What if there wasn't enough food, even at the farm, for the boy who could eat everything in Zaire? What if . . . what if . . .

- Why do you think Banza went through all the trouble of seeing the governor instead of just becoming a thief? If you were in trouble, who would you go to for help?

- If you do not have a list of emergency numbers by each phone in your house, ask your parents to help you make one. Then post them where they can be seen easily.

I Won't Be a Thief! Part 3

This woman did the only thing she could do for me. Mark 14:8, EB.

The next morning Banza climbed excitedly into the cart that would take him to the farm. It was a long ride, and with each passing minute his excitement grew so that by the time they arrived, he was squirming all over the cart, leaning out and trying to see everything all at once.

But as soon as the cart creaked to a jerky stop at the farm, a swarm of people—adults and children—rushed up to them. Banza shrank back against Bea, the wife of the nice man who had brought him to Bulaya. Where did all these people come from?

Bea gave him a reassuring hug. "You're going to like it here, Banza," she said confidently.

Banza looked around with wide, frightened eyes. Then something caught his attention. Some boys were playing a game with some kind of ball. He leaned out of the cart to get a better look. But he couldn't see well enough, so he climbed out of the cart and took a few steps toward the boys. It sure looked like fun.

"Would you like to play?" one of the boys asked.

Would he ever! Banza hardly noticed when the nice people who brought him left, but it was OK. He knew now that they worked for ADRA, and that ADRA ran this place. He waved at them, knowing he would see them again. Until he did, he would learn to play games and eat food that he didn't have to steal. And maybe, just maybe, he'd learn something at school.

Banza's long journey was over. He had a good place to stay and many new friends. Because of his obedience to God, and ADRA's good work, there would be one less thief in the marketplace.

- How was Banza rewarded for obeying God's commandment not to steal? Does God always reward us for doing good? Are all our rewards for obeying God given to us on earth?

- The next time you see someone doing a good job or resisting temptation, encourage him or her with a smile or a kind word.

"Cootie"

The Lord does not look at the things man looks at. Man looks at the outward appearance, but the Lord looks at the heart. 1 Samuel 16:7, NIV.

The bus I was riding creaked slowly to a stop. One girl got up and staggered down the aisle to get off. We had just moved to Highgate Springs, and I didn't know the girl or anything about her. As soon as she stood up, everyone on the bus started chanting, "Cootie! Cootie! Cootie!"

Not knowing what a "cootie" was, I guessed it was her name and figured she must be pretty popular. I cheerfully joined in the chant. Before the girl covered her face with a book, I could see that she was crying. She ran off the bus and into her house without looking back.

Mr. Bard, the bus driver, completely stopped the bus and stood up to face everyone. He was mad. "Stop it!" he yelled. "You leave her alone. And you—" he said, looking right at me. "I can't believe you'd do such a thing."

I shrank down in my seat. Mr. Bard had always been nice to me before, and it wasn't hard to tell I'd done something very wrong. I knew immediately what it was when my mother told me that "cootie" was a slang word for lice. The kids on the bus hadn't been calling the girl's name at all.

They didn't know Alayna, but they had decided that they didn't like her because of how she looked. They thought she was a loser. My sister Faith and I became friends with Alayna. We got to know the Alayna that the kids on the bus never saw because they judged her by how she looked instead of the person she was inside. They were the real losers.

😊 **Is there anyone you just *know* you don't like, even though you really don't *know* them? Why do you decide whether or not you like someone before you even get to know them?**

😊 **Choose someone in your class you don't know well and make an effort to get to know him or her.**

Smoke Jumpers

For waging war you need guidance, and for victory many advisors. Proverbs 24:6, NIV.

Have you ever wondered what happens when a fire starts where there are no roads, no fire hydrants, and no fire trucks? The answer is smoke jumpers.

Smoke jumpers are people who parachute into remote mountain wilderness areas to fight fires. Their mission is to prevent small fires from becoming big fires. They've been doing this since 1940.

Smoke jumpers land very close to a fire. They have to jump wearing all their gear, which weighs about 85 pounds. Using natural obstacles, such as rivers, creeks, lakes, and logging roads, they try to contain the fire. Sometimes they must dig a fire line, a dirt path several feet wide, through the vegetation.

They try to get the fire to burn out before it reaches the treetops. Once the treetops start burning, there is no way to put the fire out from the ground. Then a plane, which can drop fire retardant, must be called in to help.

Fighting a fire in the wilderness is a hard and dangerous job. Smoke jumpers have to be very brave, because a lot depends on them. They spend many hours in training to learn the skills they need to survive while fighting fires in the wilderness.

Satan sometimes starts a fire somewhere inside you that is hard to reach. Maybe it's something you don't really want to talk to your parents or pastor about. But if you try to fight the fire all by yourself it might reach the treetops and really take off. It takes courage, but call in the smoke jumpers right away while it's still a little fire.

- **What do you think would be a "fire" that Satan could start in your life? Why do you consider this a fire?**

- **Sometimes our problems start out looking little, and we think we can handle them by ourselves. When they get out of control, we're often afraid to ask for help. The next time you're facing a problem, ask for help right away and put out the fire.**

On Your Mark!

Do you not know that in a race all the runners run, but only one gets the prize? Run in such a way as to get the prize. 1 Corinthians 9:24, NIV.

On your mark! Get set!"
Your feet are positioned just right on the blocks. Your fingers are touching the ground, and your behind is sticking up high in the air. Then you raise your head and look down the 100-meter track. It's a difficult position to be in, but to win it's what you have to do.

The first step toward winning is actually quite simple: you have to *want* to win. Then comes the hard part: you have to *train.* Some people train for years and years. A few of those people even make it to the Olympics. And a very, very few of those who go to the Olympics win a medal.

In 1996 Tony put his feet on the blocks, raised his behind in the air, and cocked his head to focus on the track. Tony was racing in the Paralympics. He had been born without hands or feet, so he was wearing special prostheses. Less than a month before, Canada's Donovan Bailey had broken the world record and captured a gold medal by running the 100-meter dash in 9.84 seconds.

Tony also won his race. What's even more amazing is that it took him only about one and a half seconds longer than Donovan Bailey, the world's fastest man.

Are you so fast that you win every race you enter? Or are you so slow you come in last every time you run? Maybe, like me, you win some and lose some. Did you know there is a finish line we can all choose to cross and be winners? All we have to do is *want* to cross it. That's the first step toward becoming a winner.

- Jesus wants each one of us to choose to love Him and to be with Him in heaven. Why do you think He wants us there?

- Sometimes it's hard to stay focused on winning. Many people hang pictures of their favorite athletes on their walls to keep them inspired while they're training. To help remind yourself of your desire to go to heaven, try hanging up a picture of Jesus where you can see it often.

A Book and Its Cover

The court was seated, and the books were opened. Daniel 7:10, NIV.

ave you ever heard the expression "Don't judge a book by its cover"? It means that you can't tell what a book is about, or if you're going to like it, just by looking at the cover. You actually have to open the book up and read what's inside to know that.

There was a well-known journalist who wrote two books. One day two big boxes arrived at her house filled with her new books, hot off the press. Excitedly she tore the boxes open. In one box was a book about holiday romance . . . *but on the cover was a picture of the state capitol building in Boise!* In the other box was her book about political intrigue . . . *but on the cover was a picture of a happy couple in Hawaii!* Somehow the publishing house had mixed up the covers of the books.

My friend Robin and I had to read the same book for a book report in English. I put off reading it because it looked boring. A week later I asked Robin if she had started reading the book yet.

"Oh, yes," she said. "And it's so good!"

"It is?" I couldn't believe it. I started reading the book myself. And it was so good that to this day it is one of my favorite stories.

Whatever book you are going to read, whether it is a textbook, the Bible, a book for a report, or something just for fun, you can't tell what is inside until you read it. If you judge the book by what is on the outside, you may never find the treasure inside the pages. Some of the books with the plainest covers (like the Bible) hold the greatest treasures.

When you pick up a book, what is the first thing you notice? How are books and their covers like people?

Ask your parents to choose a book for you. Then ask them to put a book cover on it so that you can't see what it is until you've read it. How did that affect what you thought of the book before you started reading?

Did Too! Did Not!

I appeal to you, brothers, in the name of our Lord Jesus Christ, that all of you agree with one another so that there may be no divisions among you and that you may be perfectly united in mind and thought. 1 Corinthians 1:10, NIV.

"Sam, what did you do with Albert's manual?" Dillon asked as he pulled books and papers off the shelf in the clubhouse. Pretty soon he had a large, messy pile on the floor.

Getting no answer, Dillon turned to see Sam slumped in a chair with her nose in a book. *"Sam!"* he shouted again, loudly.

Sam looked up irritably. "What? I'm trying to read."

"Well, *excuuuuuse* me!" Dillon sneered. "I need Albert's manual. Where did you put it?"

"I didn't put it anywhere," Sam replied, bristling at Dillon's tone.

"Did too!" Dillon insisted, his voice getting louder and louder.

"Did not!" Sam shrieked, jumping to her feet so that they stood toe-to-toe, nose-to-nose, eyes glaring, nostrils flaring.

"You guys sound just like little kids," Zeb observed as he pushed through the door of the clubhouse and saw them. "What's the problem?"

"She took my computer manual," Dillon complained.

"He's being a jerk," Sam said at the same time.

"I've got the computer manual," Zeb said. "Remember? I took it home last night to look at it." He handed it to Dillon, who suddenly looked embarrassed.

"I'm sorry, Sam," Dillon said sincerely. "Will you forgive me?"

Sam nodded. "I'm sorry too. I shouldn't have gotten upset. Will you forgive me?"

Dillon nodded happily.

"Good," said Zeb. "Now will someone explain to me what a byte is?"

> **What is the best thing to do after you have had a fight with someone? Who should say "I'm sorry" first?**

> **It takes two people to fight. The next time you're one of the two, swallow your pride and be the first one to apologize for your part in the fight.**

Who Is Your Enemy?

Be self-controlled and alert. Your enemy the devil prowls around like a roaring lion looking for someone to devour. 1 Peter 5:8, NIV.

During the Texas Revolution, the Karankawa Indians, who lived in southern Texas and northern Mexico, virtually ceased to exist. Their final fate was because the Karankawas could not seem to do anything right.

The Karankawas had made friends with a Texas rancher named Captain Dimmit, who always treated them kindly and offered them beef whenever they came around. But when the Texas Revolution began, Dimmit went to fight for Texas against Mexico, leaving his ranch deserted. When the Karankawas came by again, they rounded up a few cattle for themselves as they had always done. They knew nothing about the revolution.

Suddenly a party of Mexican soldiers rode up. "What are you doing?" they demanded.

"It's all right," the Indians replied innocently. "We are Captain Dimmit's friends."

At this, the Mexican soldiers charged the Karankawas, killing many of them.

The Indians who managed to escape were badly shaken, having no idea what had caused the Mexican soldiers to attack them. Suddenly they met a party of American soldiers. Fearing they would be attacked again, the Karankawas decided to play it safe and shouted, "Viva Mexico!"

Hearing this, the Americans promptly attacked. The Karankawa Indian tribe had come to a sad end because they didn't know who their enemies were. A war is being waged between God and Satan. Do you know who your enemy is?

- **How are we sometimes like the Karankawa Indians? Why is it good to know who our enemies are? How can people we think are friends turn out to be our enemies?**

- **Draw a line down the center of a piece of paper. Put *God* at the top of the first column, and *Satan* at the top of the second column. List the reasons God is your friend. List the reasons Satan is your enemy.**

The Key to a Fortune

Jesus answered, "It is written: 'Man does not live on bread alone, but on every word that comes from the mouth of God.'" Matthew 4:4, NIV.

I n 1853 Jay Gould's grandfather gave the 17-year-old boy the right to make money on an invention of his. Jay was certain he would make a fortune from it and set out for New York to sell the idea.

Jay carried the invention with him in a beautiful mahogany case. Unfortunately, as he was riding the Sixth Avenue trolley, someone stole the case. The conductor told Jay that a man had picked up the case and gotten off at the last stop. Jay jumped off in a mad rush to get back to where the thief had departed the trolley. When he caught up with the thief, he wrestled the man to the ground.

Of course, by now it looked to everyone else as though Jay was the one who was trying to steal the case. When a police officer arrived on the scene, Jay tried to explain that the case was his in the first place. But it was no use. Jay and the thief were escorted to the station to sort it all out.

The issue was finally decided when Jay was the only one who could accurately describe the contents of the case. The thief was dumbfounded to learn that the only thing inside the beautiful case was a crude mouse trap. The contents were of no value to him. But the contents were valuable to Jay, because he later made a profit from his grandfather's invention.

This story reminds me of a Bible that lies on the shelf and never gets read. The words remain locked between its beautiful covers, because no one takes it down and opens it. Are you like the thief who didn't know what was inside the case? Or are you like Jay? Do you know the value of what is inside?

🙂 **Where is your Bible? When was the last time you looked inside your Bible?**

🙂 **If it is not a habit already, make looking up your Sabbath school lesson texts part of your daily lesson study.**

APRIL

Judge and Jury

So we should stop judging each other. Romans 14:13, EB.

Samantha Reese chewed on the end of one long strand of hair as she watched her friend Zeb Dalton running for all he was worth around the track. He was the fourth leg on their four-man relay. But he was in second place and couldn't seem to gain any ground.

Legs pumping, arms swinging, Zeb rounded the corner. His face was screwed up into a grimace of concentration and flushed as red as Sam's T-shirt. Slowly, ever so slowly, he began to gain on the person ahead of him—Baxter Birney. Baxter sneaked a quick look over his shoulder. When he realized that Zeb was getting closer, he spurted ahead, but it wasn't enough. Zeb drew closer and closer.

Just as Zeb was about to pass, Baxter ducked to the side, driving his shoulder into Zeb's side, sending him staggering off the track. Resuming his speed, Baxter flew over the finish line, the winner.

Zeb picked himself up and examined his scraped knee. Sam ran toward Zeb as he limped back onto the track. "Did you see what he did to me?" he cried angrily. "He did that on purpose!"

"Well, you don't know that," Sam said slowly. She was pretty sure herself that Baxter had done it on purpose, but she reminded herself to give him the benefit of the doubt.

"I do too know it," Zeb sputtered. "And I have the skinned knee to prove it."

Baxter jogged up with a smile. "Sorry about that little stumble at the end," he said. "I tripped. I told the coach you probably would have beat me if I hadn't run into you. So here." He handed Zeb the blue ribbon. "This is really yours."

Zeb gulped. "Uh, ah . . . thanks," he mumbled.

Why is it important for us not to judge other people? Can we ever be sure of what's in their heart?

The next time you are tempted to judge someone, give them the benefit of the doubt instead of jumping to conclusions.

Special on and off the Field

Let us fix our eyes on Jesus, the author and perfecter of our faith. Hebrews 12:2, NIV.

Michael Ptaschnik had already opened his presents. One of them was a Curtis Martin jersey. His ninth birthday party was almost over, and there was still no sign of one of the invited guests. New England Patriots rookie Curtis Martin had been handed an invitation in the Foxboro Stadium parking lot about 10 days before the party. If Michael had known Curtis better, he wouldn't have been worried.

"I wasn't sure if he was going to come," Michael said.

But Curtis did come. And he created quite a stir. He patiently signed autographs and even signed Michael's birthday present, the Patriots jersey with Martin's number 28 on it.

"I know how important that is," Curtis said. "If someone had done that for me when I was younger, I know what an influence it would have had. He was just amazed when I came in."

"He's such a nice guy; such an unassuming fellow," Michael's father said. "He came, he stayed, he talked, he chatted. He was like part of the family. He showed no indication of any rush—was just a true gentleman. Michael will remember this always."

Curtis has performed some awesome feats on the field, but his success hasn't gone to his head. He sees challenges in life as opportunities, not obstacles. "It's just working hard, a lot of prayers, that's all," he says.

Michael wrote Curtis a letter. "You know, Curtis, you're great on the field, but you're even greater off the field."

Finding good role models is not easy. And we have to be sure that we don't look up to our role models too much, since they are only human and can make mistakes. But there is one role model who will never let us down. Jesus. He is our ultimate role model.

🙂 **Why are role models important? Why should we be careful in choosing a role model?**

🙂 **Make a list of the qualities you most admire about your role models. How many of them are qualities Jesus has?**

Hoppin' Mad

In your anger do not sin. Do not let the sun go down while you are still angry. Ephesians 4:26, NIV.

I was new in school and probably a good target. Ellie wasn't exactly popular either. The two of us were drawing cartoons in the sand of the playground with a stick when Todd sauntered up with a smug look on his face. With one swipe of his foot he erased all our work.

Ellie and I stared at each other in horror for a second before I lost it. Leaping to my feet, I clenched my hands into fists and reminded myself that although I knew karate, I wasn't supposed to use it unless my life was being threatened. I didn't think this qualified, but I was so angry I had to do something.

I brought the heel of my shoe down as hard as I could on Todd's foot. I think it surprised him. And although he limped for the rest of the day and never again bothered us directly, I had made a permanent enemy.

Anger is one emotion that can get us into a lot of trouble if we let it. When we get angry, we either turn it outward, like I did with Todd, or turn it inward and bury it. The anger smolders there and can even make us sick if we don't get rid of it.

God knows that we are going to get angry, and He doesn't want our anger to cause us to sin. He wants us to deal with it right away. When we do, it will disappear.

First, ask yourself why you are angry. When you know why, deal with it. In my case, I could have asked Todd to leave us alone. Then if he didn't, I could have told a teacher. Had I done that, we might have become friends.

😊 **What makes you angry? Why?**

😊 **The next time you get angry, count to 10, and then find out why you are angry. Ask Jesus to show you how to deal with your anger so that it won't cause you to sin.**

Determination

So I say to you: Ask and it will be given to you; seek and you will find; knock and the door will be opened to you. For everyone who asks receives; he who seeks finds; and to him who knocks, the door will be opened. Luke 11:9, 10, NIV.

He couldn't read very well. He didn't know most of the words he was looking at. He couldn't write very well. He considered his handwriting to be atrocious. Most people might have decided that it wasn't worth the effort to try to change. Yet this man thought differently. He wanted to know what the words that he couldn't understand meant. He wanted to comprehend what he was reading.

So while he was in Charlestown Prison, he requested a dictionary, pencils, and a tablet to write on. The dictionary amazed him. It might have even scared him a little, too, and he spent the first few days after receiving it just thumbing through its pages, wondering where he should start.

But he started. He started at the very beginning and began copying. He copied the first page. He said it took him all day to do that. Then he read everything he had written several times. The next day he copied the next page. He learned about places and things. He taught himself words he had never even known existed. He eventually copied the whole dictionary.

What Malcolm X received from his will to study and learn was freedom. He was motivated to learn because when he looked at his world, he saw there were things he couldn't do simply because there was so much he didn't understand. It seems simple, but so many people never realize how much they are missing because they don't make an effort to study. Jesus says to ask, look, and knock. In other words, go for it!

🙂 **When was the last time you read a word for which you didn't know the meaning? Did you look it up, or try to figure out what it meant?**

🙂 **The next time you discover a new word, look it up. Make it a habit.**

Too Young to Save Lives?

They began shouting praise to God for all the powerful works they had seen. They said, "God bless the king who comes in the name of the Lord! There is peace in heaven and glory to God!" Some of the Pharisees said to Jesus, "Teacher, tell your followers not to say these things!" But Jesus answered, "I tell you, if my followers don't say these things, then the stones will cry out." Luke 19:37-40, EB.

If you live in Darien, Connecticut, you rely on teenagers to save your life. For 25 years Explorer Post 53, a division of the Boy Scouts of America, has had total responsibility for the town's ambulance service. Sixty teenage volunteers provide 24-hour emergency medical service. They're pretty busy, too, answering more than 1,000 emergency calls every year.

When the volunteers turn 14, they are given extensive first-aid training and are supervised by adult volunteers and paramedics, who do the tough medical procedures and give the medications. The teens train to be radio dispatchers, emergency medical technicians (EMTs), drivers, and crew chiefs.

The people in the town of Darien count on teenagers to help them in an emergency. In the same way, the people of your town and school rely on you to save them.

"But I don't have any medical training," you say.

Maybe not, but you have something even more important. You have training in eternal lifesaving skills. You know Jesus in a way that many people don't. You can help them to know Jesus too. You can answer their questions and rescue them from the disease of sin by bringing them to the Great Physician.

Won't you join God's volunteer lifesaving rescue squad now?

What does witnessing mean to you? When do you feel like you're witnessing? What kinds of witnessing are there? How is witnessing like being a volunteer in a rescue squad?

Ask your pastor about getting some information on friendship evangelism. Maybe he or she will teach a class especially geared for you and your friends.

103

Look Up!

When I look up into the night skies and see the work of your fingers—the moon and the stars you have made—I cannot understand how you can bother with mere puny man, to pay any attention to him! Psalm 8:3, 4, TLB.

Have you ever stood outside and gazed up at the stars in the heavens and thought, *Wow! I'm so insignificant. Does God even know I'm down here?* In the first place, it's hard to feel good about ourselves when we feel as tiny as dust mites, tucked away on a small planet that has been home to billions of other people. But then to look up and see the moon and stars just as David did so long ago—*wow!* We find ourselves getting smaller by the second!

One way to ruin our self-image is to think that God has forgotten all about us, especially when we look at the stars and think about all the wonderful, amazing things that God has created. How could He bother with you or me when He has so much else to take care of?

However, David looked at things from a different angle. He had worked on building a relationship with God that helped him see that God really did know him and love him. David looked at the stars in wonder because, in the first place, it was so amazing to him that God had made such an awesome universe. But there was something even more amazing to David: God gave it all to us to take care of! I think that blew David's mind, don't you?

I can see David lying on the grass and looking at the night sky. He's quit trying to count all the stars. Now he just lies there, staring. God gave everything He had created to humankind to be in charge of. Suddenly David shakes his head in wonder about a God who would think us so important.

🙂 **What causes people to have a low self-image? Do you know anyone who thinks God has forgotten all about them?**

🙂 **We absorb whatever messages we hear about ourselves, whether they're good or bad. Try reminding yourself of the good things about yourself. You are valuable in God's eyes.**

The King's Visit, Part 1

For it is by grace you have been saved, through faith—and this is not from yourselves, it is the gift of God—not by works, so that no one can boast. Ephesians 2:8, 9, NIV.

There once was a small town called Nominal, nestled in the grassy slope at the end of the winding road that led up to the king's palace. One day a messenger ran breathlessly down the long road from the palace shouting, "The king is coming! The king is coming!" Right away he drew a crowd of people.

"When is the king coming?" people wanted to know.

"The king *can't* come now!" one good woman shrieked. "My wash is hung out on the line and won't be dry for hours!"

"I am in the middle of constructing my house," a man wailed. "I can never be finished before the king comes!"

"If the king is coming, I have to learn a new song on my mandolin so that I can play him something to amuse him," a boy added.

"And I must iron my very best clothes so that I can impress His Majesty with my beauty," a young lady simpered.

The noise increased as the people clamored about what they had to do before they could accept the king's visit. They urged the messenger to tell them when the king would arrive so that they could be ready.

"I'm sorry," the messenger said. "I only know that he is coming. I do not know when."

Quickly the crowd raced back to their homes to make ready for the arrival of the king. Soon the only people left standing in the town square were the messenger and a little girl. As he sat down on a park bench to catch his breath, the messenger looked curiously at the little girl.

🙂 **What do you think of the townspeople's idea about preparing for the king's visit?**

🙂 **Use your imagination. Pretend that Jesus, the King, is coming to visit you. What would you talk about? What would you do?**

The King's Visit, Part 2

The Lord would speak to Moses face to face, as a man speaks with his friend. Exodus 33:11, NIV.

on't you have something to do before the king can come and see you?" the messenger asked.

"The best thing I can do to get ready for the king's visit is to wait here to welcome him," the girl replied.

And so it was that only one child was there to greet the king when he arrived, dressed in a simple cloak and riding an average-looking brown horse. No one paused to give him a second glance.

"Welcome to Nominal, Your Majesty," the little girl said, taking the reins of his horse and directing him to the bench in the park where the messenger had so recently rested.

"What's going on here?" the king asked gruffly, peering at the little girl from beneath bushy eyebrows.

"The people are all preparing for your visit, sir," she replied. "They had unfinished business that needed to be taken care of before you came."

"Harumph," the king grunted thoughtfully. "What about you? Why aren't you preparing for my visit? Do you think you are better than all these other townspeople?"

"Oh, no, sir!" the little girl cried. "But I have nothing that would make me worthy of your visit. Instead, I thought to wait here for your arrival and greet you so that I could spend some time with you during your visit."

"Well, young lady, I am very glad that you did, because I wanted to spend time with my subjects."

The little girl talked freely and found herself enjoying the king's visit very much. By the time he left, the king was laughing and smiling. He thanked her kindly for spending time with him before he climbed back onto his horse and headed up the road to the palace.

Do you ever miss spending time with Jesus because you are too busy doing things *for* Him? Which do you think He would rather that you do?

Set some time aside today to spend with the King, telling Him about yourself and what you've been up to lately.

Extraordinary Faith

Again the Israelites did evil in the eyes of the Lord, and for seven years he gave them into the hands of the Midianites. Judges 6:1, NIV.

The Israelites had gotten themselves into a jam. Because they weren't obeying the Lord, He allowed the Midianites to take over their land and crops. There were so many Midianites that it was impossible to count the men and their camels. They invaded the land and ravaged it. The people of Israel were hurting, and they wanted God to help them out.

So the angel of the Lord came to Gideon. "The Lord is with you, mighty warrior," the angel said.

That probably came as a pretty big shock to Gideon, who was hiding out in a winepress, threshing wheat, so the Midianites wouldn't find him and take it. Normally wheat was threshed out in the open on a hard, smooth place. So I don't think he felt much like a mighty warrior.

He probably raised a doubtful eyebrow. The Lord must be mistaken. "But Lord," he protested, "how can I save Israel? My clan is the weakest in Manasseh, and I am the least in my family" (Judges 6:15, NIV).

How many times have you thought you were the weakest, the least popular, or the least intelligent? Gideon certainly thought he was the least of all of those. But God doesn't choose people because they are the strongest, the quickest, the prettiest, or the most popular people. He knows that people who will do His work most faithfully are those who love Him and trust Him.

Gideon's faith in God grew into extraordinary faith the night he instructed his small force of men to surround the Midianite camp. When God first called Gideon to save the Israelites from Midian, Gideon had been doubtful. However, he obeyed the Lord, and during his lifetime Israel enjoyed peace for 40 years.

What qualities did Gideon have that God liked? What kinds of people does God look for to do His work?

Think about what qualities made Gideon someone God could use. Try to make those same qualities part of your life today.

107

Pulling a Fast One

The Lord said to Gideon, "With the three hundred men that lapped I will save you and give the Midianites into your hands." Judges 7:7, NIV.

Pirate Hippolyte de Bouchard was furious. Not only had three of his men been captured by Mexican soldiers and taken to the presidio (military post) at Santa Barbara, but the residents had removed their food and livestock because they knew he was coming.

In a foul mood, Bouchard left to replenish his supplies elsewhere. Three days later he returned to Santa Barbara Bay to get his men back. As Bouchard's three ships lay anchored offshore, he observed several columns of men marching at the presidio.

Bouchard calculated his chances if he were to attack the presidio. He decided he would be wiser to strike a deal for the release of his men rather than risk an attack against such a force. In exchange for his three men, he offered a hapless Mexican whom he and his pirates had captured sometime earlier. The commander of the presidio accepted Bouchard's terms under the condition that Bouchard leave Santa Barbara without causing trouble.

Bouchard agreed. But had he known the true strength of the presidio, he would surely have attacked. The force at the presidio was barely 50 men—not nearly enough to defend the presidio against Bouchard's 285 fierce pirates! Thinking quickly, the commander had ordered his men to change the appearance of their clothing every time they marched behind a dense thicket on the beach. The small force of men marched and marched. To Bouchard, who looked on from his ship, it appeared as though there were hundreds of men guarding the presidio.

Have you ever felt outnumbered because you were a Christian? Have you ever felt alone or small or insignificant and wondered *What's the use?* Gideon and his men surely felt that way. I'm sure the commander of the presidio and his 50 men felt outnumbered, too. But God is far wiser, more powerful, and more intelligent than the devil and his advocates.

🙂 **How is this story like the story of Gideon?**

🙂 **Check out Gideon's whole story in Judges 7.**

Top Priority

A wise man thinks ahead; a fool doesn't and even brags about it!
Proverbs 13:16, TLB.

What is your highest priority? TV? Video games? Playing football or roller hockey with your friends? What about studying? Is studying your highest priority? I think you will find that studying ranks pretty high. Although watching your favorite television program may be enjoyable, as far as being very important, you might say, "No, TV isn't where it's at for me."

Football, baseball, soccer, leisure reading—they are all enjoyable activities too. But they're not as important as studying. After careful thought, studying school assignments and your Sabbath school lesson ranks pretty high. If studying ranks the highest in your list of priorities, then you are like most students who have wisely thought about what is most important to them.

Then why is it so easy to become sidetracked, even when we know what we should be doing? Often the most important things are the most time-consuming and difficult, so we trade them off for activities that are easier and have immediate rewards. It might not matter much at the time, but think about what happens down the road.

By making studying your highest priority, you are planning for the future. You are making high school easier and more fun. You are building a solid foundation for college. As you study your schoolwork and your Sabbath school lesson, you are making yourself like the wise person who thinks ahead.

- 😊 **How far ahead have you started planning for your future? Do you know what you would like to do as an occupation? How do you plan to accomplish your goals?**

- 😊 **Make a list of the things that are important to you to do today. What is most important? What is least important? Try this: Number the things you have to do in order of their importance. Then begin at number one and do that. When you finish number one, then move to number two. This way you will know you are doing the most important thing.**

109

Attitude Adjustment

Jesus answered, "If you want to be perfect, go, sell your possessions and give to the poor, and you will have treasure in heaven. Then come, follow me." Matthew 19:21, NIV.

Francis undoubtedly gave the local law enforcement people in his hometown a run for their money. He was known as a ruffian and the local youth gang leader. His father was rich, so he had no financial worries. He didn't have much education, either. He spent his time satisfying his interest in what the world had to offer, not caring much for anything besides himself.

Then something happened to Francis's rotten attitude—it actually became more rotten. He ended up in prison for a year, and then became very sick. And his attitude began to change.

Francis got tired of thinking only about himself. He became depressed about his life full of riches and finally turned to God. Like the rich young ruler in Jesus' story, Francis gave up all his worldly possessions and decided to spend his life helping the poor and following Jesus.

He spent the rest of his life doing his best to follow Jesus' way of life and obey His words. Many others began to follow Francis's example of servitude and formed an order called the Franciscans. At one time in history there were as many as 100,000 Franciscan friars. Even today, the Franciscans continue to care for the poor and do missionary work. What a remarkable turnaround for the local town ruffian!

I believe Francis of Assisi helped the poor because he loved Jesus, and it made him happy to be of service to others. He had discovered that his selfish lifestyle had only let him down. Selfishness is a vicious cycle: the more things we have, the more we want. It never stops. That empty place in our hearts can be filled only with Jesus and His love. Once Francis found that out, his life became much more rewarding.

🙂 **How does following Jesus make your life rewarding? Why does helping others always make us feel good?**

🙂 **Do a good deed today without getting found out.**

"Shut Up and Let Your Sister Sing"

I will sing to the Lord, for he is highly exalted. Exodus 15:1, NIV.

I love to sing. But for years I sang solo—so low no one could hear me. It wasn't always that way. When I was growing up, I sang real loud. I liked the way my voice sounded. My mother and sister Faith were always getting complimented on their singing. It did occur to me to wonder why no one ever complimented me, but I didn't think about it much.

Then one day Faith and I were singing a song for someone and they told me to shut up and let Faith sing it alone. I was crushed! And I wondered *Was my voice really bad?* Then I felt awful, remembering all the times I had sung at the top of my lungs because I loved singing so much.

I didn't want anyone to know how bad my voice really was, but I still liked being in the church choir and singing with the juniors in my class. So I joined large singing groups in which no one would notice my voice, if I sang quietly.

As I got older, people were always asking me why I sang so softly. "We can barely hear you," they'd complain.

I wanted to tell them to consider themselves lucky, but instead I just mumbled something about my voice being small.

And then I became friends with someone who heard me sing something and liked my voice. Unbelievable! Someone actually *liked* my voice. Impossible! So I tried singing a little louder, and no one dropped dead or anything.

I'm not Amy Grant, of course, but I don't sound too bad. And I don't think God cares as much how my voice sounds as what I do with it. And you know something else? Because of my friend's encouragement, I'm not afraid to sing loud anymore. Even alone.

- **Is there something you feel you don't do well? Why do you feel that way? Do you want to improve in that area? What are some ways you can do that?**

- **Tell someone today how much you appreciate one of his or her talents.**

111

Red Corvette

And yet you have made him only a little lower than the angels, and placed a crown of glory and honor upon his head. You have put him in charge of everything you made; everything is put under his authority. Psalm 8:5, 6, TLB.

A car rolls into the driveway. Dad has been gone for two hours, and you've been wondering what's up. Something's been in the air around home, but you seem to be the only one unaware of the secret Mom and Dad have been keeping.

You look out the window. What you see is the very back portion of a car in the driveway. A red car. The side of the garage blocks most of your view, so you open the front door and go outside.

"Hi," Dad says.

Your mouth hangs open. You try to speak, but what can you say? Sitting in your driveway is the most beautiful car! A Corvette. The style you've always dreamed of. "Wha—Why—" you stutter.

"Your mom and I want you to have this for your first car," Dad says. "We worked hard to save for it. We want you to enjoy it, first of all, and second of all, to take care of it."

No way! Not a chance this would ever happen! You pinch yourself, because you are obviously dreaming. It's too much! What parents would ever give their kid a brand-new, totally perfect Corvette when he or she starts driving? The whole idea is *preposterous!*

And then it's not so preposterous when you think about what God has given you and me. You know how awesome it would feel to be handed a Corvette? Well, that's the same feeling David had when he looked at the heavens and saw all that God had made and was amazed that God would put human beings in charge of everything He had made.

What does it mean to be put in charge of all that God has made?

Part of the responsibility of being in charge of what God has made is to be responsible for your environment. Is there litter in your neighborhood? If there is, grab a trash bag and take a walk through your neighborhood one evening this week. And invite your parents along.

Spread Too Thin

To this end I labor, struggling with all his energy, which so
powerfully works in me. Colossians 1:29, NIV.

Sam burst into the clubhouse to find Dillon immersed in a
writing project, a dictionary at his elbow, a stack of papers
on the desk beside him, and a small pile of them wadded
up on the floor.

"I guess you're pretty busy," Sam observed.

Dillon looked up with a wild expression, as if he'd just become aware of her presence. "Oh, Sam, I don't know what to do!"
he wailed. "I have to finish this article for the church newsletter
by this afternoon. But I have band practice in an hour, and there's
a hockey game after lunch."

"Wow, I guess you *are* busy."

"That's not everything!" Dillon cried. "Then I have my schoolwork, and there's a Pathfinder meeting tonight. And I promised
my mother I'd mow the lawn today and told my dad I'd take my
little cousin, Jeff, to the library."

Sam shook her finger at Dillon. "You've got too much to do,"
she said.

"I know, I know," Dillon groaned. "But I just can't say no. I
mean, they're all good things, so God will help me do them all.
Right?"

Sam shrugged. "Dillon, God wants us to do good things, but
He doesn't want us to kill ourselves doing them. We've got to
have a balance. If you spread yourself too thin you could get sick.
You really need to decide which things you really want or need
to do and do those first. If you've got extra time, then take on
some extra things."

Sam tidied up the clubhouse while she talked. "Here," she
said, picking up a piece of paper. "Let's list all the things you
want to do and figure out which ones can be left out."

🙂 **What does your schedule look like? Have you ever done
so much for God that you forgot to spend time with Him?**

🙂 **Evaluate your activities. Are there any that can be
dropped to make more time for other things?**

Boy, Was His Face Red!

Abraham fell facedown; he laughed and said to himself, "Will a son be born to a man a hundred years old? Will Sarah bear a child at the age of ninety?" Genesis 17:17, NIV.

Have you ever had something really embarrassing happen to you? Christian comedian Ken Davis tells the story about a time he and his family were in church. His wife was irritated with him for some reason, and he had slipped out of the pew for a few moments. When he returned, he wanted to make everything right between them, so he put his arm around her and gave her a loving squeeze.

His wife stiffened. A little put off because she was being so stubborn about the issue, Ken looked over to say something to his wife, then noticed *he had his arm around another woman!* His wife was in the seat behind him, trying not to laugh! Boy, was his face red!

Abraham had an embarrassing moment too. God had been promising for years to make him the father of many nations. Now he was pretty old. He was 99. And his wife, Sarah, was way too old to have children.

When God told Abraham that Sarah would have a son, he laughed hysterically. God said the baby's name would be Isaac, which means "he laughs." Abraham thought that was a pretty good joke. However, God honored His promise, and Sarah did give birth to a son. Boy, was Abraham's face red!

When something goes wrong, we can either get mad or laugh about it. When it's something that makes us look bad, it can be even more tempting to get mad about it. By taking ourselves so seriously that we can't laugh when we do something foolish, we put ourselves in a mighty high position, because we all make mistakes sooner or later. But if we can laugh at ourselves when we mess up, we create a good environment in which to learn from our mistakes.

😊 **Why is it important to be able to laugh at ourselves? What circumstances make it hard to laugh at ourselves?**

😊 **The next time you find that you're taking yourself too seriously, throw back your head and laugh.**

114

The Lord Is My Shepherd?

The Lord is my shepherd, I shall not be in want. Psalm 23:1, NIV.

We don't want to be compared to sheep," a friend of mine complained one day in Sabbath school class. "Sheep are stupid! I heard a story once about a man who went to visit a shepherd, and he brought his little dog with him. The sheep were scared of the dog, and it wasn't even chasing them!"

"Yeah, and sheep are so helpless," someone else remarked. "If they lie down and their center of gravity shifts, they can't even get up!"

I don't think God compares us to sheep because they are dumb or helpless. I think it's to show the relationship between the shepherd and the sheep. Shepherds take very good care of their sheep. They go to the field ahead of them to pull out any poisonous plants; remove their heavy wool; water them at calm springs so that the running water won't saturate their wool and drag them under the water to drown.

And shepherds spend a lot of time with the sheep. They're with them all the time. They protect them from predators. They quiet them in a storm. They care for them.

Take a minute to read Psalm 23. And then read this little version of the same psalm, written by my friend Dave Foote.

The Lord is my jockey;
    I shall run fast.
He gives me hormones to build my muscles;
    He gives Lasix before a race to get rid of excess waters.
He guides me to the inner lanes, for His name's sake.
    He leads me past the roaring stands to excite my adrenaline.
Yea, though I break my leg, I will not fear.
    He will end my life painlessly with a bullet.
And I will dwell in the barn of my Lord
    Until my usefulness is gone.

😊 **What is the difference between the real Psalm 23 and the "psalm" that Dave Foote wrote? Which relationship would you rather have with God? Why?**

😊 **Write your own version of Psalm 23.**

Anyone for Hockey?

Wisdom, like an inheritance, is a good thing and benefits those who see the sun. Ecclesiastes 7:11, NIV.

ey, Sam! Want to play hockey?" Zeb called as he sped into Samantha Reese's driveway, made an exaggerated leap to clear the curb, spun around, and skated backward down the sidewalk in front of her house. He was wearing about 40 pounds of safety equipment: wrist braces, knee pads, elbow pads, helmet, face mask, and gloves.

Samantha paused on the front porch, a science book in her hand. She had just come outside for a breath of fresh air before going back to her room and studying for another half hour. "I'd like to go, Zeb," she said, "but I really need to study."

"You can study later," Zeb argued.

Sam thought about Zeb's suggestion. Then she smiled. "I can't skate right now, but I will later. I promised myself that I would study first, because it's the most important. Then I can do whatever I want to do later. Do you still want me to come and play later? I'll only be a half hour."

Zeb did a figure eight in the driveway. "Sure, Sam. No problem."

A half hour later, as Sam bladed up to where the hockey game was supposed to be, no one was skating on the asphalt. She found Zeb sitting in the grass in front of his house. "What's up?"

Zeb looked up from his Bible class textbook. "Oh, hi, Sam. I got to thinking about what you said—about studying being more important. I guess I think the same way, but it just seemed like too much work. Hockey sounded like a lot more fun."

"So why aren't you playing hockey?" Sam asked, raising an eyebrow.

"I will in a second. I'm almost finished reading," Zeb said, grinning. "The rest of the team thought it was a good idea too. They went home to study, but they'll be back any minute."

🙂 **Did Sam make a wise choice by studying first? What decision would you have made? Why?**

🙂 **Plan a schedule that helps you remember to make studying your most important activity.**

116

Know What You Are Talking About

Always be prepared to give an answer to everyone who asks you to give the reason for the hope that you have. 1 Peter 3:15, NIV.

Whenever a new soldier appeared among his guards, Frederick the Great would ask three questions: "How old are you? How long have you been in my service? Are you satisfied with your pay and treatment?"

One time a young French soldier decided to enlist. This particular soldier didn't know any German. However, his captain, realizing the young man would be questioned by Frederick the next day, drilled him on the three German answers he should give, in the exact order the king had always asked the questions.

Unfortunately, this time the king didn't ask his questions in their usual order. He began with the second question first. "How long have you been in my service?"

"Twenty-one years," said the soldier.

Finding this confusing, considering the young man's apparent youth, Frederick said, "How old are you?"

"One year, if it please Your Majesty," answered the soldier.

Frustrated at the soldier's baffling answers, Frederick shouted, "You or I must certainly be bereft of our senses [nuts]!"

This seemed the appropriate time for the young soldier to answer the third question about time and pay. With all sincerity he said, "Both, if it please Your Majesty."

Frederick thought the young soldier was trying to make a fool of him. Not until the young man explained in French that he did not understand a word of German was the mystery solved.

Knowing what we believe and telling it to someone else are two different things. Sometimes we get confused or nervous. Being able to explain all the doctrines of your church is not the most important thing. Being able to introduce the person asking the questions to your Best Friend, Jesus, is.

- **Has anyone ever asked you a question about what you believe? How did you answer them?**

- **Whenever someone asks you a question you don't have an answer for, offer to find out. Then be sure you do.**

Spectacular Spelunker

He lifted me out of the slimy pit, out of the mud and mire; he set my feet on a rock and gave me a firm place to stand. He put a new song in my mouth, a hymn of praise to our God. Psalm 40:2, 3, NIV.

Have you ever been in a cave or a pit? I'm talking a *big* pit—one as deep as a 40-story building is high. Can you imagine going into one? Leah Brown can. Although she is only 12 years old, Leah is so experienced at climbing that she helped to save a stranded spelunker. She's also broken five world records for speed, and she holds the woman's world record for the 120-meter climb.

Spelunking (spee-LUNK-ing) is another name for exploring caves. Spelunkers sometimes wear harnesses attached to ropes secured at the top of the cave and lower themselves down into it. They pull themselves back out by the rope.

Maybe you've never lowered yourself by a rope into a cave to explore it, but you've probably fallen into a few pits in life. There are pits all over the place. There are pits called greed, selfishness, vanity, despair, laziness, hopelessness, and lots more. Sometimes you don't fall very far; maybe you land on a ledge and a friend or parent helps you out. But sometimes you fall into a pit and no one can help you out but God.

What do you do?

When soldiers bury land mines in a field, they make a map to show where the mines are buried so that they can get through the field safely if they need to. It's the same way with the pits Satan has dug. We can't see them, but God knows where they are, and He's given us the Bible for a map. By reading the Bible we'll find out where they are and how to get around them safely. And if we fall into a pit God will pull us out with the strong rope of prayer and the harness of faith.

● **Which pits do you fall into? How do you get out?**

● **This week, try setting your alarm clock 15 minutes earlier and read the Bible before you go to school.**

An Opposite Reaction

But the wisdom that is from above is first pure, then peaceable, gentle, willing to yield, full of mercy and good fruits, without partiality and without hypocrisy. James 3:17, NKJV.

Newton's third law of motion says this: For every action, there is an equal and opposite reaction. When you take off in a passenger jet, the force that pushes you forward comes from the exhaust gas being expelled from the jet engine. In a turbojet engine, air is compressed as it enters the engine. Then the compressed air is mixed with fuel and ignited. The gases expelled from the engine give thrust, which pushes the aircraft forward.

Like a jet engine, when you speak angrily to someone your negative actions push them farther away from you. That may not seem like such a bad idea at the time. You may never want to see that person again, so the farther away they are, the better.

"But the wisdom that is from above is first pure, then peaceable, gentle, willing to yield, full of mercy and good fruits . . ." The wisdom from above is from God. It's a solid, proven theory. Just as there is an equal and opposite reaction that pushes people away with harsh words and hateful actions, Jesus' theory of gentleness and peace and mercy will draw people to us.

Jesus never turned anyone away with hateful words or actions. He never poked fun at anyone. He never picked fights with people who disagreed with him. Whenever He spoke, He spoke with love and kindness. He was always gentle and peaceable. People always wanted to be near Him. If we practice the same gentleness, people will want to be near us, too.

- What effect did Jesus' kind words have on people? What picture can you see in your mind's eye about the people Jesus came in contact with? Were they happy? Were they sad? Were they turned off by Jesus?

- If you know someone you don't get along with very well, try extra-kind words the next time you see him or her and see the change in your relationship.

Susanna Wesley: The Mother of a Faith

Whatever you do, whether in word or deed, do it all in the name of the Lord Jesus, giving thanks to God the Father through him. Colossians 3:17, NIV.

As a pioneer in the Christian faith, Susanna Wesley was never privileged with a life of relaxation, ease, and comfort under God's protective hand. In fact, it seems that Susanna had more than her fair share of hard work and personal tragedies to cope with. Susanna's husband, Samuel, could not seem to financially support his family. So at times their finances got so bad it was left to Susanna to find a way to provide food for their children. Worse still, Samuel was thrown in jail because he couldn't pay his debts. But by far, Susanna's worst tragedies were the loss of about half of her 19 children who died before adulthood. After all that, why would anyone want to go on?

Susanna was born January 20, 1669. Her father was a pastor who apparently passed on to his youngest daughter a deep interest in religion, for when other children were playing, Susanna spent her time thinking about religious matters. Throughout her life she believed that everything she did should be done to Christ's honor and glory. She not only believed that way, but she practiced her beliefs, too. She often prayed that whatever she did as she went about her daily life would be done as if she were in God's presence.

Susanna Wesley struggled on, in spite of hardship and sorrow when other people might have given up. Why did she decide to go on trusting in God? Susanna did more than obey God—she loved Him with all her heart and had faith that He was by her side even when she was enduring so many trials.

- **Have you ever thought about living as though Jesus were right there beside you? What kinds of changes would you make in your actions if you showed Jesus around your school today?**

- **As you go through the day, consider your actions and your thoughts. Do them as if Jesus were beside you. At the end of the day, ask yourself if you acted differently.**

Like a Rock

Let this encourage God's people to endure patiently every trial and persecution, for they are his saints who remain firm to the end in obedience to his commands and trust in Jesus. Revelation 14:12, TLB.

Though she suffered many personal tragedies, Susanna Wesley stood like a rock in her faith and continued to trust God. Even through the deaths of her children and the family's severe financial burdens, Susanna continued to grow spiritually and teach her children the love of God. Every evening she gathered her family together for family prayers. And on Sunday evenings she conducted services in her home.

Susanna was also a schoolteacher to her children. She taught them six hours a day for 20 years, and through her devotion and love of learning helped them develop a passion for education.

Yet, as busy as Susanna was in raising and teaching her children, she faithfully set aside two hours each day for private devotions during which she studied and prayed by herself. When troubles seemed to grow, she prayed harder and trusted in God more.

In a house as full of children as was Susanna's, privacy was sometimes hard to come by. When she wanted to be alone with God, Susanna would sit in a chair and put her apron over her head, letting the children know she was praying and giving herself a little privacy.

Twice the Wesleys' home burned, adding to Susanna's trials. The second time, however, the family lost everything they owned when their house burned completely to the ground. At one point it looked as though they might lose another child during the fire. Six-year-old John was trapped inside as the house became engulfed in flames. But during the last few seconds before the roof caved in, he managed to find his way to the window and was rescued.

🙂 **Why do you trust God? Why are you a Christian? Is the life of a Christian always easy?**

🙂 **Jesus wants to be with you every moment of every day, even when you're having a bad day. Remind yourself often today that Jesus loves you and stands beside you.**

The Seeds of a Faith

See that what you have heard from the beginning remains in you. If it does, you also will remain in the Son and in the Father. 1 John 2:24, NIV.

Inspired by his mother's love for God and her devotion in spiritual matters, John Wesley grew to hold fast the faith his mother had instilled in him through her Christlike example and the love for God that she taught and showed all her children. Later, as John grew into manhood, he taught and won souls to Christ.

John and his brother Charles visited with the poor, the sick, and those who were in prison. Their mother had had such a profound religious influence on them that they never wavered from their faith later in life. When John decided to go into the ministry, his mother encouraged him in his pursuit. He went on to become a great preacher and later founded the Methodist faith.

Charles was also becoming known. During his life he composed more than 4,500 hymns. Because of their adherence to the methods by which their mother practiced her faith and brought up her family, people began calling John and Charles "Methodists."

Susanna Wesley kept her faith, even through tremendous trouble. When things seemed to get worse instead of better, she prayed harder. She never gave up. She never stopped loving God. Through her guidance and teachings she planted the first seeds of a Christian faith that would later become the Methodist movement.

It's easy to believe in God when things are going good. But when life gets turned upside down and our faith in God is tested by hardship, just as Susanna Wesley was tested by the hardships she lived through, only knowing God keeps us from turning our backs on Him and giving in to Satan's pressure tactics.

What people are making a positive influence in your life? How are they a positive influence? What lessons do they teach? What kind of life do they live?

Do you see yourself living through the last days? Can you imagine the hardships you will have to endure? Take time to pray and study God's Word each day.

Math, Sunny Side Up!

I searched everywhere, determined to find wisdom and the reason for things. Ecclesiastes 7:25, TLB.

What is the sum of all the numbers between 1 and 100? How quickly do you think you can figure it out?

More than 200 years ago a teacher asked that same question of his students. He believed it would keep them busy for a very long time. However, one boy in the class, Karl Friedrich Gauss, came up with the answer in minutes. He would later become one of the greatest mathematicians in history.

Gauss could have approached the problem the way his classmates did—by simply using the conventional method for arriving at the answer. It would have taken a long time, just as the teacher expected. Instead, Gauss put the creative part of his mind to work along with the knowledge he already possessed about the rules of math.

He saw that if he took the two end numbers, one and 100, and counted equally forward from one and backward from 100, the sum would equal 101. For instance, if he counted to eight from one, and counted eight backward from 100, he would come up with 8 and 93. Added together, eight plus 93 equals 101. Gauss saw that every pair of numbers added up to 101 and that there were 50 pairs of numbers. He took 50 times 101 to arrive at the answer: 5,050.

It is important to learn the rules of math, but that doesn't mean math has to be boring. Knowing the rules can help you know how to be creative in solving problems. Gauss looked at the problem and decided there might be an easier, more fun way to solve it. You can use the same approach every day.

God gave us a wonderful gift when He created us with the ability to reason and be creative. But the abilities God has given us are of no value if we don't use them.

☺ **Why do you like math? Why don't you like math? What can you do to help yourself enjoy math more?**

☺ **Instead of thinking math is a pain, have fun with it. Look for creative solutions to problems.**

Krummholz

We also glory in tribulations, knowing that tribulation produces persever-ance; and perseverance, character; and character, hope. Romans 5:3, 4, NKJV.

"Do you know what *krummholz* means?" I asked my friend. "It's a cake you tried to bake that turned out so dry it crumbled into millions of tiny pieces," my friend ventured. "Ha, ha. Very funny. No. Wrong. *Krummholz* is a German word that means 'crooked wood.' The gnarled and twisted trees that struggle to grow high in the mountains above the forest and just below the alpine region are called krummholz."

I have a lot of admiration for the krummholz trees. They aren't dwarfed, crooked, and gnarled because they are supposed to be. By accident their seeds got blown onto the high rocky re-gions of the mountain, where fertile soil is scarce.

From the time the krummholz begin to grow, they battle for survival against fierce winds and bitter, unpredictable weather. Many times krummholz are assaulted by killing frosts in the spring and a very short growing season—not more than 10 weeks.

Many people are just like krummholz. They may have seem-ingly insurmountable obstacles to overcome in their lives. Maybe they have been born with a birth defect. Maybe they have devel-oped an incurable disease. Maybe, through an accident, they have become disabled. And not all krummholz people have phys-ical obstacles. Some krummholz people have suffered emotional trauma or abuse.

The dwarfed krummholz trees with their wood twisted and gnarled by the harsh elements will never stand as tall or look as healthy as the trees that grow below them in the forests. But they are much richer with character because of the harsh elements they have survived.

Just like the krummholz trees, a krummholz person who loves and trusts God may rejoice even in the bad times, for per-severance produces character, "and character, hope."

😊 **Why does the Bible say that bad times build character?**

😊 **Do you know anyone who is having a particularly bad time right now? If so, think of a way to share today's text.**

Pentagon Command

Therefore I tell you, do not worry about your life. . . . Who of you by worrying can add a single hour to his life? Matthew 6:25–27, NIV.

ello, Lori? This is—"

"You have reached—"

"Oh, no, not the answering machine," I groaned.

"—Pentagon command. Transmit destruct sequence. Sequence correct, T minus one minute and counting." *Beep.*

"Cute, Lori, really cute. Call me when you get a chance."

There was a time when I wouldn't have thought Lori's message was cute at all.

When I was 12, we lived in a really small town. It was more like a rest area between Vermont and Canada. It was also, as I learned, painfully close to the Air Force base in Plattsburg.

"If there is ever a nuclear attack on Plattsburg," one of my teachers said cheerfully, "we're history. But don't worry about it. It's not likely to happen any time soon."

Not likely? I wanted to grow up, not blow up.

I worried about it for a week before I finally decided to ask my pastor.

"You don't have to worry about being blown up by a bomb," Pastor Nelson assured me. "Today, tomorrow, or 50 years from now you could be hit by a bus and die, but you're not worried about that, are you?"

"Noooo . . ." I admitted reluctantly.

"There are a million ways to die, but if we worried about them all day we'd be so depressed we wouldn't do any *living.*"

I won't say that I didn't think about nuclear war any more, but I *was* able to start eating supper again. I still haven't been hit by a bus or blown up by a bomb, but I don't worry about that either. My life is in God's hands, and I believe He'll take care of me.

🙂 **What kinds of things do you worry about? Why?**

🙂 **The next time you are worried about something, write it down and put it in a box. Take it out one week later. Was it really worth worrying about?**

Diversity

Consequently, you are no longer foreigners and aliens, but fellow citizens with God's people and members of God's household. Ephesians 2:19, NIV.

I heard it on television. "Erase the hate!" several kids shouted before the station switched back to its regular programming. They were talking about racism. Their suggestion? Concentrate on the positive side of being different.

It's a great idea. And guess what? It's easy and fun. Appreciating diversity is one of the many exciting lessons God has given us to learn. Unfortunately, many people fear anyone who is different.

Knowledge doesn't always come out of a book. We learn by listening, watching, and doing, too. Talk to your friends and classmates who are from a different culture. Ask them questions about their culture. Share differences from your culture, too. People from different cultures are unique in so many wonderful ways: they read, think, and write differently. They eat differently. They talk differently.

Our differences help make us who we are. They are what give each one of us our own unique style. Learning about different cultures helps us understand why other people think the way they do. It helps us understand where their unique style comes from. As we learn about our differences, we soon feel closer to each other because we understand one another better.

Learning about other cultures from new friends and schoolmates is not only fun, it is also valuable because it helps us know how to get along with each other. If we all concentrate on the positive side of being different, we can "erase the hate!" No one has to be afraid of people who are different.

☺ **When Jesus was on earth, how did He relate to people He met? Did He accept their customs? Did He accept other people's way of life? Can you name some instances in which Jesus went out of His way to respect the customs of the people He met?**

☺ **When you have a chance to meet someone from a different culture, do! Ask questions about their culture. You will be surprised at the interesting things you learn.**

From Tragedy to Triumph, Part 1

We are hard pressed on every side, but not crushed; perplexed, but not in despair; persecuted, but not abandoned; struck down, but not destroyed. 2 Corinthians 4:8, 9, NIV.

I t was a hot July day on the Chesapeake Bay. Joni Eareckson was swimming with her sister and some friends. The water was murky, and as Joni cut the surface in a clean dive something happened that changed the course of her life forever. Her head hit the bottom of the bay, breaking her neck and paralyzing her from the neck down.

Fortunately, Joni's sister Kathy saw her, but she didn't realize Joni was in trouble. From beneath the water, Joni heard her sister ask if she was looking for shells. When she didn't answer, Kathy grabbed her and pulled her to the surface. She was rushed by ambulance to the hospital, where doctors operated on her neck.

During the time Joni was in the hospital, she agonized over why God had allowed this to happen to her. Was He punishing her? Was He trying to teach her some great cosmic lesson? At one point she became so depressed that she wanted to commit suicide. She even asked a friend to help her, but her friend refused. Eventually Joni recovered enough to be allowed to go home.

Wouldn't it be sad if that had been the end of Joni's story? But it wasn't. Joni faced fierce personal and spiritual struggles. She wrestled for answers. She wasn't willing to give up without understanding what had happened to her and what it meant in her life.

It is very easy for us to go through life believing in surface things about God. Yes, God loves us. Yes, sin is a bad thing. Yes, we should love others as we love ourselves. Most of the time nothing comes along that makes us question these things. But when Joni broke her neck, suddenly everything was much more important.

Why do you believe the things you do? How well do you really know God? If Jesus came back to earth right now and was standing beside you, how would you introduce Him to a friend?

Ask your pastor for a copy of what Adventists believe. Look it over, and then state why *you* believe each doctrine.

127

From Tragedy to Triumph, Part 2

Praise be to the God and Father of our Lord Jesus Christ, the Father
of compassion and the God of all comfort, who comforts us in all our
troubles, so that we can comfort those in any trouble with the
comfort we ourselves have received from God. 2 Corinthians 1:3, 4, NIV.

Eventually Joni faced this question: Did she trust God
enough to stop asking "Why, God?" and accept that God
was in control? Joni decided to trust God, because He was
worthy of her trust.

In rehabilitation she learned to draw and paint by holding a
pencil or paintbrush in her mouth. As people took an interest in her
drawings, many asked why she always signed them with a PTL.
The initials stand for "praise the Lord" and are Joni's way of pointing to the love of God in all things, even in what happened to her.

A well-known artist today, Joni Eareckson Tada is the president of JAF Ministries (Joni and Friends). Her ministry reaches
out to people with disabilities and their families all over the
world with the good news about Jesus. Joni proves every day that
with God disabilities are defined by the way in which you view
them—either as obstacles or stepping-stones.

"Wouldn't it be exciting if right now, in front of you, I could
be miraculously healed and get up out of my chair and on my
feet?" Joni once asked an audience of 1,600 young people. "What
a miracle! If my body were suddenly and miraculously healed, I'd
be on my feet perhaps another 30 or 40 years, then my body
would die. From the standpoint of eternity, my body is only a
flicker in the time span of forever. But far more exciting and
wonderful, in the long run, would be the miracle of your salvation—the healing of your own soul. You see, that's more exciting,
because that's something that will last forever."

- **What obstacles do you face? How do you see them?
How, with God's help, can they become stepping-stones
to even greater achievements?**

- **To get some idea of Joni's ability, try drawing a picture
while holding a pen in your mouth.**

Reading Exercise

Sow your seed in the morning, and at evening let not your hands be idle, for you do not know which will succeed, whether this or that, or whether both will do equally well. Ecclesiastes 11:6, NIV.

"Bye, Mom! 'Bye, Dad! Have fun!" Toby Larson called after his parents.

Toby rolled his lithe body to one side and slid out of the straps of his backpack after he entered the day-care room. He leaned the backpack against the wall and pulled out a storybook his mom had bought him for his birthday at the local Adventist Book Center.

Toby's mom and dad went to the gym three nights a week to exercise. Sometimes Toby went with them to work out. But on Wednesday nights he didn't go to exercise with Mom and Dad. He went for another purpose. And tonight was Wednesday night.

Toby had some special friends waiting for him in the day-care center at the gym. For several days Toby had been searching for a way to be a witness. Then a fabulous idea struck him. He decided to try reading to the younger kids at the day care and see if they liked it.

Most of the kids gathered around in a half circle the first night Toby read. The second Wednesday night, even more kids gathered around. Toby discovered that his newfound friends remembered exactly what had happened in the stories the week before. Pretty soon Toby's parents were finding out from other parents that they had to come to exercise whether they felt like it or not, because their children wanted to come and hear Toby read.

Toby had not only found a fun way to witness, he made lots of new friends who counted on him each week. And what's more, Toby was helping to keep a lot of parents in shape. He couldn't help chuckling when Mom and Dad told him that.

😊 **What are some of the things you do to witness to people? How does it make you feel when you witness?**

😊 **If you don't have a witnessing program right now, try thinking of one. Ask your parents to help. Begin by looking for fun things to do.**

Listening Counts

Though seeing, they do not see; though hearing, they do not hear or understand. Matthew 13:13, NIV.

I didn't get it."

"Well, of course you didn't get it," Daniel told me. "You weren't listening."

"I heard every word Mrs. Allen said in class."

"Yeah, but were you listening? *That's* the question," Daniel replied. "Listening means you did more than hear what Mrs. Allen was saying. It also means that you understood what she said and that you made it meaningful to yourself. What did the teacher say?"

"Well, ah . . ."

Daniel sighed. "That's what I thought. You weren't listening, because if you had been listening you would have remembered what Mrs. Allen talked about."

Daniel was right. I guess I wasn't listening very well. Maybe not at all. I was looking out the window part of the time, wishing I were out in the warm spring weather playing baseball. I was drawing designs when I should have been writing notes. I *heard* Mrs. Allen just fine, but now that I try to remember what she said, it just seems as if she droned on and on like a swarm of bees.

Ever discover that the easiest things to remember are the things that are the most interesting to you? That's because your mind is doing more than just hearing what is being said. It's reaching out for the information rather than letting it pass through your short-term memory to be lost a minute, an hour, or a day later.

I decided that I would ask God to help me listen more effectively. I also decided to make what I was hearing more meaningful to me.

- Where is your mind when you are listening to your teacher? Do you remember most of what the teacher was talking about in class?

- Find an interesting way to apply the information you are learning in class to your life. Once you make information interesting to yourself, it is easier to remember.

Macaroni

When God created man, he made him in the likeness of God. He created them male and female and blessed them. And when they were created, he called them "man." Genesis 5:1, 2, NIV.

I've got a box of macaroni in my pantry. As weird as it sounds, it helped me understand something about individuality.

Amazingly enough, I like being myself. The macaroni helped me decide that. Here's how: All the pieces in that box look the same! They don't just look the same, they act the same! If I were hanging out in a box of macaroni, I'd be having a real identity crisis right about now.

Yeah, I know that being different is no joyride, especially when everyone else in the world is trying to imitate the most popular kid in school, the latest, greatest movie star, or the hottest singing artist.

OK, so I'm looking back inside this box of macaroni, and well, I've pretty much convinced myself that being different isn't so bad. In fact, being myself and being different might even have some really positive high points.

I figure that God had a plan when He designed me. He knows my physical characteristics and personality quirks, and I think He says, "Hey, this guy's got a lot going for him, and he's got a lot going for Me, too. I can use someone like that!"

So there's no sense in my wishing I were like a piece of macaroni, stuck in a boxful of macaroni that's all exactly the same. I like being me. And I like the fact that you are different than I am, and your friends are different than you are. It makes the world a whole lot more fun than a box of macaroni.

🙂 **What are some of your unique characteristics? Why do some people want to be like someone else rather than themselves?**

🙂 **One way to appreciate your own uniqueness is to learn to appreciate other people and to help them feel good about themselves. Today tell someone that you appreciate his or her differences. Learn to see how these differences complement your differences.**

131

You're Worth Millions

God created man in his own image, in the image of God he created him; male and female he created them. Genesis 1:27, NIV.

When I was in high school, we had something called a "senior auction." The seniors were "sold" to the highest bidder—other junior high and high school students—for one day. While many of the details are hazy to me now (like what on earth we used all that money for), I do remember that I was sold for the highest amount of any of the seniors (to a junior high boy who had a crush on me).

I suppose I remember that detail because to me it said I was worth something—not just the $25 that was paid for me to wear a sandwich sign and read proclamations in study hall, but something that had no price. Which probably accounted for the fact that I drew the line at singing in the school lobby.

How much are you worth?

A movie star popular during World War II had her legs insured for $1 million. Would you like to see another pair of million-dollar legs? Look down at your own. Will they take you where you want to go? Would you trade them for $1 million?

How about your eyes? Would you trade your eyes for $1 million? Or your hearing? Would you trade that for $1 million?

See that? You're already worth $3 million, and I haven't even gotten started yet. Like yourself better already, don't you?

There is one Person to whom you are priceless. He would pay anything to redeem your soul so that you can spend all eternity with Him. In fact, He loves you so much that He traded the life of His only Son to purchase you. What do you think of that?

Think about this: if you're worth millions, how much is someone you dislike worth? If God loves everyone equally, how should you love everyone? If you are priceless to God, how should you treat yourself?

Do something nice for yourself today. You deserve it.

Do Unto Others

Do to others as you would have them do to you. Luke 6:31, NIV.

Samantha Reese bit her lower lip in concentration. She had almost finished her homework assignment, and then she was going on a bike ride with some friends. She wrote in the last answer with a smile and snapped her book shut with a satisfying *thud*. But before she could leave her room, the phone rang.

"Hello?" she said, expecting it to be Zeb, wondering where she was.

The person on the other end of the line coughed before answering. "Sam? It's Baxter. Could you do me a favor? I've got a cold and won't be able to go to school tomorrow, but my science project is due. Would you come get it and take it to school for me tomorrow?"

Sam groaned. Baxter lived way out of the way. If she went to his house she wouldn't be able to go on the bike ride, and she'd been looking forward to it all day. Still, if it were *her* science project and she were asking *Baxter* for the favor, she'd want him to say yes. She could still remember Mr. Evans' stern warning about getting the project done on time.

"Sure. I'll have my mom bring me over to get it as soon as I can," she told Baxter.

Zeb wasn't happy about it when she called him to explain that she couldn't go on the bike ride. "Why don't you let him turn it in late?" he whined.

"Because he'd get a lower grade," Sam explained.

"Well, it's his own fault for procrasta— procracina— for not getting it finished on time," he grunted. "Besides, he wouldn't go out of his way for you."

Sam giggled. "Well, maybe that's why the Bible doesn't say 'Do unto others the way you think they'd do unto you.' I'll see you tomorrow, Zeb."

🙂 **How do you treat other people? If they treated you the way you treat them, would you be happy or unhappy? Why?**

🙂 **Today, treat someone the way you would like to be treated if you were in their place, and not the way they deserve.**

133

No Need for Darkness

Walk while you have the light, lest darkness overtake you; he who walks in darkness does not know where he is going. John 12:35, NKJV.

We had ridden 20 miles, and there were still 10 more left before we would be at our vehicles. But night was coming, and if we were going to find a camping place that pleased us, now was the time to do it. Dad turned Magic, his 4-year-old gelding, off the trail to hunt for a camping spot.

The spot he found had just the right amount of protection and grazing area. But on his way back to share the good news, Dad brought Magic across a flat rock beneath a stand of tall pines. There must have been a year's supply of needles blanketing the rock. The needles were dry and as slippery as ice on the rock when Magic's hooves hit them. Instantly Magic crashed onto his side, crushing Dad's foot between him and the rock and breaking it.

Instead of spending the night, we decided it was best to ride out in the darkness, although I doubt either of us knew just how dark it would become. Often during the next 10 miles, I would put my hand inches from my nose to test whether or not I could see it. Each time I was amazed—I couldn't see anything at all!

Luckily, our horses knew the trail well enough to take us back to the vehicles. We were totally lost, in complete and total darkness, aware only of the motion of our horses. I prayed many times to God that we would find our way out.

The darkness we experienced on that ride was total blackness, void of any light because of the mountains and trees towering over us. It is as close as I care to come to the darkness of being without Jesus, the Light of life. On the mountain we didn't have any choice about the darkness that surrounded us, but you and I have a choice every day to live in darkness or light. Choose to live in the light today.

🙂 Have you ever been in darkness so total that you couldn't see even your hand in front of your face? How did you feel?

🙂 When you read your Bible, think about God and His Word as being the Light of life.

A Million-dollar Gift

But a Samaritan, as he traveled, came where the man was; and when he saw him, he took pity on him. He went to him and bandaged his wounds, pouring on oil and wine. Then he put the man on his own donkey, took him to an inn and took care of him. The next day he took out two silver coins and gave them to the innkeeper. "Look after him," he said, "and when I return, I will reimburse you for any extra expense you may have." Luke 10:33–35, NIV.

Tammie Murphy, a cash control clerk for ALSAC-St. Jude's Hospital, got a big surprise when she opened a plain white envelope, postmarked Dallas, with no return address. Inside the envelope was a $1 million winning game piece from McDonald's Monopoly promotion.

St. Jude's Hospital specializes in the treatment and research of children's diseases, such as cancer, AIDS, and sickle-cell anemia. Patients are treated, even if they are unable to pay.

Although McDonald's doesn't allow game pieces to be transferred, when they learned of the circumstances, they decided to honor the anonymous gift with a $1 million donation.

"We consider all the gifts we receive, large or small, as special. Clearly, this donor believed in our cause. For that reason we think of this gift as a holiday miracle," said Richard C. Shadyac, national director of ALSAC-St. Jude, the hospital's fund-raising unit.

If you had found that winning game piece in your McDonald's garden salad, what would you have done? Let's say that instead of $1 million, you get an unexpected $20 from Great-aunt Bertha. What will you do with it?

- How much are you responsible for in helping people in the world who are less fortunate than you are? What are some ways you can do that?

- Call the Adventist Development and Relief Agency (ADRA) at: 1-800-424-ADRA and ask them to send you some coin keepers. When they are full, you can drop them in the offering plate at church or mail them back to ADRA.

135

No Room in the Inn

Share with God's people who are in need. Practice hospitality. Romans 12:13, NIV.

One day Thomas Jefferson was traveling through Baltimore. He stopped at the main hotel in town. He was traveling unattended, so he entered the lobby alone to see about accommodations for the night. The owner studied him carefully and decided that he was only a farmer. He promptly informed Jefferson that there was no room for him.

Giving the hotel owner a second chance, Jefferson again asked if there was a room. He received the same reply.

Not long after Jefferson had mounted his horse and ridden away, a wealthy gentleman entered the same hotel. He told the hotel owner that the man who had just left was the vice president of the United States.

Shocked, the owner immediately sent his servants out to find Jefferson and tell him that surely there was room for him, and that he could have the very best of everything the hotel had to offer.

But Jefferson had already taken a room at another hotel. He sent the servants back with the message that if there was no room for a dirty farmer, there was also no room for the vice president.

If there is no room in your heart for the kid who wears clothes from the secondhand store, if there is no room for the least popular student in your school, if there is no room for someone of a different race, how can there be room in your heart for Jesus?

- Has your family ever invited people into your home who needed a place to stay? Have you ever helped a family who didn't have enough food or clothes?

- Check with the person or persons in charge of the Community Services organization in your church and see if there is anything you can do to help. You might even know of a family in your community who needs assistance. Make a connection.

Preparing for the Future, Part 1

The fear of the Lord is the beginning of knowledge, but fools despise wisdom and discipline. Proverbs 1:7, NIV.

Whether you are preparing for a test at the end of the week or a final test at the end of the year, or you are teaching yourself good habits to help you take tests in high school and college, it can all start right now.

David started. David's older brother, Kevin, who was just finishing his first year of college, gave David some helpful tips to turn into habits. David decided to try them out, especially after reading today's text. What could he lose?

"David," Kevin said, "I had to learn how to prepare for tests the hard way. I failed my first couple exams before I realized I had never developed good study habits."

Wow! David thought. *Kevin never failed any tests when he was in high school!*

"First, I had to learn how important reviewing is and how to review effectively," Kevin said. "I couldn't just read the notes I had taken in class during the past couple weeks right before a test and expect to remember everything. I had to start reviewing my notes as soon as I took them. If I had a few minutes after class, or later in the day, I took out my notes and went over them again. I started scheduling five minutes, 10 minutes, or even 15 minutes a day to review my notes. Reviewing every day really helped me remember."

David nodded. "That makes sense, Kevin. I've started taking notes in class to help me remember what my teachers were talking about. I think I'll start reviewing my notes every day too."

"Good, David," Kevin said with a grin. "You are a lot wiser than I was at your age. You are also teaching yourself discipline."

- What are some of your good study habits? What are some of your bad study habits? How can good study habits help you study the Bible?

- As you finish this year, get a jump on some good study habits that will help you next year. Begin by taking notes in class, and review them often.

In Disguise

For I am convinced that neither death nor life, neither angels nor demons, neither the present nor the future, nor any powers, neither height nor depth, nor anything else in all creation, will be able to separate us from the love of God that is in Christ Jesus our Lord. Romans 8:38, 39, NIV.

Ever missed anyone a whole lot? In 1692 a woman missed her husband, Richard, so much that she decided to go look for him. Richard had been away at war. Apparently she had been missing him terribly, because when she decided to go look for him, she at once felt relieved to actually be doing something about her loneliness.

She took one of her husband's suits and put it on (she was about the same size as Richard). She cut her hair. She enlisted in the army. No one seemed to know that she was a woman. She was so happy thinking about being reunited with her husband that she was not even worried about the danger of fighting in a war.

Mrs. Walsh did find her husband. She asked him not to tell anyone who she was, and they stayed in the army together. Not until 13 years later was it finally discovered who she was.

It's hard to miss someone we don't know, because we don't know anything about him or her. But when we are friends with someone who leaves, all of a sudden we miss that person's smile, laughter, ideas, and way of doing things. Most of all, we miss the warm feeling we have inside when he or she is around. That's how much Jesus hopes we will miss Him. But we have to *know* Him first.

🙂 **Is there someone in your life whom you miss a lot? What are some of the things you miss the most about this person?**

🙂 **Make an effort each day to make Jesus a close friend. In prayer, tell Him how much you miss Him.**

A Partner in Trials

See, I have refined you, though not as silver; I have tested you in the furnace of affliction. Isaiah 48:10, NIV.

Ioannis Metaxas was a general who ruled Greece back in the 1930s. One day he was asked to test a new "flying boat" at an air base. General Metaxas took the plane up for a short flight before preparing to make a landing. Just before he touched down on the runway at the air base, the base commander, who was sitting beside him, spoke up.

"Excuse me, General," he said. "It would be better to come down on the water. This is a flying boat."

The general, who was about to drop the wheelless plane onto the runway, gunned the craft upward, circled around, and landed neatly in the water. Before he got out of the plane, he turned to the base commander and said, "Thank you, Commander, for preventing me from making a stupid blunder." Then he opened the door, jumped out, and sank into the water.

Oops.

General Metaxas couldn't seem to get it through his head that he was in a flying *boat*. If the base commander hadn't said anything and allowed the general to land the boat on the runway—and the general had lived through the experience—he probably would not have made the same mistake again. But he was saved by the quick comment of the base commander . . . only to forget once again that he was actually in a boat.

It's the same way with the trials we go through. We are quick to pray "Lord, help me out of this trial" and miss the entire point of trials. Trials teach us something. We should focus on what we can learn from the trial. It's nice to be saved from going through a trial, but if we don't learn anything, it doesn't help us much.

😊 **When you are going through a trial, what do you pray for? Why does it make a difference where your focus is?**

😊 **The next time you are going through a trial, remember that God leads us into deep water, not to let us drown, but to teach us how to swim.**

Investment for Life

What good is it for a man to gain the whole world, yet forfeit his soul? Mark 8:36, NIV.

Thirty years ago an eager investor thought he would make a lucrative real estate deal in the town of Arles, located in the south of France. Apparently a 90-year-old woman lived in an apartment the investor desired to own.

The deal was that the investor would pay the elderly owner $500 a month for the rest of her life in exchange for her apartment when she died. After all, how long could she live? She was 90 years old! He was only 47. *Shortly,* he might have thought, *the apartment will be mine for a fraction of what it's worth.*

It is common practice in France to make arrangements with elderly real estate owners to pay them a monthly income for their property until they die. Such an arrangement gives the owner a monthly income to live on. Then, after the owner's death, the buyer receives the property, hopefully at a bargain, no matter how much money was invested.

Ninety years old? Surely the woman could not live much longer. But she did. She lived 30 more years. At 120 years of age she became the world's oldest living person. The investor, who once thought he might have received the apartment he desired at a fraction of its worth, ended up paying $184,000 for it, far more than the apartment was really worth. Then he died at the age of 77.

The investor thought he had a sure deal. Every day many people all over the world think the same thing. They might risk all they have to get what they desire on this earth. They might even give up their friends, their family, and God. But in the end they will have lost everything the world has to offer. They might even lose eternal life with God. God is the only sure deal. All we have to do is invest our life in Him.

🙂 **What is the wisest investment you can make on this earth? How can you invest time in God?**

🙂 **Make a list of ideas on how to invest in God and put it on the refrigerator or your bedroom door, where you will be reminded about your biggest investment often.**

All Wet

Then Jesus came from Galilee to the Jordan to be baptized by John. Matthew 3:13, NIV.

Y ou're not getting me into that water," Sam said firmly.

"Oh, come on, it's not that bad," Michaela assured her. "Really."

"You don't understand," Sam wailed. "I'm scared of the water."

"I understand that perfectly," Michaela said calmly. "That's why I'm here, so we can practice for your baptism this fall."

Sam walked hesitantly into the water and stood there, drawing circles on the surface with her fingertips. "I don't know why I have to get wet to be baptized," she complained. "What does God care if I get wet, as long as I follow Him?"

"I don't think getting wet is the point," Michaela said. "The point is to demonstrate your commitment to God."

"Well, why can't I do that without getting wet?" Sam demanded.

"Well, for one thing," Michaela said, "we're following Jesus' example. And for another thing, if there were some way to be baptized without water it wouldn't be called baptism, now would it?

"Jesus showed His commitment to our salvation by dying for us. It wasn't easy for Him, but there was no substitute."

Sam nodded. "And there's no substitute for baptism either, huh?"

"And don't forget—when Jesus died on the cross, He was all alone. But Pastor Peters will be holding you all the time, and you'll be under the water for only a second," Michaela reminded Sam as she put her arms around her to help her into the water.

Sam gave her friend a quick hug. "Thank you for doing this with me. I know I won't be nearly so frightened of going under the water if we practice it a few times."

Michaela smiled. "No problem. What are friends for?"

- **Have you been baptized yet? What was the experience like? If you haven't been baptized, discuss baptism with your parents or pastor.**

- **Write out your baptism story. If you haven't been baptized yet, interview other people about their experiences and write them down.**

Gulf Stream Christians

Don't let anyone think little of you because you are young. Be their ideal;
let them follow the way you teach and live; be a pattern for them in your
love, your faith, and your clean thoughts. 1 Timothy 4:12, TLB.

The Gulf Stream, a warm water current that flows from the Florida Straits across the Atlantic Ocean to Northern Europe, is so huge that it is larger than all the rivers in the world combined. The Gulf Stream is like a river. The only difference is that it flows through the sea instead of on land. The Gulf Stream is visible from above because its clear, indigo-blue color is sharply contrasted by the green-grayish waters of the ocean.

Because the Gulf Stream originates in warmer regions, its waters are warm. Its warmth tends to affect the climate of many places in the world. Winds that pass over the Gulf Stream in Northern Europe gain warmth from the warmer waters and carry that warm, moist air over parts of Norway, Sweden, Denmark, the Netherlands, and Belgium. These parts of the world that get the warmer air have milder winters than places just as far north, all because of the warm Gulf Stream water.

For many people, their only association with Christianity is what they learn from the examples you and I show them. If we are Gulf Stream Christians, those people will feel the warmth of our love. They will see a difference between the cold, harsh world and being a follower of Christ.

Don't think that only adults make a difference in the world. In some countries little children preach the gospel and hold revivals. It doesn't matter what your age is. It just matters where your heart is.

How are our actions able to make a difference in the lives of people we don't even know? Do you remember a time when your actions affected how someone thought about you, or Christians in general?

Print copies of today's verse and share it with your Sabbath school class.

Good Trees, Good Fruit

No good tree bears bad fruit, nor does a bad tree bear good fruit. Each tree is recognized by its own fruit. Luke 6:43, 44, NIV.

Trevor Davis was a shining star in the crown of Millmont Junior High School. He was the best athlete, the best scholar, and the best musician. And he was probably the cutest boy in school.

The only problem with Trevor was that he wasn't very reliable. He showed up late for practice. He usually forgot to turn in his homework unless he was reminded. He sometimes told you one thing and then did the opposite. Not that he did it on purpose—that was just the way Trevor was. One time Jenny Sanders had to walk the three miles home because Trevor promised her a ride and then forgot about her.

Jeff Daniels wasn't a good athlete, an excellent scholar, or a good musician. And he looked pretty bad. He needed a haircut, and some shampoo on a regular basis wouldn't have hurt anything either. And those clothes! Well, with a good washing . . .

But when teachers wanted something done, they asked Jeff to do it. If he said he was going to be somewhere, you could count on Jeff to show up. His wasn't the loveliest voice in the choir, but he was always at practice and on time. And he sang with as much enthusiasm as any choir director could hope for.

Jeff was too shy to act, but he worked harder than anyone else making the props whenever there was a play. And even though he was quiet, most of the students at Millmont considered him their friend.

On the outside, Trevor looked good. But when you got right down to what he did, it wasn't so good after all. Jeff, on the other hand, would have fooled you. He looked kind of messy on the outside, but his actions showed that he had a good heart.

- What do you think the Bible verse means when it talks about "fruit"? What kind of fruit do you produce?

- Write out today's Bible verse on a piece of paper. On the back of the paper write *Thanks for bearing good fruit.* Then give it to someone you appreciate.

143

Preparing for the Future, Part 2

How wonderful to be wise, to understand things, to be able to analyze them and interpret them. Wisdom lights up a man's face, softening its hardness. Ecclesiastes 8:1, TLB.

emember Kevin and David from last week (May 11)? Well, as soon as Kevin walked through the door one afternoon, David called him upstairs.

Kevin poked his head in the door of David's room. "Yeah? What's up?"

"I was wondering if you could give me some more pointers on studying for tests," David said.

Kevin came in and sat down. "Sure thing. I review the notes I take in class every day, plus what I read in my reading assignments. But I also review those same notes and assignments every week. That takes me longer. I spend as much as an hour on each class. But it's good for me to take so much time, because it helps me really grasp the ideas and concepts I'm trying to learn."

"Hmmm," David said. "You want to make sure that all the information you've listened to, written down, and read makes sense. It's sort of like putting a puzzle together."

"Right, David! During my weekly review I'm making sure all the pieces of information I have memorized fit together so that I really understand what I am supposed to be learning. Do you have your Bible handy? I want to read you a text I like to remember just before I do my weekly reviews."

Kevin opened a Bible to Ecclesiastes 8:1. "How wonderful to be wise, to understand things, to be able to analyze them and interpret them. Wisdom lights up a man's face, softening its hardness."

David got his notes together. "I have some tests just before school is out for the summer. I'd better make sure I understand what I've been learning. Thanks, Kevin."

😊 **How did doing weekly reviews help Kevin? How will it help David, and how can it help you?**

😊 **Try doing weekly reviews of your notes and reading assignments so that you really understand what they are about.**

144

A Little Too Late to Be Good

Let him who does wrong continue to do wrong; let him who is vile continue to be vile; let him who does right continue to do right; and let him who is holy continue to be holy. Revelation 22:11, NIV.

Every war has stories of officers who, while they were engaged with the enemy on the battlefield, were killed by their own men. On purpose.

I'm reminded of one particular officer who knew that he had treated his men badly. Before attacking the enemy, he turned to them and apologized. I can well imagine his sincerity as he asked them to forgive him for his past behavior. He asked that should he be killed in battle, it be from the bullets of the enemy. He told his men that if he lived through the battle he would change his ways.

How many times have you treated someone badly? I know I have lots of times. And how many times have you thought, *Oh, I'll change tomorrow. I'll be nicer tomorrow?* Did tomorrow ever come? Were you nicer the next day than you had been the day before? It *is* possible to change.

For some people that day will never come, and then Jesus will come back, and it will be too late. Make up your mind to invite Jesus into your heart today. Some things just won't wait.

Fortunately, the officer and his men fought well in the battle. And the officer was very much relieved to have lived through it. However, as he turned to his men and raised his hat for a cheer, he was shot in the forehead and killed. Apparently the officer's promise that he would be a better leader if he lived came a little too late. No one believed him.

- 🙂 **How many times have you treated someone badly without thinking about what you were doing? How did it make you feel when you realized how rotten you had been?**

- 🙂 **Whom have you been mean to recently? Resolve right now to be the cause of lifting people's spirits, rather than crushing them.**

145

The Best Medicine

A cheerful heart is good medicine, but a crushed spirit dries up the bones. Proverbs 17:22, NIV.

Denise Rogers could hardly pull herself out of bed in the morning. *I don't have any friends. No one likes me. I don't even like myself,* she thought.

Finally Denise did get out of bed after hitting the snooze button on her alarm clock for the fifth time. But she never did go to school. She told her mother she was sick and stayed at home that day. The next day she felt worse inside than she had the day before. But she forced herself to get up, go to school, and suffer through the day.

On that day, however, Denise made a great discovery for herself. Instead of going outside during class break, she stayed at her desk. After her classmates had gone, she approached her teacher, Mrs. Lockett, and asked if they could talk. Denise knew that Mrs. Lockett was someone who cared about people.

After they talked the first time, Mrs. Lockett scheduled the same time the very next day for them to talk again. She also urged Denise to come and talk to her anytime she felt down and lonely.

Denise discovered that talking to someone she could trust helped her feel better. Mrs. Lockett helped Denise realize that she wasn't alone. Most of us have questions about who we are and what we're doing here. And everyone has feelings of loneliness.

It's not unusual to feel lonely or depressed. But don't stay that way; it's not healthy. Find someone to talk to. Read God's promises in the Bible. Make a list of your blessings. Try to find at least 10 of them every day. And praise God for everything from air to sunshine. You won't stay depressed for long!

😊 **Have you ever wanted to stay in bed and not face the day? What made you feel like that? How did you get over it?**

😊 **God always loves you and wants to help. Talk to Him when you feel depressed. He also gave you friends and people here on earth to help you. Find someone you trust to talk to when you feel down and lonely.**

Little White Lie

My mouth speaks what is true, for my lips detest wickedness. Proverbs 8:7, NIV.

Samantha Reese was just about to slip out the door and head down to the clubhouse to meet Dillon and Zeb when her mother's voice froze her in place.

"Sam, did you call Aunt Sylvia to invite her over for dinner?"

She'd forgotten that Mom had asked her to call. Aunt Sylvia was really nice, but she could talk your ear off. Sam had once left the phone on the chair for 10 minutes while she went to her room to get something, and when she came back Aunt Sylvia was still talking and hadn't even known she'd gone. Of course, Mom had told her not to do that again.

The point was that if Sam stopped to call Aunt Sylvia now, she'd never make it down to the clubhouse. On the other hand, Mom wouldn't let her get out of the house until she did. Sam was very tempted to tell her mother she'd already done it. After all, she could call from the clubhouse and no one would ever know . . .

Except *she* would know. Sam took a deep breath. "No, Mom," she confessed. "I forgot to call Aunt Sylvia."

"Well, I want you to do it before you leave," her mother replied.

Sam groaned. Aunt Sylvia answered the phone on the third ring and sounded out of breath.

"Oh, *Samantha!*" Aunt Sylvia exclaimed with her usual enthusiasm. "You just caught me. I was on my way out the door."

"Mom asked me to call and invite you to dinner," Sam said politely. "But if you're leaving, then I guess you can't—"

"I'd *love* to!" Aunt Sylvia exclaimed. "Sorry I can't talk, though. Gotta run. See you in a little bit. 'Bye."

Sam hung up the phone with a smile. She hadn't lied, she'd made the call, and she still had plenty of time to go to the clubhouse. "Thank You, Lord," she whispered as she hurried out the door.

- Are some lies worse than others? Are there more ways to lie than just by what you say?

- Give someone a call and tell them how much you appreciate them.

You Gotta Read It!

Jesus' disciples saw him do many other miracles besides the ones
told about in this book, but these are recorded so that you will
believe that he is the Messiah, the Son of God, and that believing
in him you will have life. John 20:30, 31, TLB.

A man who had received a handsome leather Bible for his
birthday decided that since he had no use for God, he
would dispose of the Bible on his way to go fishing. He
packed a lunch, grabbed his fishing pole, tackle box, and, of
course, the Bible.

On the way, the man stopped on a bridge that crossed the
stream he planned to fish from. Tossing the Bible into the water,
he continued on his way.

Sometime later, as the man stood on the bank of the stream,
he felt a tug on his line. He reeled in his catch—only to discover
that he had snagged the very Bible he had discarded at the bridge,
its pages warped and soggy. The man put it with his tackle box
and later returned home with it, where he left it in the garage.
Later that evening, the man's wife discovered the Bible and tried
to dry it out. By now the pages were stiff, but still quite readable.

One day the Bible was placed in a box and stored away.
Several years later, after the man and his wife had died, the Bible
was discovered again, still packed away in the box. Neither the
man nor his wife had ever read it.

A crazy story? Think about it. How many times have you
looked at your Bible and thought *I should take it down and read it;
it's not doing any good lying on the shelf?*

Don't wait for your Bible to jump off the shelf into your
hands. Take it down today and read what God has to say.

- 😊 **Did you expect the man or his wife to read the Bible?
  Why do so many people never read their Bibles? How
  many Bibles do you have in your home?**

- 😊 **Have you noticed Bibles in the homes of your friends?
  Ask them what their favorite texts are. Share your favorite texts from the Bible with others.**

Look, Honey, God Healed Elvis! Part 1

Are not two sparrows sold for a penny? Yet not one of them will fall to the ground apart from the will of your Father. Matthew 10:29, NIV.

I wanted an aquarium, but it took a while to convince my husband. "I want to put it on my desk and watch the fish while I write. Besides," I pointed out, "they're supposed to help reduce stress."

"So are the dogs," he reminded me. (We had four at the time.)

In the end, I got the fish. First, just one big goldfish I named Gil, and a catfish I named Jonah. Jonah got stuck in the net about a week later and had to be cut out. The trauma turned out to be too much for him, and he died. Then I added Elvis and Priscilla, two perky barbs.

Two days later I was dismayed to see Elvis acting strangely. He swam in crazy circles, gulping air and backstroking around the bowl. Depressed, I put him in a smaller bowl and told my husband he was dying too.

The more I watched Elvis gulping and floating, the more depressed I became. I put my chin on the edge of the bowl and watched his perfect little gills pumping furiously. The tiny fins pedaled against the water, swimming backward, staying close to the surface.

Before my husband left for work, he prayed with me and added, "And please heal Elvis, if it's Your will. Amen."

Heal Elvis? What could God care about a little fish? After my husband left I stared into the bowl again.

"You do care, though, don't You, Lord?" I asked. "You care about this little fish, just as You care about the sparrows. You know he's dying, and You could heal him if You wanted to. But why would You bother about a tiny fish?" I didn't have much hope for Elvis.

🙂 **Why do you think that God cares about even the little things? Have you ever prayed for something you thought was really insignificant in the scheme of things? What happened?**

🙂 **Take time to talk to God about even the little things today. Then pause for a moment and see what He has to say.**

149

Look, Honey, God Healed Elvis! Part 2

If you, then, though you are evil, know how to give good gifts to your children, how much more will your Father in heaven give good gifts to those who ask him! Matthew 7:11, NIV.

I didn't doubt that God *could* heal Elvis—it was a question of *would* He heal him. I didn't think it was likely that God was going to bother with such a little thing when there was important stuff going on in the world.

I'm glad I was wrong. Two hours later Elvis was a completely healed fish. Not only was he swimming right side up; he wasn't gulping air and backpedaling. He was zipping around the small bowl as if to say, "Hey, let's have some room to move. Put me back in the big bowl."

To some people a recovered fish might be a little thing indeed, but it wasn't for me. I hate to see anything die, even my houseplants. The healing of Elvis reminded me that nothing is too insignificant to be brought before the Lord's throne. Nothing is too small for God to love or too impossible for Him to do.

I couldn't wait for my husband to get home so I could tell him, "Look, honey, God healed Elvis!"

People often wonder why God will miraculously cure a little girl's cat, and allow a boy to die of cancer. I don't claim to know. In a world full of sin many unpleasant things happen. God has the power to change them all. Sometimes He does. Sometimes the greater miracle is none at all.

One thing I am positive about is that God can bring good out of every bad circumstance if we will only trust in Him and ask Him to show it to us.

☺ **Why is it that God sometimes doesn't answer prayers, no matter how hard you pray, or how hard you believe? How do you think God feels when bad things happen to us? What do you think He does?**

☺ **Keep a prayer journal. Make a note of your prayers and how they were answered.**

Keep Your Mind in Tune

If you want to know what God wants you to do, ask him, and he will gladly tell you, for he is always ready to give a bountiful supply of wisdom to all who ask him; he will not resent it. James 1:5, TLB.

School is almost over. Congratulations! What are you going to do with your summer break? No one is laying school assignments on you. No tests. No textbook reading. No math, history, geography, social science, science. So? What are your plans?

Although this is the end of learning in a classroom for the next three months, it's not the end of learning. As you are discovering, learning is fun. It also happens from the time you get up in the morning until you go to bed at night. Even as you lie in bed before going to sleep, you may be sorting information as you think about what you did during the day.

There are a few things you might try to keep actively learning this summer. If your family is planning a vacation this summer, take along a notebook to use as a journal. (You may do this already. Keeping a journal is a great idea anytime.) Record your day's activities. If your family is planning a trip to a zoo, an animal park, or an aquarium, think of these trips as great learning opportunities. If you are traveling to another country, be sure to learn as much as you can about that country's manners, customs, and history.

Now that you have some extra time, why don't you try an in-depth Bible study, using some of the study techniques you learned this year? Choose a topic or a question and see how much you can find out about it. Use a Bible dictionary and concordance to help you out. Write out what you discover in a journal or in a notebook.

What were your favorite subjects this past school year? What made them fun? Why? Was there any subject you wished you could have studied more about?

Plan to observe more of your world. When you discover something that is particularly interesting to you, go to the library and research it. Keep your mind in tune.

Love Account

Love is patient, love is kind. It does not envy, it does not boast, it is not proud. It is not rude, it is not self-seeking, it is not easily angered, it keeps no record of wrongs. Love does not delight in evil but rejoices with the truth. It always protects, always trusts, always hopes, always perseveres. Love never fails. 1 Corinthians 13:4-8, NIV.

Allen set up an account—a unique account that gave him an excellent return on his investment. What was so unique about Allen's account was that the interest on his money came before he ever deposited a dime!

Whenever Allen did something for someone else, he deposited anywhere between a nickel and a dollar, depending on how much love he put into his good deed. If he did it grudgingly, it was worth only a nickel. If he did it willingly, out of love, he put in a dollar.

The way Allen's plan worked was actually quite simple. Whenever he did something for someone with love in his heart, he felt better inside. And to Allen, that good feeling was worth something. The better the feeling, the more it was worth. So every time he did something with a lot of love, he increased how much he put in his offering for God.

Allen put money in his love account, then each quarter, when Thirteenth Sabbath came, he gave the money from his love account as an offering. Allen doubled the worth of his helpfulness. But even more exciting to Allen was the interest he was earning on his love account before he put money in the bank!

What an exciting idea!

There may be some people who don't quite understand why. Allen gives an offering for each act of kindness *he* does. Here's how Allen explains it: "Jesus told us to love our neighbors as ourselves. This is my way of doing that."

🙂 **Why was the money in Allen's "love account" so special to him?**

🙂 **Set up a special "love account" like Allen's in your Sabbath school class. At the end of the third quarter give your special offering for the Thirteenth Sabbath project.**

Angels Among Us, Part 1

If you make the Most High your dwelling—even the Lord, who is my refuge—then no harm will befall you, no disaster will come near your tent. For he will command his angels concerning you to guard you in all your ways. Psalm 91:9-11, NIV.

Faole came from a tribe in New Guinea, where killing and murder were common occurrences. In fact, a boy wasn't considered a man until he had killed someone, and he couldn't get married until he was a man. Well, after Faole killed a man for the first time, he went a little nuts and didn't stop killing. It wasn't long before everyone in the area was afraid of him.

Then he became a Christian and was very sorry for what he had done. When a White missionary opened a new mission station in the village of Maibikee, he asked Faole to help operate it. Faole and his family moved there. The people of the village loved them. Wonderful things happened there. They built a new village and a church. Faole loved flowers and planted them everywhere.

Well, not everyone was happy about the changes in the village. A few miles away was another tribe who didn't like all these changes. They were worried about them, but didn't know what they could do to stop them. One day the chief of that village died suddenly.

The villagers tried to find someone to blame. But there was no one. The man hadn't been killed. He hadn't been sick. He just died; but this didn't seem at all reasonable to them. They decided that someone must have cast a spell on him—and that person should be punished.

Finally they decided that Faole's village, and especially Faole himself, was responsible, because they had abandoned the old customs and practices. The only way to break the spell, they thought, was to raid the village and kill everyone—most of all, Faole and his family. Fifty strong warriors were sent to do the job.

🙂 **Why do you think people are often afraid of change? What do you think when something changes?**

🙂 **Flowers are probably starting to come up where you live. Pick a bunch and give them to your parents.**

153

Angels Among Us, Part 2

The angel of the Lord encamps around those who fear him,
and he delivers them. Psalm 34:7, NIV.

*O*ne man in the village wasn't sure that killing everyone in Faole's village was the right thing to do. He liked the changes, and he wished the same things would happen in his village. So risking his own life, he set out to warn the White missionary that the warriors planned to kill Faole. On the way he met a man from Faole's village and told him to tell the people to flee because there was trouble. Two days later, exhausted, he reached the missionary and told him that Faole was going to be killed.

The missionary left immediately to go to the village. He was very surprised to see Faole, smiling and happy. The missionary questioned Faole and found that on the night of the raid he had known something was wrong, but didn't know what. Worried, he had gathered his family around him to pray.

Opening the Bible, he happened to see this verse: "The angel of the Lord encamps around those who fear him, and he delivers them" (Psalm 34:7, NIV). *Well,* he thought, *who am I to doubt God?* He asked God to forgive him for doubting, and then slept peacefully through the night.

The missionary decided to visit the warriors' village to investigate. When the 50 men had reached Faole's house, they had found it guarded by many men in white standing in a ring around it. The warriors had waited all night, but the men never left. Finally they crept back home at daybreak in disgrace.

The men of the village were convinced that the White missionary and many of his friends had guarded Faole's house. The missionary couldn't convince the men that he had not been in the village, but on the coast, two days' march away.

"The Book that belongs to God," Faole says, "He is very much true. 'The angel of the Lord encampeth round about them that fear him, and delivereth them.'"

🙂 **Whom do you think the men in white were? Do you think you've ever seen an angel?**

🙂 **Get a book about angels and read more about them.**

An Anonymous Letter

Listen, for I have worthy things to say; I open my lips to speak what is right. Proverbs 8:6, NIV.

I wrinkled my nose. "Phew!" I whispered to my friend Pam as I sat down next to her on the bus. "Smells like a grass fire in here again."

She giggled. "You could say that."

I tried to angle myself so that I could see behind me without seeming too obvious. A couple of the boys in my class were smoking marijuana on the bus. Again. It had been going on for a week, and the bus driver had apparently decided not to do anything about it.

Karen, a kid from the elementary school, got up from her seat in the back of the bus and made a big show of moving to the front, loudly proclaiming how it stunk. I agreed.

I wanted to tell the principal, but I didn't dare. Instead, I decided to type a letter and not sign it. I sent the letter to the vice principal and waited to see what would happen.

It didn't take long. When the letter arrived, he called the troublemakers into his office. They were not happy. Suspicion fell on Karen. Since she had to walk a mile home from school after the bus dropped her off, they decided to follow her and beat her up on her way home.

Terrified that my plan had backfired, I called her brother, Bryan, and told him what was going to happen. He left his job and picked her up at school. The next day he stopped and offered me a ride to school. In the car with him was one of the boys who had been smoking the marijuana! Bryan was assuring him that his sister hadn't told on them.

No one ever did find out who wrote the letter, but they never tried smoking pot on the bus again, either.

Do you think it is always important to get credit for the good things we do? What are some circumstances when it would be better to remain anonymous?

Write an anonymous letter to your principal pointing out the things that are good about your school.

155

God's Time-out, Part 1

But the Lord provided a great fish to swallow Jonah, and Jonah was inside the fish three days and three nights. Jonah 1:17, NIV.

Do you remember "time-out"? That's when you'd done something you weren't supposed to, and an adult would plunk you into a kitchen chair, facing the wall, and set the kitchen timer. When the timer went off, you could come out.

Time-out gives kids time to reflect, to think about what got them into trouble in the first place. It also gives them time to cool off and to feel sorry for what they did so they can apologize.

God uses time-out very successfully. Are you surprised? Remember Jonah? God told him to go to Nineveh, but instead he ran away. He was disobedient. He was ignoring God. Then God said, "Time-out!" Not having a kitchen chair handy, God put Jonah inside the belly of a great fish.

Now Jonah had nowhere to go and nothing to do but think about what had gotten him there in the first place. Which is what Jonah did. After three days the "kitchen timer" went off, the Lord spoke to the fish, and it vomited Jonah onto dry land.

Another case of time-out is found in Numbers. Moses chose some men to spy out the land that the Lord had given them. When they returned, they told stories about giants and filled the people with fear so that they wished they were dead—or at least back in Egypt.

And God said, "Time out!"

So the Israelites wandered around in the wilderness, bored and alone for 40 years. Then the buzzer went off and they entered the Promised Land—40 years later, but hopefully much wiser.

Sometimes God still uses time-out to set us straight. If you think about it, you can probably think of a time when He put you there.

😊 **Has God put you in time-out lately? Why did He do it? What did you learn from it?**

😊 **Read the stories about Jonah (the book of Jonah) and the Israelites (Numbers 14:1-10, 30-35). Can you think of other times when God used time-out?**

God's Time-out, Part 2

Immediately what had been said about Nebuchadnezzar was fulfilled. He was driven away from people and ate grass like cattle. His body was drenched with the dew of heaven until his hair grew like the feathers of an eagle and his nails like the claws of a bird. Daniel 4:33, NIV.

King Nebuchadnezzar thought he was a pretty terrific person. Walking around one day, he looked out on his kingdom and puffed up with pride. "All this is for my glory and my majesty," he said.

And God said, "Time-out."

So the mighty king roamed the fields like a wild animal, probably being chased by little boys with sticks and old women with brooms. He had nothing to do except stay alive and wait. And at the end of that time the "buzzer" on the "kitchen timer" went off, and Nebuchadnezzar's reasoning returned to him.

Have you experienced a time-out in your own life? Have you run up against a wall and asked "What next, Lord?" Frustrated plans, lack of communication, dry seasons in our lives, are all God's way of trying to get our attention. Have you ever felt that your prayers didn't reach any farther than the ceiling before coming back unanswered? When we barrel ahead, intent on our own pursuits, He is right behind us like the toddler's mother, ready to reach out and grab us by the suspenders.

"Time-out! Stop. Listen to Me. Think. What are you doing? Is it in harmony with My will? Or are you going to hurt yourself?"

And sometimes we sit there, like the toddler, not understanding why we're there or what has happened. And as soon as our time is up, we're off and running again, only to be brought back again and again until we learn our lesson. How much better it would be for us to listen and learn well the first time.

😃 **What is the purpose of correction, or discipline? Does God discipline us out of spite, or love? How can you tell?**

😃 **Read the story about Nebuchadnezzar in Daniel 4:29-37.**

Race for Life, Part 1

The angel of the Lord asked him, "Why have you beaten your donkey these three times? I have come here to oppose you because your path is a reckless one before me. The donkey saw me and turned away from me these three times. If she had not turned away, I would certainly have killed you by now, but I would have spared her." Numbers 22:32, 33, NIV.

God has used animals for some pretty amazing purposes. Sometimes the animals even seem to listen to Him better than we do! For example, I'll bet Balaam felt pretty foolish when he found out that his donkey had saved his life.

Many stories are about dogs saving the lives of people. One such dog was named Balto.

Gunnar Kaasen and his friend Charlie were holed up in a tiny cabin while a blizzard raged outside. It was 28 degrees below zero out there, and both men hoped the storm would soon stop. Beside them on the table was a package wrapped in furs that had arrived by dogsled. Nineteen teams of dogs, working in relays, had already carried the package more than 600 miles. It was still 53 miles to Nome, Alaska, where the package was desperately needed.

A diphtheria epidemic had broken out in Nome, and many people were stricken. Some had already died. If the epidemic couldn't be checked, it would spread throughout the territory, killing thousands of people! The package contained the serum that would save the people from the awful disease.

There were no trains in Alaska in 1925, and airplanes couldn't get off the ground because of the blizzard. The only way through was with dog teams. Gunnar took one last look out the window and decided he would wait no longer.

With Charlie's help, he hitched up his dogs. He knew he was risking his life and theirs, but dying people were relying on him. His job was to take the serum 35 miles to the town of Safety, where another dog team would take it on to Nome.

🙂 **Why do you think God uses animals to help Him accomplish things? Does that make you think of animals differently?**

🙂 **Got a dog? Or know someone who has? Give it a bath!**

158

Race for Life, Part 2

So he did what the Lord had told him. He went to the Kerith Ravine, east of the Jordan, and stayed there. The ravens brought him bread and meat in the morning and bread and meat in the evening, and he drank from the brook. 1 Kings 17:5, 6, NIV.

Gunnar knelt beside Balto, a large black dog with one white foreleg. "It's going to be a tough run, Balto," he said, rubbing the dog's chest. "But we can make it, eh, boy?"

Balto was the lead dog because he was the smartest and most experienced of all the dogs. Gunnar climbed onto the sled runners and gave the command, "Mush!"

Balto leaped forward, and the 12 dogs behind him surged ahead. Gunnar decided to follow the shore, where he thought he would make better time than if he went inland. The cold wind slapped at his face, stealing his breath. Its icy fingers made their way through his sealskin parka and pants.

Besides the whipping white snow, the only thing Gunnar could see was the string of dogs pulling the sled. But he had traveled this trail many times and knew where he was going. They were making good time and reached Topkok River when Balto suddenly stopped.

Gunnar worked his way to the front and was dismayed to see that Balto had run into an overflow, where the water had come up through the ice. Balto's wet paws would have to be dried so they wouldn't stick to the ice and tear as he ran. Gunnar spent precious time drying off Balto's paws; then they started out again.

They crossed the river and began to climb Topkok hill. At the top they ran into the teeth of the storm, a battering 80-mile-an-hour wind. The snow was like a cloud of bitter cold that blocked out everything. Gunnar couldn't even see the wheel dog, who was nearest to the sled.

- Do you think Gunnar should have risked his life and the dogs' lives to save so many people? Do you think God was with him, even though he may not have been aware of it?

- Do you live in a place where it snows? Check out some dogsled races.

159

Race for Life, Part 3

Abraham looked up and there in a thicket he saw a ram caught by its horns. He went over and took the ram and sacrificed it as a burnt offering instead of his son. So Abraham called that place The Lord Will Provide. Genesis 22:13, 14, NIV.

Gunnar couldn't go back, and he couldn't stop. He had to trust Balto to follow the trail. Although the dog could see no better than Gunnar, his nose told him this was the trail hundreds of dogs had followed in the past. So Balto ran on.

At the town of Solomon there was a message for Gunnar, telling him to wait until the blizzard was over. No man or dog could possibly make it through the storm. But Balto didn't know about the message, and followed the trail right past Solomon.

They finally made it to the town of Safety, where another driver was supposed to take over for them. But because Gunnar wasn't expected until after daylight, no one was awake. Rather than waste time waking up the driver and waiting for him to hitch his team, Gunnar decided to keep going. Nome was 21 miles away, and he knew his team could make it.

Seven and a half hours after they started, Balto led the team into the snow-covered streets of Nome. They had come 53 miles in the worst weather imaginable. The sled dogs were panting and exhausted. Two were half frozen and limping. Gunnar's face was half frozen. But they had won the race for life!

Gunnar staggered up the line of dogs and collapsed beside Balto and wrapped his arms around the dog's neck. "Balto," he wept, "you're one fine dog. You got us through."

Ten months later Gunnar and Balto made the trip to New York City to watch the unveiling of a statue that had been paid for by many people in New York, honoring Balto and the other 150 brave dogs who helped to win the race for life to Nome. The statue stands in Central Park in New York City.

😊 **Have you ever had to trust an animal with your life? Do you think you could?**

😊 **Volunteer some time at the local animal shelter.**

Top-hat Party

A good tree cannot bear bad fruit, and a bad tree cannot bear good fruit. Every tree that does not bear good fruit is cut down and thrown into the fire. Thus, by their fruit you will recognize them. Matthew 7:18-20, NIV.

Samantha closed her eyes while Zeb put a hat on her head.
"Now what am I supposed to do?"

"You ask people yes or no questions and try to guess who you are," Zeb explained. "Your name is written on a label on your hat."

Sam teetered her way into the living room, where some of her other friends were gathered around a table, eating cookies and drinking punch. They were all wearing hats. "Hey, Keisha, would you tell me if I was a good person?"

Keisha glanced at Sam's hat. "Nope, you weren't."

"Am I a man?" Sam persisted. "Was I royalty?"

"Nope and yep."

Puzzled, Sam wandered around the room with her punch.

"Baxter, was I married?"

"Yes."

"Did I die peacefully?"

"Nope."

"Was I"—Sam gulped—"murdered?"

Baxter read the name on her hat once more before replying. "Well . . . I guess you could say so. It was pretty disgusting."

Sam made her way back to the table where Zeb was. "I know who I am," she said proudly. "I'm Jezebel, aren't I?"

Zeb smiled. "You're good at this. Yes, you're Jezebel."

- People know us by how we act. In the Bible, actions are compared to fruit. What do your actions say about you? What can you do if they aren't what Jesus would want them to be?

- Have your own top-hat party. Make sure you have the hats and labels made up ahead of time. (And cover up any mirrors that are around!) Have a small prize for the winner.

Oops!

The way of a fool seems right to him, but a wise man listens to advice. Proverbs 12:15, NIV.

Shortly before the turn of the twentieth century three partners in the oil business, Hardison, Steward, and Thomas Baird, decided to build an oil tanker to transport their oil. Hardison was in charge of the project. For safety considerations, Baird instructed Hardison to build the hull of the tanker out of iron. While Baird was on a trip, however, Hardison contracted to have the ship built with a wooden hull. Upon its completion, the *W. L. Hardison* became the first bulk oil tanker in the Pacific, capable of carrying 6,500 barrels of oil.

On June 25, 1889, while taking on crude oil near the Ventura Pier, an inexperienced first mate decided to check the level of the oil by lowering a lantern into the hull. It was a mistake he was lucky to have survived. The *W. L. Hardison,* however, did not. Billows of black smoke poured into the sky as the ship burned and sank.

Hardison made a mistake. He built an oil tanker with a wooden hull, even after being told to build it of iron. The first mate made a careless mistake by lowering a lantern into a tank full of oil.

The Bible is full of people who made mistakes. From Adam and Eve to Paul. From the children of Israel to the Corinthians. We all make mistakes.

Isn't it wonderful that after all the mistakes we make, God still loves us and wants us with Him in heaven? Isn't it wonderful that He will forgive us when we are sorry for our sins and ask His forgiveness?

- **Have you ever done something you felt you couldn't be forgiven for? Is it hard for you to imagine that God could forgive you just because you are sorry?**

- **If someone has done something to hurt you or to make you mad, ask God to help you forgive them.**

162

Ultimate Forgiveness

Everyone who believes in him will have their sins forgiven through his name. Acts 10:43, TLB.

*C*harles Stanley, in his book *The Gift of Forgiveness,* relates a story from an evangelism course he had taken. The lesson was on God's grace and forgiveness.

As Stanley's professor handed out the final exam, he cautioned everyone to read it all the way through before beginning. There was even a warning on the exam itself telling the students to read the whole exam before beginning.

As Stanley and his classmates read the exam through, it became painfully obvious to each of them that the test was impossible to pass. It was far more difficult than they were prepared for.

But wait! On the last page there was a note. It told them that they had a choice: they could either do the exam, or they could merely sign their name at the bottom and receive an A.

Stanley recalls how stunned they all were. But slowly, one after another, each student signed his or her name and turned in the exam.

The professor later told of the reactions he had gotten in the past. There were students who, after reading only a few pages, would become angry, give up, and turn their papers in before ever getting to the part that said all they had to do was sign their name to receive an A. Others would struggle through the exam for the whole two hours of class before finally reading the message at the end. One stubborn student read the exam as he was told to do, saw that all he had to do was sign his name, and then decided that he didn't want a free gift. He did the exam anyway and received a C+ instead of an A.

Forgiveness is God's gift to us. When we are sorry for our sins, all we have to do is ask God to forgive us.

😊 **How can you receive God's gift of forgiveness? God's grace is free—you only have to ask.**

😊 **On each of seven 3 x 5 cards, write one of your favorite texts that has to do with forgiveness. Share one at family worship each night for a week.**

163

Sometimes It's Hard

So take a new grip with your tired hands, stand firm on your shaky legs, and mark out a straight, smooth path for your feet so that those who follow you, though weak and lame, will not fall and hurt themselves, but become strong. Hebrews 12:12, 13, TLB.

Grant Peters and his father were scouting out some logging roads on their motorcycles. An hour earlier Mr. Peters said he wanted to explore one of the roads they had found, so he made a right turn onto what looked like a well-used dirt road. But as the two rode farther and farther, the road became more difficult to negotiate. Grant rode his bike over as many of the downed trees as he could and followed his father around others. But the fallen trees were getting more and more frequent, and Grant and his father were becoming more and more tired.

Finally Grant pulled over to rest. He took off his helmet and wiped the sweat out of his eyes. "I think I've learned something, Dad," he said thoughtfully. "I've been thinking a lot lately about being a Christian example to my friends at school."

Grant's father removed his helmet. "What have you come up with?"

"Well, going to public school isn't always easy. It's hard to act like a Christian sometimes." He nodded back up the road. "It's sort of like this trail we're on. Sometimes the trail is really easy. Then it gets hard. Sometimes it gets easy again. And then it gets really hard the more trees there are to cross or go around."

Grant's father nodded in agreement. "You're right. It is a lot like being a Christian. But no one ever said it was going to be easy all the time. That is what you are getting at, isn't it?" he asked.

Grant rolled his eyes and laughed. "Yeah, Dad, that's what I'm getting at."

🙂 **Why is being a Christian example sometimes hard for you? When is it easiest?**

🙂 **Read today's Bible verse every morning until you memorize it. After you read it, pray for God to help you share your Christianity.**

Bible Billboard

I will come and proclaim your mighty acts, O Sovereign Lord; I will proclaim your righteousness, yours alone. Psalm 71:16, NIV.

Have you ever seen a billboard? There aren't any in my state, but I've been in other states that have billboards all over the place. Some of the billboards are for advertising. Some have good messages, and some have bad messages. They say whatever the person who bought the billboard wants it to say, but most of them are trying to sell something. And because they are so big, everybody has to look at them.

Sometime ago people got the idea of using T-shirts as billboards. Sports manufacturers, chain stores, neighborhood baseball teams, and other people who wanted to advertise their products started putting them on T-shirts, baseball hats, and other pieces of clothing that people wear. One man even started a line of T-shirts publishing his own stories, because he got sick of reading the usual T-shirt material!

In this world we have many ways of advertising something we want to say. We put it on billboards, on the radio, on television, in the newspaper, and now even on the Internet. As Christians we can take advantage of these avenues of communication to spread the message that *we* have. Jesus is coming soon, and He loves us very much.

Some Christian companies make very catchy T-shirts with Christian messages, but you can design your own. To make it interesting, have a T-shirt design contest in your Sabbath school, church, or school. Then advertise *your* message wherever you go.

- Why do you think advertisers put their products on so many things? How do you think advertising helps people sell things or influence others? Have you ever bought something because you saw it advertised somewhere?

- Find some plain white cotton T-shirts, and get fabric paints at a craft store. Following the directions on the paints, decorate your T-shirt with your message about God. Include some of your favorite Bible verses. You have something wonderful to advertise.

Flying Sling

Then he took his staff in his hand, chose five smooth stones from the stream, put them in the pouch of his shepherd's bag and, with his sling in his hand, approached the Philistine. 1 Samuel 17:40, NIV.

While everyone was eating breakfast around the fire, Mark took his father's sling into the trees surrounding Sawtooth Lake to practice. He wanted to practice alone, because the rocks never seemed to fly exactly where he wanted them to go. In fact, he could never really be sure they were always going to go in the direction he hurled them.

Mark was having fun firing rocks off at the calm, crystal-blue lake through the trees. After a while he felt he had mastered the art of using a sling almost as well as David the shepherd had. Then he picked the smoothest rock he could find. He braced his legs to hold himself steady and swung the sling around his head— *faster, faster, faster . . .* And then he let go. The rock missed every tree. It flew straight and true toward the lake. But Mark wasn't impressed as he watched helplessly while the rock traveled through the air—still nestled inside the sling. Somehow the loop had slipped off his finger. When the sling finally landed, it looked as though it had landed far out in the lake.

As Mark made his way to the edge of the lake, he wondered how he would tell his father he had lost the sling. But most of all, he prayed that he would be able to get the sling back. When he reached the lake, he discovered the sling floating near the shore. He didn't even have to get his feet wet to retrieve it. Immediately he thanked God for helping him. Of course, the question did come up about why the sling was wet, but Mark's father seemed to understand, almost as if something similar had once happened to him.

- **Can you think of a time when you thought something was going to turn out far worse than it did? Were you praying that God would help you out? Do you think God did help?**

- **When someone needs your understanding, try putting yourself in his or her place. Later, ask yourself how it helped the situation.**

166

A Good Last Name

A good name is more desirable than great riches; to be esteemed is better than silver or gold. Proverbs 22:1, NIV.

Ever wonder where last names came from? People didn't always have two names. Generally people used only one name. Then around 1066 surnames began to come into use to help identify people better. Having only a first name got to be a little frustrating when there were two Davids, three Marys, and four Johns in the same town.

One common way to identify someone was by the work he or she did. John the baker became John Baker. David, who protected the town and hunted with his bow and arrow, became David Archer. Other ways to identify someone might have been to tack on a name that told where the person came from or who his or her father was. For example, Peter, whose father's name was William, became Peter Williamson.

Most people have a first name, a middle name, and a last name. Some people go by several names. A name is important. It gives us identity. When people think of you or me, they think of our names. When we ace a test, run for a touchdown, hit a home run, sing in church, or play an instrument for special music, our names are announced, shouted, and praised.

Unfortunately, names also identify murderers, drug dealers, and thieves. A bad name can be remembered just as easily as a good name. Sometimes a bad name is remembered more easily! And a bad name is hard to overcome. How would you feel if someone who had the same name as yours was suddenly showing up in the newspapers for doing something bad?

When people think of your name, what do you want them to remember? Good things? Or bad things? Godly things? Or worldly things? Are you working on having a good name?

- **What does it mean to you to have a good name? How can you keep a good name?**

- **Every time you write your name, think about who is your example, and then mentally add the word *Christian* after your name.**

167

A Sticky Situation

These commandments that I give you today are to be upon your hearts. Impress them on your children. Talk about them when you sit at home and when you walk along the road, when you lie down and when you get up. Deuteronomy 6:6, 7, NIV.

ey, Sam, what's up?" Zeb asked as he knocked on her open bedroom door and came in.

Sam jumped guiltily and hid something behind her back. "Don't you believe in knocking?" she asked irritably.

"I did knock," Zeb replied. "Your mom said you were studying and to come right up. What are you doing? Something illegal?"

Sam snorted. "Of course not! I'm upholding the law and the promises of God."

"Well, what is it?" Zeb asked, clearly becoming frustrated.

"You can't tell anyone. Promise?" Sam showed him a pile of sticky notes. Each one had something written on it.

"It's a bunch of sticky notes. I see them all over the place," Zeb said.

"But," Sam pointed out triumphantly, "what kinds of things do you see written on them?"

Zeb shrugged. "I don't know . . . Reminders to do chores or take out the garbage or that someone called, I guess."

"Exactly! And my sticky notes have Bible promises on them. I'm going to stick them all over, where my parents can see them."

"Why? Are you afraid they don't know what's in the Bible?"

"No, silly! The verses are to encourage them."

"Wow! That's a neat idea," Zeb said, admiration in his voice. "Can I do some?"

"Sure," Sam said, handing him a pad of sticky notes and a pen.

- **Why do you think it's important to read and think about God's Word every day? Why does God want us to read the Bible in the first place?**

- **Buy your own pad of sticky notes and place Bible verses and promises for your family and friends around the house. Some suggested places: pillowcases, mirrors, lunch bags, and dinner plates.**

Nolan's Big Accomplishment

I pray that you, being rooted and established in love, may have
power, together with all the saints, to grasp how wide and long
and high and deep is the love of Christ, and to know this love that
surpasses knowledge—that you may be filled to the measure of
all the fullness of God. Ephesians 3:17-19, NIV.

Nolan was 22 years old when he got his first job. It wasn't
because he didn't *want* a job that he had been unable to
find a real one until he was in his 20s. It was because no
one wanted to hire him. To hire Nolan would require a lot of time
and patience on the part of his employer, because Nolan had a
disability. He had Down's syndrome.

Down's syndrome happens when there is a defect in one of
the chromosomes. A child born with Down's syndrome will
have severe obstacles to overcome, including mental retarda-
tion, stunted growth, and possible abnormalities of the heart,
intestines, and teeth.

Nolan's first job was in a pizza restaurant. He vacuumed the
floor and made sure everyone had a clean table to sit at. When
any of his fellow employees needed help, Nolan was right there
to help in any way he could. It wasn't always easy for Nolan to
learn what to do, but Nolan's coworkers showed him a lot of love
and patience as they helped him learn his job.

I was there when Nolan received his first paycheck. For a moment he just stared at the piece of paper. Then he waved it in the
air for everyone else to see, his face glowing with pride. Nolan's
friends at the pizza place all got a hug before Nolan left that day.
As I watched him walk out the door with his head held high, I
doubted there had ever been a moment in Nolan's life when he
had been more proud.

- How do you react toward people who have a disability?
  Are you patient and understanding? Do you help them
  get the best out of life?

- Is there someone in your school who is disabled? Ask
  how you can help. There are many things you can do
  that would be greatly appreciated.

169

A Picture of God

Now we see but a poor reflection as in a mirror; then we shall
see face to face. 1 Corinthians 13:12, NIV.

Have you ever seen God? I did. No joke. It was a cold weekend in February at a place called Warm Lake in Idaho.

My wife and I had decided to go for a walk, so we bundled up in our heavy coats, warm boots, and mittens. All the previous week Warm Lake had been locked in subzero temperatures. But on Sunday morning, as we stepped out of our cabin, we noticed the weather had changed. It was warmer. A weak storm front had moved in, bringing with it a light snowfall.

We found a trail where we could walk without sinking in snow up to our knees and headed off toward the lake. Along the way, we doused each other with handfuls of snow or tried to wrestle each other into the deepest drifts we could find. By the time we reached the lake, we both resembled snowpeople.

Our warm breath mingled with the falling snow as we gazed out over the frozen lake. We were surrounded by tall mountains, covered with ranks of tall pine trees heavily laden with snow. The air was still, and the clouds ranged in color from blue-gray to white as they hung low on the horizon. They seemed to be hovering low enough to protect that beautiful winter wonderland.

That's where I saw God.

Sometimes I forget how easy it is to believe in God and His awesome power. But that isn't the only thing I need to remember. As I gazed at that scene at Warm Lake that February morning, I remembered something else that is even more important. Our God created us in His own image, and He also takes pleasure in the things that we enjoy because we are like Him. I imagine He enjoyed that morning as much as I did.

🙂 **What are some of the beautiful places you have been that are your favorites?**

🙂 **Start your own photo album of your favorite places. Mark the ones in which you felt especially close to God.**

All Are Precious in His Sight

I praise you because I am fearfully and wonderfully made; your works are wonderful, I know that full well. Psalm 139:14, NIV.

His name was Schooner Bill, and Dorney met him on her way to work each morning. He would stop short, sashay to one side, and bow low, saying, "Friend." The other remarkable thing about Schooner Bill was that he wore a different type of hat every day. The people where he worked would give him a different person's hat each day. It didn't matter to them—or to Bill—if it was a woman's hat or a man's hat. He wore either happily.

Dorney always felt pleased after she'd met Schooner Bill, and she once thought that it was very kind of the Lord not to make everybody alike. *Why didn't He?* she wondered.

After giving it some thought, she decided that when we saw people like Schooner Bill we would ask why there was someone like him. Then we'd ask Why is there this? or Why is there that? Next we'd be thinking about God, because He made everything.

Schooner Bill is just a character in a book, but Leslie Lemke is real.

When May Lemke took in a baby who was considered a hopeless case, she didn't give up hope. Baby Leslie had a multitude of problems. He was blind and had cerebral palsy and mental disabilities. May worked with Leslie every day, believing in him.

One night May woke up hearing beautiful piano music. Thinking she'd left the radio on, she went to investigate, only to find Leslie sitting at the piano playing a piece of music he'd heard that day. He went on to play other pieces after hearing them only once and began giving concerts when he was 22.

God didn't intend for people to have to live with disabilities. Disabilities are a result of sin's destruction of the human body. But with God's help, many people rise above their disabilities to do much more than they would have accomplished if they had been born "normal."

😊 **What do you think of when you see a disabled person?**

😊 **Bake a batch of cookies and visit a school for special-needs children.**

171

Den of Robbers

"It is written," he said to them, "'My house will be called a house of prayer,' but you are making it a 'den of robbers.'" Matthew 21:13, NIV.

Timothy Bartell had gone to the same church ever since he was a week old, when his parents carried him through the door. That was 14 years ago. Many of the church members had watched him grow up. They smiled and shook his hand every Sabbath morning in the foyer.

One Sabbath as Timothy dropped into a church pew beside Carl, he pulled a stack of 10 baseball cards out of his jacket. "Here are those cards I wanted to sell, Carl. You want to look at them?"

Carl nodded. "Sure do!" he said eagerly. Ten minutes after the pastor started speaking, Carl slipped Timothy $2 for the baseball cards.

Now jump back 2,000 years in time.

As you enter the Temple, just ahead of the Man called Jesus, you see Timothy Bartell at a table where there is the heaviest flow of pedestrians. He's got doves to sell to the weary travelers who have come a long distance and were unable to bring a sacrifice. He's also exchanging foreign money for local currency, but with a hefty charge added on. Oh, Timothy's got a good business going right there in the Temple. Raking in the money. Getting wealthy.

Instead of feeling the joy of God's presence, you can't help feeling sadness. But then you look back at Jesus. An unexplained hush falls over the crowd.

Timothy is folding up his money, getting ready to put it in his pocket, when a shadow falls over him. He looks up into the pained face of Jesus, who speaks only one word.

"Why?"

😊 **What are some ways church can become like a "den of robbers" on Sabbath morning? What are some things that can keep the presence of God out of church? Why do you like to go to church?**

😊 **Before you leave church this Sabbath, take a moment to think: *Would Jesus have been comfortable in my church this morning?***

Taking a Stand!

Now let the fear of the Lord be upon you. Judge carefully, for with the Lord our God there is no injustice or partiality or bribery. 2 Chronicles 19:7, NIV.

That unexplained silence is almost deafening. A tinkle of coins can be heard in someone's pockets. A chair squeaks, a wooden leg clatters along the floor as someone bumps the table. But all eyes are on the Man called Jesus.

Has anyone ever picked on your sister or your brother or your best friend? Maybe someone says something derogatory or insulting about your parents. What's worse, they don't even think twice about it! It's as if they do it all the time! So what difference does it make? They're not even sorry! And when they insult your friends or family, it's a personal insult to you, too. It's time to stand up and defend your family and your friends! So you stand up and speak out!

As you gaze at Jesus, you realize that at that moment He feels exactly the same way. The people are basically making fun of *His* father! *Your* heavenly Father! They are making fun of everyone who truly loves God, too. You see the hurt in Jesus' face, and at that instant you understand that Jesus is going to defend God and those who love Him. He's going to make some changes!

Aren't you glad you came to the Temple to be in God's presence and spend time worshiping Him, instead of being one of the money changers Jesus is suddenly so furious with?

- How can reverence in God's house be ruined today? How does it make you feel when you know someone has come to church to be close to God, but someone else acts irreverently?

- When you go to church this Sabbath, make a list of reasons you like to go to church. Then make a list of reasons you think Jesus would like to come to your church. How do your lists compare?

Pet Therapy

A generous man will prosper; he who refreshes others will himself be refreshed. Proverbs 11:25, NIV.

S am hopped out of the car as soon as it stopped. Pulling a wiggly little puppy out of its crate, she gave it a quick hug, scratching it under the chin.

"Do you want to take the puppy or the kitten?" her mother asked, then smiled. "Oh, I see you've already made your selection. I'll take the kitten."

Sam gripped the puppy tightly as they walked up the front steps of the retirement home. "Mom?" she asked in a small voice. "Are you scared?"

Mrs. Reese stopped short. "Scared? What of?"

Sam gulped. "Well, we don't know any of these people."

"Don't worry, Sam," her mother assured her. "The people at the humane society come here with the animals all the time, and the residents love it. Now, let's hurry. We have to get the animals back to the humane society in a couple hours."

At first Sam tagged after her mother, shyly offering the puppy in her arms to anyone who seemed interested in petting it.

"Oh, what a beautiful baby you have," an elderly woman gushed, patting the puppy's head, while it tried desperately to lick her hand.

Sam giggled. "He likes you."

"And I like him," the woman said. "Thank you for bringing him by for a visit."

"You're welcome," Sam replied, a light, happy feeling welling up inside her. There was nothing frightening about this. In fact, it made her feel good—so good she couldn't wait to do it again.

🙂 **How does it make you feel when you do something nice for someone? Why?**

🙂 **Call your local humane society or animal shelter and see if they have a pet therapy program and if they accept the help of volunteers.**

174

Tall Prejudice

Charm is deceptive, and beauty is fleeting. Proverbs 31:30, NIV.

S he has a really long neck. But her head is sorta small compared to the rest of her body. And her legs aren't the same
length, either," Tawnya said as she sat down at the picnic
table beside her brother Jeff.

Wow! Now, that's ugly, Jeff thought. *Poor girl.*

"You should have *seen* her!" Tawnya said.

Jeff chuckled. "No, thanks. Sounds too gross for me." *Besides,
I'd probably end up just staring, and she'd see me staring, and then
I'd feel uncomfortable,* he thought.

Tawnya frowned as she sipped her pop. "You don't want to
see her?"

"No, I don't."

Tawnya shook her head. "But we came all this way. You were
really eager to go to the San Diego Zoo."

Jeff shook his head earnestly. "Sorry, but I don't want to see
her. Besides, why do you insist that I should go look at her? I
doubt she wants anyone staring at her."

Tawnya gritted her teeth in frustration. *Sometimes boys are
really too weird,* she concluded. "I *don't* think it matters to *her* at
all. I'm sure she's used to it. Besides, that's what she's here at the
zoo for . . . so people can look at her."

"That's sick," Jeff replied. "I mean, what's this world coming
to if people stand around staring at a girl just because she's ugly?"

Tawnya nearly let out a scream. "I'm not talking about a *girl!*
I'm talking about a giraffe! I think she's the most beautiful animal
God created. Her neck is so long and sleek. Her head looks so delicate and pretty. And even though her front legs are longer than
her back legs, she walks more gracefully than a queen. You're just
so hung up on ugly versus pretty that it makes you prejudiced."

- Do you ever get so hung up on how people look that
  you become narrow-minded about their other qualities?

- Instead of fitting other people into categories, such as
  whether you consider them ugly or pretty, focus on
  what makes every person beautiful.

Sticks and Stones

All kinds of animals, birds, reptiles and creatures of the sea are being tamed and have been tamed by man, but no man can tame the tongue. It is a restless evil, full of deadly poison. James 3:7, 8, NIV.

Sticks and stones can break my bones, but names will never hurt me."

Ever hear that little rhyme? When I was going to school, anytime someone called you names or picked on you, that was the little song you sang to them to show that it really didn't hurt. Yessiree, your skin was as tough as shoe leather.

Except that it *did* hurt. Teasing happens a lot. Especially in schools.

"Great jacket. I wish I'd worn my sunglasses; it's so bright it hurts my eyes."

"Where'd you get those shoes? From your grandmother?"

"What kind of name is Hossenpfeffer? Sounds like horses and feathers. What are you, half chicken and half horse?"

Teasing can get pretty nasty too. Sometimes it's easier to pretend you didn't hear. You may even be tempted to return the teasing.

Some kids teased Rachel Bradley, of Doylestown, Pennsylvania, one day, and she realized that words *can* hurt. But Rachel didn't give up or pretend it didn't hurt. Instead she decided to help other kids who were being teased at school.

Rachel started the I Don't Care Club at her school. She held meetings to help kids cope with teasing. At the meetings they talk about how they can deal with the kids who tease them, but one of the best parts is making new friends.

"Many kids get teased," Rachel says. "If there's one little thing about you that's different, other kids pick up on it."

Standing up to unkindness can be hard, but if you ask Him, Jesus can help you love even people you find unlovable.

🙂 **Can you think of a time when someone's words hurt you? What can you do to make sure that your words don't hurt someone?**

🙂 **The next time you take a walk in the woods, pick up some sticks and stones. Glue them on a poster and hang it in your room to remind you to say kind things.**

Roscoe

To the man who pleases him, God gives wisdom, knowledge and happiness, but to the sinner he gives the task of gathering and storing up wealth to hand it over to the one who pleases God. Ecclesiastes 2:26, NIV.

I first met Roscoe in a dark corner of the Monterey Bay Aquarium, on the second floor. Roscoe had a broad, friendly face and wide nose. From what I could tell about him, he was pretty happy. I called my wife over to introduce her to him.

"Roscoe, this is Sue, my wife . . . Sue, this is Roscoe, the otter."

Roscoe might have smiled. I'm not sure. He did a couple somersaults for us before swimming down to the bottom of his 55,000-gallon tank. Then, in a matter of seconds, he was back again, doing rolls and somersaults. He would float on his back and rub his fur. His somersaults caused air to blow into his fur. All the while he seemed to be enjoying the attention. Otters like to play.

Yet what seemed like mere fun and games to us was also survival for otters, because while an otter is rolling and rubbing, it is also grooming itself to keep its fur clean, warm, and waterproof.

Roscoe is just one of the sea otters who came to the aquarium as an orphan to be nursed back to health. But when it came time to turn Roscoe loose, he returned six days later, tired and skinny, because he had never learned how to survive in the wild.

Roscoe's experience is a good example for us too. The world is no place for a halfway Christian. There are too many traps. Too many distractions that will take our eyes off Jesus. There are all kinds of worldly entertainment, but none that will bring us closer to God. There are even people who may deceive us. But if we learn to survive by careful study and sincere prayer, Jesus will become our strength.

- **Are you sincere about God? Or are you more concerned with having fun and forgetting about building a solid relationship with God?**

- **Make up your mind to read one chapter of the Bible each day. When you finish each book of the Bible, check it off in the index.**

Where Jesus Walked

The Son of Man came eating and drinking, and they say, "Here is a glutton and a drunkard, a friend of tax collectors and 'sinners.'" Matthew 11:19, NIV.

It seemed odd that of all people, Jim found a friend in Pastor Mike, an Adventist minister. Jim was about as far from God as a man could get. It was almost as though he tried to be as crude as possible toward Pastor Mike, especially when they first met.

When Jim met Pastor Mike, he tried pretty hard to turn him off by acting even more rotten than usual. But Pastor Mike didn't let Jim's irreverent attitude turn him away. Pastor Mike was used to being around people who didn't know anything about God or didn't care if they knew anything about God. Sometimes people just didn't know that there was a better life for them. How would they learn about God if no one came to them and told them?

That attitude was the cornerstone of Jesus' ministry too. Jesus sought out the people who didn't know a better way so He could show them the love of God. Who else would do it? Jesus hung around people who swore, lied, cheated, and sold their bodies. He showed them how much He loved them. That had become Pastor Mike's philosophy too.

Slowly Jim found out who God was through Pastor Mike, and his life began to change. He became a follower of Jesus. When Jim had to move, his rowdy friends threw him a goodbye party. Jim invited Mike to come to the party to meet his friends. Hesitantly Pastor Mike went. He didn't want people from his church to misunderstand why he would be at such a party, but standing up for Jim was more important.

Jim introduced Pastor Mike to his friends. He told them about how knowing Jesus made his life better. Jim's testimony prompted several people to tell Pastor Mike their own problems. Eventually many were baptized into the church.

🙂 **Are people who don't know Jesus happy? Why not?**

🙂 **You can witness just by showing non-Christians through your happiness that there is a better way to live.**

178

Kids Who Help!

What good is it, my brothers, if a man claims to have faith but has no deeds? Can such faith save him? Suppose a brother or sister is without clothes and daily food. If one of you says to him, "Go, I wish you well; keep warm and well fed," but does nothing about his physical needs, what good is it? In the same way, faith by itself, if it is not accompanied by action, is dead. James 2:14-17, NIV.

Last week I picked up my paper and began to wade through a glut of stories about corrupt politics, nationwide violence, and local car accidents. I didn't expect happy news, and sure enough, I didn't get any. At least, not until the last section, where the headline "Kids Who Help" caught my eye.

Luke and his 12-year-old sister, Anne, are helping out at a local retirement home. They bring cookies, help people in wheelchairs, play games with some of the residents, and sometimes just sit and visit. Luke and Anne are not the only kids getting involved, either. Many kids are volunteering to help out in nursing homes, food drives, fund-raisers, and humane shelters.

What's the deal?

Besides helping other people, kids are helping themselves. Becoming involved takes the attention away from self and directs it outward toward others. Becoming aware of other people's problems teaches compassion. Sharing someone else's life experience teaches empathy (the capacity for participating in the feelings or ideas of another). Today's kids want to focus less on themselves and more on others. They want to make a difference.

- 😊 **If you were to choose a volunteer project, what would you choose? Why?**

- 😊 **If you want to make a difference and become a volunteer, you might try checking out these organizations: Neighborhood Housing Association, Parks and Recreation, nursing homes, Easter Seal Society, humane societies, hospitals, YMCA. Check with your pastor for other ideas. Organize your youth group to volunteer together.**

179

Precious Partnership, Part 1

*Whoever loves his brother lives in the light, and there is nothing
in him to make him stumble. 1 John 2:10, NIV.*

In 1861, after already having three daughters, William found himself to be the proud father of his first son, William, Jr. Another son, Charles, was born in 1865. Although young Will and Charles loved their sisters, they found a much deeper connection with each other and soon became inseparable.

Major medical advancements were happening at the same time Will and Charles were growing up. Their father, whose goal was to see that Will and Charles would continue to grow with the medical times, traveled to New York's Bellevue Hospital to expand his own knowledge of medicine. After observing their father's dedication, it was only natural that Will and Charles would become doctors, just like their father.

Will graduated from the University of Michigan in 1883 and returned to Rochester, Minnesota, to practice medicine with his father. Five years later Charles graduated from Chicago Medical College and also returned to Rochester to practice surgery with his brother and father. A year later, in cooperation with the Sisters of St. Francis, William, Sr., and his two sons opened St. Mary's Hospital.

Until 1905, William, Jr., and his brother Charles performed all surgeries at St. Mary's. Their knowledge about surgery helped originate many of our modern surgical procedures. During World War I, Will and Charles served as chief consultants to the United States Army concerning surgical services, later being commissioned as brigadier generals in the Medical Corps Reserves.

But that is only half of the story of these two brothers, who were very close in life and profession. They also found happiness in helping people.

🙂 **Do you have brothers or sisters or friends you are very close to? Why are you close?**

🙂 **Find out how many of your classmates want an occupation in which they can help people. Which occupation was the most popular? Was money more important than service?**

Precious Partnership, Part 2

This is how we know who the children of God are and who the children of the devil are: Anyone who does not do what is right is not a child of God; nor is anyone who does not love his brother. 1 John 3:10, NIV.

William, Jr., and Charles, the two brothers who were so close from childhood, had also become teammates in medicine. As physicians they published more than 1,000 scientific papers and established new surgical procedures. What people usually didn't know, however, was how the two brothers helped people behind the scenes. It was little known that when nearly one third of their patients would receive their medical bills, the words "paid in full" would be written across them. What a relief to the patients who did not have the money to pay their bills!

And what about those who had money? Their bills reflected only what they could afford. But the brothers' generosity did not stop there. They also gave every dollar they collected on bills that were more than $1,000 to help other sick people.

I wonder if, while they were growing up, Will and Charles had any idea how many people they were going to help? It is doubtful that they could have made such an impact on the medical world if they had not decided to work together with such dedication to help others.

Will and Charles were not only close in life, they were close even in death. It came as a surprise when Charles died of pneumonia on May 26, 1939. To Will, who was already sick, the loss of his brother made him lose interest in life, and on July 28 of that same year he passed away also.

Because they were so close, neither of the brothers ever accepted an honor without prefacing his acceptance speech with the words "My brother and I . . ."

Through a willingness to help others, two brothers founded the Mayo Clinic.

🙂 **What are your dreams for the future? Do they include helping other people?**

🙂 **Discuss with your family ways you can help people right now.**

Treasure Hunt

I have hidden your word in my heart that I might not sin against you. Psalm 119:11, NIV.

Wake up!" Sam sang as she bounced into her parents' room and popped the shades up.

Her father groaned and rolled over. "Is the house on fire?"

"Nope," Sam replied cheerfully.

"Then let me sleep in," he pleaded.

"Sorry, Dad, not today. Mom, wake up. I have a surprise for you both." Sam hopped impatiently from one foot to the other as her parents yawned and looked at her with sleepy eyes.

"Here are your directions." Sam handed them each a piece of paper. "When you find the first clue, it will tell you where to find the next one, and so on," she explained.

"What is this, exactly?" her father asked, scratching his head.

"It's a treasure hunt," Sam said. "There's buried treasure waiting for you at the end." If she thought this bit of information would catapult them from their beds, she was mistaken. But eventually they each headed off in a different direction.

"I found something!" her dad called excitedly from one end of the house.

"Me too!" her mom said.

Her dad's last clue was to look in the phone book, and when he did, he found a bookmark with a Bible verse on it. Her mom wandered in from another room holding a similar bookmark.

"Thank you, sweetie," her mom said, giving Sam a hug.

Sam beamed. "You're welcome. I was reading about hiding the Word in your heart today, and I thought with a bookmark you wouldn't have so much trouble finding it again!"

😊 **Do you think God likes it when we have fun learning His Word? Why do you think it's important to memorize Scripture?**

😊 **Send your own parents or friends on a treasure hunt. At each spot hide a clue, or directions, to the next spot. At the end have a nice bookmark with a Bible verse on it. You can buy them or you can make your own.**

Veto Violence

Whatever is true, whatever is noble, whatever is right, whatever is pure, whatever is lovely, whatever is admirable—if anything is excellent or praiseworthy—think about such things. Philippians 4:8, NIV.

Wiley E. Coyote is after the Road Runner again. He orders some supplies from Acme Company and builds another machine to outsmart, outrun, or outdo the swift Road Runner. For a moment it looks as though he's going to finally get his hands on the Road Runner. But, alas, the Road Runner stops, Wiley races on and gets run over by a train, or falls off a cliff, or gets beaned by a large chunk of rock.

Violence is no laughing matter. When thinking of television violence, you probably wouldn't include the hundreds of cartoons out there. No one gets hurt, so it's supposed to be funny, right?

Ask 14-year-old Virginie Lariviere, whose younger sister was murdered by an unknown attacker. Because she believed that her sister's killer might have been influenced by violence on TV, Virginie decided to do something to change that.

She wrote a petition to the people in government, asking them to pass laws that would reduce violence. With her parents' help, she gathered support and presented her petition to the prime minister. It held 1.3 *million* signatures.

Maybe the violence in cartoons will never inspire someone to commit murder, but violence is on the increase, both on television and on the streets. Coincidence? Not many people think so.

Use today's text to test everything you allow into your mind. Everybody needs a laugh now and then, but don't let yours come at the expense of someone else's pain.

- In your opinion, how much of the television you watch would be what Paul had in mind when he wrote today's verse? Can you find a verse in the Bible that tells what happens to us because of the things that we see around us?

- For one week monitor all the shows you watch on TV, and write down any time violence occurs, even if it's supposed to be funny. At the end of the week talk over the list with your parents.

183

What a Save!

But when he saw that the wind was boisterous, he was afraid; and beginning to sink he cried out, saying, "Lord, save me!" And immediately Jesus stretched out His hand and caught him, and said to him, "O you of little faith, why did you doubt?" Matthew 14:30, 31, NKJV.

When the German fighter planes suddenly attacked, Makepeace tried to evade them by putting his plane into a nearly vertical dive. The quick maneuver, however, came as a sickening shock to his passenger.

Captain J. H. Hedley, an American, was flying with Canadian pilot Makepeace over German territory on January 16, 1918. When Makepeace dove his plane, Hedley was not prepared and was yanked from his seat in the open cockpit plane.

Makepeace knew Hedley had disappeared, but there was nothing he could do about it. He had those German fighters to worry about, so he continued his steep descent. But when Makepeace finally leveled out several hundred feet later, Hedley suddenly reappeared! Hedley had landed on the tail of the airplane, where he clung for dear life until he carefully climbed back into his seat. Apparently the steep dive Makepeace had thrown his aircraft into created enough suction to tow Captain Hedley along behind.

Just like Captain Hedley, who fell out of his plane, then landed right back on it, Jesus wants you and me to know that He always wants to get us back if we become lost. When Peter was walking on water, he lost faith for a moment when he looked at the angry waves, and instantly he began to sink. But when he cried out to Jesus to save him, Jesus did just that!

Jesus is never far away. That is important to remember if we take our eyes off Him. He is always ready to reach out and catch us. He is always ready to get you and me back.

☺ **Can you remember a time when you forgot about Jesus? What helped you to think more about Him again?**

☺ **Sit in a chair. You can see the chair; you know it's there. It's holding you up. Now cover your eyes with a blindfold. You can't see the chair. Is it still there? Is it still holding you up? How do you know, if you can't see it?**

United We Stand

How good and pleasant it is when brothers live together in unity! Psalm 133:1, NIV.

ometimes kids aren't given the credit they deserve for the influence they have on others. Consider your own group of friends. Why are they your friends? Why are other kids not your friends? Is there anyone you would not want to be friends with just because of what other kids say about them, even though you don't really know them?

There are probably kids in your school you consider to be leaders. What they say influences others.

Orlando, a 14-year-old African-American who attends the Benson Village School in Vermont, decided that he was going to run for president of the student council. Why? Because he was concerned about the fact that younger and older students were divided.

"Grades 7 and 8 got along pretty good, and grades 5 and 6 got along pretty good, but there wasn't very much intermingling between grades 7 and 8 and grades 5 and 6," Orlando said. "I wanted people to get together and know one another."

And that was precisely what he did. Under his direction the students held a grades 5 through 8 mystery game, and together they raised $80 for a local Christmas fund. Orlando believes that he won the election because of a friendly attitude.

"I don't hold grudges against people. I may not like people, but I still walk up and talk to them."

As Christians we all have a responsibility for unity. After all, unless we are all working together, we won't get nearly as far. See what you can do to bring others together today.

- **Why do you think unity is important? What can you do personally to help provide unity among the people you know?**

- **Take a good look around your school. Are there students who are excluded from activities because of the way they are perceived by the group? If so, invite them personally to join you in your activities. You'll be glad you did.**

185

Pursue Peace

Pursue peace with all people, and holiness, without which no one will see the Lord. Hebrews 12:14, NKJV.

Ben slammed the back door. "Never touch my stuff again!" he yelled over his shoulder to his sister, Lisa.

Uncle Jamie was just walking into the kitchen at that same time. "Whoa! You sound like a roaring lion," he said.

Ben stopped. He liked being compared to the king of beasts, except that Uncle Jamie wasn't comparing him with a lion's strength. He was comparing his yelling with a lion's roar. Somehow that didn't sound like a compliment. "Sorry, Uncle Jamie."

Just then Lisa charged angrily through the back door. She slammed the door even harder than Ben had. Suddenly she saw Uncle Jamie. She quickly made a face at Ben and tried to leave.

"Hold up a second," Uncle Jamie said quietly. "I want to talk to both of you." He ushered them into the living room. "I can see that you two are very angry with each other. Personally, I like peace and harmony, so I was wondering how long it will be before I can expect peace in this house again."

Ben glared at his sister. "Never!"

"Same here!" Lisa shot back.

Uncle Jamie cleared his throat. "You know, Ben, I said you sounded like a roaring lion. But even a lion knows enough to keep peace within the group. Lions make an effort to smooth out any tension in the pride. When they wake up, they greet one another to reinforce their social bonds. They do the same thing before they hunt, and again when they reunite. Lions survive by living and working together peacefully. Don't you think that is what Jesus has in mind for us human beings, too?"

Ben looked at his sister.

Lisa looked back at her brother.

"I guess if lions can keep peace, we can too," Ben said.

🙂 **How do you work out differences in your home? Why is it important to defuse tension in your family?**

🙂 **Be a leader in your home by talking through disagreements.**

No Dumping Allowed

A gossip betrays a confidence, but a trustworthy man keeps a secret.
Proverbs 11:13, NIV.

Sam was thumb wrestling with Zeb when Sara scooted onto the cafeteria bench next to her. She wiggled her thumb, trying to lure him into a position so she could pin down his thumb. Sara cleared her throat just as Sam pinned Zeb's thumb under her own. "Ha!" Sam cried triumphantly. "I won!"

Sara cleared her throat again. Sam looked at her suspiciously. "Did you want to say something?"

Sara jerked her head toward Zeb. "Does he have to be here?"

Zeb stood up with his food tray. "*He* was just leaving anyway," he said. "See you later, Sam."

Sara watched until Zeb made it all the way to the garbage can before she whispered, "Did you hear about Jenny?"

Sam wriggled uncomfortably in her seat. She wasn't sure she wanted to know about Jenny. "No. What about her?"

Sara's voice dropped so low that Sam had to bend forward to hear her. "She flunked the math test. She was crying about it, and everything. She told me not to say anything to anyone, but I know she wouldn't mind if I told you. Can you believe she flunked that test, though? It was so easy!"

Sam picked up her books. "That's too bad," she said. "I know Jenny studied hard for that test. See you later, Sara."

"Wait! I haven't told you what happened to Rachel yet."

"That's OK," Sam said. "If it's important, I'm sure Rachel will tell me herself. 'Bye." *I learned one thing,* Sam said to herself as she walked to her locker. *The next time someone asks me if I heard about someone, I'm going to tell them, "No, and I don't want to."*

😄 **What do you do when someone tries to pass on gossip? If they talk about other people, do you trust them with any of your secrets?**

😄 **Don't be a victim. The next time someone tries to dump a garbage load of gossip in your head, tell them, "Sorry, no dumping allowed."**

Mr. T

So God created the great creatures of the sea and every living and moving thing with which the water teems, according to their kinds. Genesis 1:21, NIV.

What do you think it would be like to get up early every morning—at dawn—and patrol a beach? You're looking for turtles in trouble. You have to check on their nests and dig out any hatchlings that are in trouble. Sound like fun?

Thousands of sea turtles owe their lives to 15-year-old Christian Miller's daily patrols. Sea turtles live in the ocean, but they return to the beach to lay their eggs. When the baby turtles hatch, they need to return to the sea. Since they usually hatch at night, they find the water by the moonlight reflecting off it.

That is, unless they see artificial lights in another direction. Then they head away from the beach toward almost certain death.

Seven years ago Chris found a dead baby turtle in the sand near his home in Palm Beach, Florida. He took a course in rescuing turtles and got a permit to handle them. He also helped officials to document the dangers of artificial lights.

Some animals are endangered because they have something such as fur or ivory that people want. Others are endangered because of ignorance or prejudice, or because people are starting to push them out of their living space.

Maybe there are no sea turtles near your house, but how about other animals that get bad raps? Bats, snakes, squirrels, and pigeons generally are considered little better than pests. Learn how to help them, and then educate people you know.

You can make a difference.

- **Why is it important for us to care for wild animals? Does God really expect us to save whales and manatees and turtles? Why or why not?**

- **Did you know you can adopt a whale or a manatee or other endangered wild animal? Get more information from nature stores. Or how about buying a bird or squirrel feeder? Can you make or buy a bat house? Local animals need help too, especially through the winter.**

"I Don't Get It"

This is the message you heard from the beginning: We should love one another. 1 John 3:11, NIV.

Jeremy shuffled along beside his friend as they hung a left into the Max Blaster Video Arena at the mall. Electronic explosions blended with the sounds of racing cars and synthesized voices from the more than 25 games scattered around. Immediately Jeremy's heart began to beat faster. Kids were all over the place, toggling joysticks and slapping buttons.

"Now, *this* is fun!" With a big grin, Derek slapped Jeremy on the back as he zeroed in on a vacant game.

Yeah, it's fun, but not that much, Jeremy thought. Something was troubling him. Something that had happened a few minutes earlier. "Derek, remember that woman who was carrying all those packages when we came into the mall?"

Derek lined up three quarters and dropped the fourth in the video game. "Yeah, sure. What about her?"

"I don't like what we did."

Derek was staring at the game. "We didn't *do* anything."

"That's just it," Jeremy said. "We didn't *do* anything. We didn't stop to help her pick up her packages when she dropped them. And if we had at least held the door open for her, she wouldn't have had so much trouble trying to get out, and she might not have dropped her packages in the first place. It's just been bothering me, that's all."

Derek shrugged. "So what? Are you going to play, or not?"

- What do you do when you have the opportunity to hold the door for a stranger? How does it make you feel to do small acts of kindness? What are some of the reactions you get when you hold the door for people?

- When you go to the mall with your friends look for opportunities to hold the door for people. Take turns.

Turboduck

Submit yourselves, then, to God. Resist the devil, and he will flee from you. James 4:7, NIV.

The first time I saw them, we were paddling our canoe on Kent Pond. As we slipped quietly into a small bay, a mother duck slid off a rock and into the water, paddling and quacking. A dozen little ducklings plopped into the water behind her.

"I think we can reach them if we paddle fast and then coast in," my husband, Rob, suggested.

We dug our paddles into the calm water, pulling and straining to get up enough speed. Mother Duck watched us anxiously.

"OK, coast!" Rob commanded.

I pulled my paddle out and rested it, dripping, on the gunwales as we drifted closer to the baby ducks. When we could almost touch them, Mother Duck squawked loudly, beat her wings, and flew a short distance away. The babies, being unable to fly, leaned forward onto their chests, their tiny legs churning the water behind them as they suddenly became turboducks.

Wouldn't it be great if we ran from temptation and evil as swiftly as those little ducks paddled away from the threat of our canoe? Here are five strategies for resisting temptation:

1. Say NO! out loud when you are tempted. When Satan tempted Jesus, He said, "Get behind me, Satan."

2. Say you're being tempted to cheat. Repeat a Bible verse ("You shall not steal [information]"). Strengthen yourself; rebuke Satan.

3. Get out. Remove yourself from the scene of the temptation.

4. Prevent the temptation in the first place. When your hand is inside the refrigerator on the plate of chocolate cake is not the time to start resisting. Resist the moment the temptation enters your head.

5. Pray for help. Jesus was tempted too. He can help us.

In what ways can you resist and flee the devil?

Feeding wild ducks is fun. Get cracked corn at an animal feed store. Watch their funny antics as they feed with their heads underwater and their bottoms sticking up.

Love Your Planet

God saw all that he had made, and it was very good. And there was evening, and there was morning—the sixth day. Thus the heavens and the earth were completed in all their vast array. Genesis 1:31–2:1, NIV.

God looked around and saw that everything He had made was very good. Can He say the same thing when He looks at His creation today? Centuries of misuse have left our planet crippled by waste, pollution, and smog. We take too much, give too little, and throw away everything. Think about this:

• The garbage thrown away each year in the U.S. could fill enough 10-ton garbage trucks to reach halfway to the moon. That's 120,000 miles away.

• Every day the average person in the U.S. produces a little more than four pounds of garbage.

• The paper from offices, schools, and homes that gets trashed each year could build a 12-foot-high wall stretching from Los Angeles to New York.

We're stewards of the earth. We're in charge of taking care of it. When you see all the smog and trash, you may wonder if we're doing such a good job. One person might not seem to be able to make much difference, but we have to start somewhere.

What about that soda can in your hand? How about that paper lunch bag? That old school notebook?

It seems much easier to throw away than to recycle, but trash doesn't just disappear. It's just buried under the ground. Archaeologist William Rathje dug through one of the world's largest landfills and found 40-year-old hot dogs that still look like hot dogs.

Let's start taking care of the earth God gave us to live in until He comes back and makes it all new again.

😊 **Does your household recycle? Why or why not? List 20 things you can do to make the earth a more beautiful place.**

😊 **Organize a "Green Up" day in your neighborhood. Get everyone together with big garbage bags, gloves, and rakes and clean up the neighborhood. Relax later with a neighborhood picnic.**

191

A Good Listener

Accept one another, then, just as Christ accepted you, in order to bring praise to God. Romans 15:7, NIV.

Jennifer Maenaka has made a name for herself as a caring friend. Ask anyone who knows Jennifer, and they'll tell you: Jennifer genuinely cares about everyone. Helping people, though, wasn't something Jennifer always knew how to do.

She says, "I used to find myself judging people by their decisions and actions. But now I understand that everyone has their own life to live."

Jennifer is an accepting person. She has learned to be a good listener and friend by accepting people no matter who they are.

Jennifer is Japanese-American. She knows what it's like not to fit in. So she helps kids who are new at her school by inviting them to do things with her. She wants to make everyone feel welcome.

"I think it's important for people to know there are those who always care, under any circumstances," Jennifer says.

When Jesus met people, He accepted them for who they were. He didn't expect them to be someone else before He cared about them. He didn't ask them to become robots so He would like them better. Jesus took time out to listen and understand people's problems. He does the same thing today.

One of the wonderful things to remember about Jesus is that He grew up, just like every boy and girl does. He had the same problems you have today. When someone needs a friend to be a listener, treat that person as Jesus would—with understanding and acceptance.

🙂 **What makes someone a good listener? Are you a good listener?**

🙂 **If you know of any new kids in your subdivision, church, or school, invite them to hang out with you.**

Mountaintop Experiences, Part 1

I lift up my eyes to the hills—where does my help come from? My help comes from the Lord, the Maker of heaven and earth. Psalm 121:1, 2, NIV.

I've been hiking for a long time. In fact, I climbed my first mountain, Camel's Hump, when I was 3 years old. I don't remember the view from that mountain, but there were many to follow. There were views from the tops of mountains in Vermont, Maine, New Hampshire, and New York.

This past summer I climbed Mount Mansfield with only my dog for company. We camped at the base and made the climb the next morning. I was carrying a small torso pack with water. Indy carried saddlebags. They were pretty large ones, although they didn't have much in them except an empty water bottle we planned to fill on the way back to camp.

When we got toward the top of the mountain, I realized we had a big problem. The trail followed a very steep and rocky ledge between, around, and over huge jumbled rocks covering the entire surface of the mountain. A misstep would send a person tumbling down the side of the mountain.

Quite a distance from the top, Indy balked at going between two large rocks with his pack. He backed up until I was afraid he would slip his collar and fall right off the mountain! I tried everything to get him to follow me, knowing he could make it, but he refused to budge.

A trail guide who happened to be following behind me waited impatiently, and then finally said, "You'll probably have to carry his pack. Without it he can make it easily."

I agreed with him and took off the dog's pack. Sure enough, Indy bounded up the trail. Unfortunately, I had to carry his pack.

- When you see a mountain, what do you think of? When you are at the top of a mountain, looking down, what do you think of? Why do you think the Bible often mentions the mountains as protectors?

- The next time you go for a hike and see a great view, take a picture. Then start a photo album of your mountaintop experiences.

193

Mountaintop Experiences, Part 2

Come, let us go up to the mountain of the Lord, to the house of the God of Jacob. He will teach us his ways, so that we may walk in his paths. Micah 4:2, NIV.

Even though we were walking along the top crest of the mountain, it still took us a long time to reach the highest point. When we did, we flopped down gratefully and rested. We could see all the way to Canada to the north, New York to the west, New Hampshire to the east, and Massachusetts to the south. It was fall, and the leaves had turned, leaving the entire view a brilliant patchwork of orange, red, and yellow. It was beautiful.

Another time I hiked with my parents to the top of Algonquin Mountain, in the high peak region of the Adirondacks. It was winter, and several times on the way up I began to get hypothermia, which is a low body temperature. Near the top I almost slipped over the side of a cliff. The metal crampons strapped to my boots didn't grab the ice, and I began to slide on the ice toward the side. My mother grabbed my hand and pulled me up.

When we reached the top, we could see for miles. Ten minutes later a blizzard kicked up and we couldn't see our hands in front of our faces.

The mountaintop experiences in life match the ones at the tops of real mountains. They are all different. Sometimes you can struggle for a long time and be rewarded by a great view. Sometimes you struggle just as hard, only to reach the top and get stuck in a blizzard.

We're all going to go through hard times, trials, and struggles. But when we travel with Jesus, He will reward us with a beautiful view at the end of the journey.

- **What's the hardest part about getting to the top of the mountain? What would you think of the world if there were no mountains to break up the flatness?**

- **Check in your community to see if there is a local hiking club that you could join. Or organize a hiking group at your church. Plan hikes that everyone can participate in and some challenging ones for you and your friends.**

Where Does Happiness Come From?

Jesus answered, "Everyone who drinks this water will be thirsty again, but whoever drinks the water I give him will never thirst. Indeed, the water I give him will become in him a spring of water welling up to eternal life." John 4:13, 14, NIV.

I worked as a counselor at camp the summer before my senior year in high school. One of the people I remember most vividly was Mr. B. He was an elderly Black man who had come to blind camp. Mr. B doesn't stand out in my mind because he was blind, but because he was happy from the inside out.

The terrain around camp was unfamiliar to Mr. B, so we led him around. He was fun to talk with. We ate with him and listened to his stories. We took him out on the dock so he could fish. And he rode on the boats, too. Mr. B enjoyed life, and he enjoyed sharing it with everyone.

I wonder what Mr. B's life would have been like without God. Would he have been as happy? I doubt it. There are very few people who know what happiness is. Even people who have 20/20 vision and strong, healthy bodies are sometimes not very happy.

The answer is accepting Jesus as your personal Saviour. Have confidence in your relationship with Him. If you know Jesus and give your heart to Him, then you will be happy knowing that even the ugliest problems you may encounter in this world can be overcome. You have Jesus standing beside you.

I would rather be blind, paralyzed, and dying and know Jesus as my Saviour than have all the riches in the world. I would rather die with Him in my heart than live without Him, because this world *will* pass away, and with it will go all the suffering sin has caused.

- Why are so many people who don't know Jesus unhappy? Out of all the things this world has to offer, is there anything that can make you as happy as knowing Jesus loves you and wants you in heaven with Him?

- It is easy to forget Jesus when troubles come. Begin your morning by asking Jesus to be with you today. Ask Him to help you do only things that will glorify Him.

Round and Round

At that time Samuel said to them, "If you are really serious about wanting to return to the Lord, get rid of your foreign gods and your Ashtaroth idols. Determine to obey only the Lord; then he will rescue you from the Philistines." 1 Samuel 7:3, TLB.

Every morning as I drive to work, a little black-and-white dog starts spinning in circles. I assume that it will eventually decide to stop spinning and run out and chase my car. But it never does. It just spins and spins and spins.

The first time I saw it, it startled me. I swerved, half expecting the dog would run out in front of me. The second time I saw it, I was amused by its antics. But the third, fourth, and fifth times . . .

It was getting old. It was becoming irritating. It started reminding me what our lives are like apart from God.

Doesn't that little black-and-white dog know that spinning around in circles every time a car goes by looks ridiculous?

And then it dawned on me that if that little black-and-white dog knew for sure what it wanted to do, it probably wouldn't be spinning in circles. It didn't know where it was headed.

Sometimes people are that way too. They don't know which direction they're headed. They start out thinking they want to be Christians, but they find friends who lead them away from Jesus. They find the kind of entertainment that has a big sign that reads: "Admit one only." So Jesus is left standing outside. Too many worldly pursuits get in the way.

Do you know where you are headed? Is being with Jesus in heaven a goal? If it is, it's time to stop spinning in circles. Point yourself toward Jesus.

Do you sometimes feel as if you are spinning in circles instead of getting closer to Jesus? Why do you feel that way?

Listen to Christian music. Read material that tells you more about who Jesus is. Wear a smile. Be helpful. Treat others with love and kindness, just as Jesus would. Try that for a week. Then ask yourself if you are still spinning in circles.

10 JULY

Eyes for the Blind

So we fix our eyes not on what is seen, but on what is unseen. For what is seen is temporary, but what is unseen is eternal. 2 Corinthians 4:18, NIV.

It was love at first sight. He had chocolate-brown eyes, jet-black hair, and the cutest pink tongue with a black spot right in the middle. He loved to snuggle up in my arms and just fall asleep.

His name was Indy, and he was a beautiful black Labrador retriever. But he wasn't ours. He belonged to a guide dog school. We were just raising him until he was old enough to go to school. I didn't know how I was going to give him up.

He had a blue jacket that he wore whenever I trained him. It had the name of the guide dog school on the side and told everyone that he was a guide dog in training. He was a great dog. There wasn't anything he didn't like to do, unless it was taking a bath or getting his nails clipped. He wasn't into personal hygiene.

And then the fateful day came when he had to go to school. I loaded him into the van with the other dogs and cried all the way home. Every now and then we'd get a postcard from the guide dog school, telling us that he was doing great, playing with the other puppies, and learning well. Even though I missed him, I was proud of what he was going to do. I knew that his new blind owner would really appreciate him. He was going to help someone "see."

Each of us can do the same thing. There are many people around you, kids in your school, kids who live on your block or in your neighborhood, who are "blind." They've never seen Jesus. You can be their guide. You can help them "see" something of eternal value.

Then Indy flunked out of guide dog school, and he came back to live with us. But he still reminds me of the important job I have to do.

Is there more than one way to be "blind"? Which is worse, physical blindness or spiritual blindness?

List five ways you can tell your friends about Jesus. Choose one to do each day.

"This One Is on Me"

Set your minds on things above, not on earthly things. Colossians 3:2, NIV.

One morning at work my boss, Aileen Andres Sox, editor of *Our Little Friend* and *Primary Treasure*, confessed that she had been stopped by a police officer for making an illegal turn while she was driving home from work the night before.

When Aileen saw the flashing lights behind her, she pulled over and waited patiently. The police officer walked up and asked to see her driver's license and vehicle registration.

"Do realize you made an illegal turn?" the officer asked.

"I did?" Aileen asked in surprise. Then she realized that she couldn't remember stopping at the stop sign. She apologized and admitted that indeed she must have failed to come to a complete stop.

The officer took Aileen's license and registration back to his car to run his usual check. A few minutes later he returned. But before he handed Aileen's license and registration back, he asked, "Do you always listen to KTSY?"

Now, that was an odd question! Then Aileen remembered the KTSY sticker on the bumper of her car.

"Yes, I listen to KTSY all the time," she replied.

The officer smiled and handed Aileen her driver's license and registration. "Then this one is on me," he said politely. "Please drive more carefully from now on."

God touches people's lives in ways you and I may never know about. But He does touch lives. Aileen likes how God gave her evidence of His working in her community.

KTSY is a popular Christian radio station. It touches the hearts of people from many different religions. It touches the hearts of people who are still searching for God.

- **Does your family listen to Christian music? How does Christian music bless your family? Why do you like songs that praise God?**

- **If you have friends who listen to secular music, ask them to try listening to music that praises God. Ask them to try it for a day, a week, or even a month. What are the results?**

Modeling Roles

Can a blind man lead a blind man? Will they not both fall into a pit? A student is not above his teacher, but everyone who is fully trained will be like his teacher. Luke 6:39, 40, NIV.

Do you have any role models?

Role models are people (generally sports heroes or singers or actors) whom other people admire. Clay Crosse is the kind of person who might be one of your role models. He is a very popular Christian singer. But even people you consider to be your role models have role models of their own.

"I've got plenty of role models," Clay says. "People I grew up with—Sunday school teachers and youth pastors who really molded me into what I am. They're the people I look up to in life. I don't necessarily look up to the athletes and the stars. I tend to look at the common man who serves the Lord and takes care of his family as the ultimate role model in this world."

Role models are sometimes chosen for their goals. Most want to succeed and go as far in their career as they can go. That's a worthy goal, but the success that the world has to offer won't last. The real success stories are people who want to make a difference for Jesus.

"My goal, musically, is to move the listener closer to a belief in Jesus Christ," says Clay. "A lot of people who listen to my music already share my belief that Jesus Christ is the Lord of this world, the Lord of their life. But others who hear it probably don't. I hope to move them closer to that, and I hope to encourage those who do believe to develop a stronger faith."

We have to be careful of the role models we choose. We also have to remember that role models are only human and might let us down. Jesus is the only role model we can always count on.

😊 **What kind of people do you admire? Why do you admire them? Who should be our ultimate role model?**

😊 **Write out an ad that says:** *Wanted: One Role Model.* **Using the Bible, list all the qualities of a godly role model.**

Curve Ball

So I find this law at work: When I want to do good, evil is right there with me. Romans 7:21, NIV.

Tod shook his head.

Anita folded her arms and narrowed her eyes. "Everybody knows it. I can do it, and you can't hit it!"

"It's an optical illusion," Tod argued halfheartedly. "It doesn't really curve."

Anita sighed. "Come on. I'll explain it to you." She led Tod over to the school bleachers and sat him down. "OK, it's sort of complicated. Are you ready?"

Tod rolled his eyes. "Yeah. Go ahead. I'll see if I can keep up."

Anita held the ball in front of Tod. "To make a baseball curve, what I do is make it spin when I throw it. Because of friction, the ball carries air around it as it spins through the air. That means that some of the air the ball passes through is going against the flow of the air the ball is carrying around it. That creates static pressure. But also, on the other side of the ball the air is going the same direction as the air that is spinning around the ball. So there is less static pressure on that side. The spinning ball naturally wants to move toward the side where there is the least static pressure."

"So it actually curves away from the side that has the most resistance," Tod said with an "Ah, I get it!" look on his face. "Something like a Christian's life too, huh?"

Now Anita looked puzzled. "Say what?"

"Sometimes, even though I'm a Christian and want to follow Christ, I do what is easiest for me instead of what Jesus wants me to do."

🙂 **Is your life with Christ sometimes hard? Why is it hard? Who causes the resistance?**

🙂 **Draw a picture of a spinning baseball and a line toward your favorite illustration of Christ. When you are tempted to give in to peer pressure because it seems easiest, or when you are tempted to stop studying your Bible, ask yourself if you are curving toward the side of least resistance.**

A Firm but Gentle Hand

The wolf will live with the lamb, the leopard will lie down with the goat, the calf and the lion and the yearling together; and a little child will lead them. Isaiah 11:6, NIV.

I have always loved animals. When I was growing up, we had cats, dogs, goats, and horses. How many animals do you have? Do you love and care for each one?

President Lincoln had been out visiting an Army telegraph station in Washington when he came across three lost kittens. He stooped and picked up one of the kittens. "Where is your mother?" he asked.

When someone told Lincoln that the kittens' mother was dead, he picked up the other two and set them all in his lap, where he gently stroked their fur. He said to them, "Kitties, thank God you are cats and can't understand this terrible strife that is going on," referring to the Civil War.

Colonel Theodore Bowers was standing nearby. Lincoln called him over and gave him instructions to see that the kittens were treated kindly and given plenty of milk.

Often during all the stresses Abraham Lincoln shouldered, he sat alone with those three kittens. He was a man of great power and responsibility, yet he found comfort in three of God's smallest creatures.

The very hand that signed the Emancipation Proclamation, which freed the slaves, would tenderly stroke the fur of those stray kittens. The man who led a country listened to three little kittens purr their appreciation.

Is it any wonder Jesus created pets for us to love and care for? Can you imagine Jesus picking up a chubby little lion cub on the first Sabbath after Creation and scratching its ears? Can you see Him smile a warm, tender smile?

😊 **Why do you think God gave us pets? Do you think He gave us pets to help teach us responsibility and love? How do pets help us relax? How do pets make us feel love?**

😊 **Take a few minutes to show your pets some attention right now. See if you can discover why it was important for President Lincoln to pet those kittens.**

201

Lucky Lisa?

Consider it pure joy, my brothers, whenever you face trials of many kinds, because you know that the testing of your faith develops perseverance. Perseverance must finish its work so that you may be mature and complete, not lacking anything. James 1:2–4, NIV.

Have you ever seen someone and thought, *Well, they've got everything. They've never been through what I'm going through. They don't have problems like mine?*

Lisa Bevill gets that reaction sometimes. Lisa is a very popular Christian singer with what looks like a Cinderella life. But it wasn't always easy for Lisa. Her parents were both ill when she was growing up. Her father died in her arms when she was 19, and her mother died right after Lisa came back from her honeymoon. She grew up fighting suicidal thoughts no one knew about.

"People come to me and say, 'You've never been through anything,'" Lisa says. "And I say, 'Well, let me tell you—I have.'

"I was on the cover of *Brio* magazine; it was one of the first serious articles I ever did. I just basically told about the struggles I'd gone through. When the article came out a year later, I was flooded with mail from young girls. They all said they'd read the *Brio* article and what an impact it had in their lives, because they looked at the pictures of me that had been doctored up and they said, 'Well, it's really hard for me to believe that you felt suicidal about the way you looked and that you think you're fat.'"

On the outside people's lives can look pretty close to perfect. After all, they're famous, rich, successful, or whatever. How can they have problems, go through trials, or need help?

But we all go through trials and need help. God's help. Because while we look only on the outside of people, God can see our hearts. And only He knows how to put things right.

🙂 **How can appearances be deceiving?**

🙂 **Practice "unprejudice." Don't judge someone by the way his or her life looks. Instead, get to know that person. It may not turn out to be the way it seems.**

Sticking Together

So in Christ we who are many form one body, and each member belongs to all the others. Romans 12:5, NIV.

The three flag football players huddled up. There were only a few minutes left in the game, and Angie, Steven, and Joe were losing by a touchdown. For a while they had led the game, but suddenly their whole game plan seemed to have fallen apart. Angie was mad at Joe. Steven was mad at Angie. And Joe was mad at both Steven and Angie.

"Why don't you just hike the ball to me?" Angie asked Joe. "I'll run for a touchdown. I'm the fastest runner anyway."

Steve shook his head. "No way! Last time you ran the football they were expecting it, and you got slapped on the back before you got two yards. Quit trying to be a hero."

Angie narrowed her eyes at Steve and clenched her teeth.

"Joe," Steve said, ignoring Angie, "I'm the best receiver. Just throw the ball and I'll catch it and get the touchdown."

"I know I'm a good quarterback, but don't you think they'll be expecting me to throw the ball to you, Steve?" Joe pointed out.

"I've got an idea," Angie said firmly.

"And what's *that*?" Joe and Steve asked together.

"Each of us has been trying to win the game alone by concentrating on what each of us is best at. But we haven't worked together at all. Why don't we concentrate on being a team, instead of on who is the fastest runner, the best receiver, or the best quarterback? Let's do the unexpected. Together."

It's not surprising that Angie, Steven, and Joe were losing their game. They weren't acting like a team anymore. Each was sure that with their own special abilities they could win the football game alone. But they were having a hard time realizing that they needed one another too.

Why is it so hard to work together sometimes? Does too much personal pride make it hard to be a team?

Make a list of your friends' names. Be sure to leave several lines between each name. Now write under each name the abilities each of your friends has.

Fast Friends

A man of many companions may come to ruin, but there is a friend who sticks closer than a brother. Proverbs 18:24, NIV.

Chad Walters was 20 years old. He had a wife and a new-born son. He had a home and a good job. But as he sat in his chair, he was thinking back through his life. He remembered Kenny, his best friend when he was in first grade. They had had a lot of fun riding bikes together and going to each other's birthday party. But somehow that friendship had disappeared when Chad started going to a different school and met new friends. And Kenny had made new friends too.

Then Chad remembered his friend Steven, from grade school. They had been friends the first year Chad had switched schools. But their friendship eventually became a memory as they grew older and each went to a different school in seventh grade.

Chad thought about his friends in junior high and high school. But he had lost contact with even most of those friends after graduation. Everyone had gone his or her own way. Some had gone to college or found jobs in faraway states.

He thought about the friends he had made in the past couple years. Some of those friends had disappeared too, so Chad was wondering how people kept friends. After all, how hard could it be?

Usually friends have a common interest. Maybe two friends like to ski or jog or play racquetball. But if they stop doing those things together, their friendship might gradually taper off. That is normal. Everyone changes in different ways during the growing-up process.

Chad made new friends in the neighborhood where he had moved. His new friends are very important. But he still keeps in his heart the friendships he made when he was growing up, because he believes that even though he doesn't know where some of his old friends are anymore, they're still his friends.

- **How many friends did you make while you were growing up? Do you know where all your old friends are? Do you miss them?**

- **Ask your parents if you can write to some of your friends you don't get to see anymore.**

Footprints in the Snow

For this reason he had to be made like his brothers in every way, in order that he might become a merciful and faithful high priest in service to God, and that he might make atonement for the sins of the people. Because he himself suffered when he was tempted, he is able to help those who are being tempted. Hebrews 2:17, 18, NIV.

I see her almost every day along my jogging route. I don't know her name, but the very fact that we're out there alone while the rest of the neighborhood hides within the warmth of their homes seems to tie us together. We shout things back and forth like "We're crazy to be out here" or "Nice weather." Then we jog on, stronger because we know we are not alone.

One day I was jogging in a mild snowstorm. A blanket of white carpeted everything. No one was on the street, and nothing stirred in the frozen landscape. I felt totally alone and longed for the familiar face of my jogging companion.

I reached the halfway mark in my jog without having seen her. Turning around, I made my way home. Snow smoked across the meadow to my left, and I ducked my head to avoid the icy blast of the wind. That's when I saw them. Footprints in the snow.

I smiled. Suddenly I didn't feel so alone. My friend had been there ahead of me. The proof was in the snow at my feet.

Sometimes it's like that with God, too. I feel all alone, isolated from everything. I look up at the sky and ask, "Where are You?"

"I'm right beside you," He replies, "where I've always been."

He came to earth and traveled this way ahead of me. He isn't just a God who rules in detached majesty on a throne far away. He walks the walk and talks the talk. And we are never alone.

- Why is it that sometimes when we're going through tough times, God seems far away? Who is responsible for our suffering? God or Satan?

- Practice the presence of God. Imagine Him eating breakfast with you, going to school with you, being by your side all day.

Great Separate

David longed for water and said, "Oh, that someone would get me a drink of water from the well near the gate of Bethlehem!" 1 Chronicles 11:17, NIV.

A bishai and Benaiah huddled in the darkness outside the enemy Philistine camp in the Valley of Rephaim. With them was another warrior under David's command. Abishai swept narrow, calculating eyes over the Philistine camp. He let his mind wander back to the time when he had singlehandedly fought 300 enemy soldiers and killed them all. What would happen tonight? he wondered. A wrong footstep, a guard who happened to look the right direction at the wrong time . . . There were far more than 300 men to fight here if they were discovered.

The second man, Benaiah, crouched low, his battle-scarred, handsome face hidden by the shadows. He grinned ruefully to himself. His thoughts returned to the two giants he had fought against, and how he had won. And then there was that lion in the pit. How crazy he'd been to risk killing it. And how crazy the three of them were now to attempt to draw water from the well of Bethlehem, right in the middle of the Philistine camp!

The third man also thought it was crazy for the three of them to attempt to sneak into the Philistine camp to get water to quench David's thirst. Maybe he could sneak in, get the water, and hurry out by himself.

They were three of David's 30 greatest warriors. If they were alive today, each of them would probably have received a medal of honor several times.

God wants us to be strong, confident warriors for Him. He will give us strength to do great things alone, as he did for David's men. But like those three men who risked their lives so boldly by sneaking into the Philistine camp, He also wants us to learn to work together.

Does God want strong people in His army? Why is it important to develop our abilities and talents? How can we use our abilities as a team?

Did you make a list of all your friends' abilities? Now put your name on the list and write down your own abilities.

Working Together

So the Three broke through the Philistine lines, drew water from the well near the gate of Bethlehem and carried it back to David. 1 Chronicles 11:18, NIV.

What were they doing there? David thirsted for water from the well of Bethlehem, so three of his men decided they would sneak into the Philistine camp, which was in Bethlehem, and draw water from the well.

They didn't go separately, those three mighty men. They crept down to the Philistine camp together. They had fought bravely and won major victories by themselves, but they were risking their lives *together* this time.

Can you imagine the beads of sweat on their foreheads? Can you hear their hearts pounding in their chests? Can you feel the tension sweep through them every time they hear metal scrape, wood creak, or a guard's footsteps?

Abishai might have said, "Look, you guys don't have to do this. Let me go alone. It's better that only one of us dies if something happens."

"No!" the other two whisper back forcefully. "We're doing this together!"

Sounds like the original three musketeers, doesn't it?

David was shocked when those men returned with the water. He must have imagined all the terrible things that could have happened had they been discovered, for he could not bring himself to drink the water those three brave men had risked their lives for. The Bible says, "He poured it out before the Lord. 'God forbid that I should do this!' he said. 'Should I drink the blood of these men who went at the risk of their lives?'" (verses 18, 19, NIV).

- How does it make you feel when you work with your friends to accomplish a goal? Maybe it's a school project, a baseball or volleyball game, or singing in the school choir. Do you feel good doing great things as a team?

- Now that you have a list of your abilities and your friends' abilities, look it over and write down all the things you could do if you all worked together as a team.

Going Ballistic

Be completely humble and gentle; be patient, bearing with one another in love. Make every effort to keep the unity of the Spirit through the bond of peace. Ephesians 4:2, 3, NIV.

I approached the hill, striding hard and fast. In front of me was a long downhill run. This run was going to be ballistic. I could feel it. Where I live, in a rural part of Vermont, there are no bike paths where I can skate. I have to skate on the very hilly roads. I pass within feet of cars. You could say it's a dangerous sport, but I know what I'm doing, and I wear full protective gear.

And I didn't always skate like this. When I learned how to skate, it was toward the end of winter. Snow had melted off the road, and snowbanks lined it. I ended up in a snowbank more than once. In-line skaters call wiping out "bacon in the pan." I was probably more like "snowman in the drift."

When I first started skating, I didn't like it much. The skates felt like giant cement boots strapped to my feet. I never thought I'd be brave enough to go down a big hill. There was a time when I wasn't even sure I'd master stopping.

The Christian life is sometimes a lot like that too. You think you're starting to get somewhere, then all of a sudden you end up headfirst in a snowbank. Or there's a sin you just can't stop doing, even though you know you should. Or you figure you'll never get strong enough to do some of the things other people do.

If I had given up on skating, I wouldn't be able to jump curbs now, or skate down huge hills. We have to look at our Christian journey in the same way. Even the apostles didn't start out working miracles. Our relationship with Jesus will get stronger and stronger each day, until soon we'll be high-impact Christians, living and loving enthusiastically for Jesus.

- **Does anything ever make you feel like giving up on being a Christian? What's the most important thing to do when you feel like that?**

- **Learn something new. Try skating or painting or sculpting. Notice how you gain confidence with experience.**

208

The Hidden Cake, Part 1

"As surely as the Lord your God lives," she replied, "I don't have any bread—only a handful of flour in a jar and a little oil in a jug." 1 Kings 17:12, NIV.

On the morning of his birthday a peasant was surprised to receive a beautifully decorated cake from his landlord. It was a magnificent treat, so the peasant stored it away until after his meager evening meal of dry bread and thin soup.

But that evening, as the peasant was preparing his soup, a weary traveler happened by.

"I don't mean to intrude," said the traveler, "but do you mind if I share your meal? I am very hungry."

Not wishing to appear rude by turning the hungry traveler away, the peasant set two places at his small table. But he decided he would wait until the next day to eat his cake.

As was his custom after his evening meal, the peasant gathered the dry crust from his bread and tossed it to the dog that lay in a corner near the table. The traveler noticed this, but he did not speak. Soon the traveler continued on his journey.

The next day another traveler happened by who was also hungry and weary. Again the peasant left the cake in the cupboard and served only his usual fare of dry bread and thin soup.

Then, as was his custom after his evening meal, the peasant gathered the dry crust and tossed it to his dog. The second traveler noticed this. "I will be sure to speak to your landlord about your generosity," he told the peasant.

The peasant was pleased that the traveler had noticed he spared a few crumbs for the dog.

On the third day another traveler appeared. Again the peasant selfishly kept his cake hidden in the cupboard, planning to eat it the next day. Irritably he fed the traveler, ate his own thin soup and dry bread, and tossed the dog a few dry crumbs.

🙂 **If you were the peasant, would you have happily shared your cake? Why is it hard to share? What are some of the things you have the hardest time sharing?**

🙂 **Make a cake! Give it away, or share it!**

The Hidden Cake, Part 2

Elijah said to her, "Don't be afraid. Go home and do as you have said. But first make a small cake of bread for me from what you have and bring it to me, and then make something for yourself and your son." 1 Kings 17:13, NIV.

O n the fourth day the peasant waited expectantly. But no one came. He ate his evening meal alone, and then very eagerly removed the cake from the cupboard. Sadly, after so long a time the beautiful frosting had turned rancid, and the cake itself was too spoiled to be enjoyed. The peasant angrily threw his cake onto the ground for his dog and stomped off to bed.

The next morning, before the peasant returned to the fields, a handsome carriage came by. Three richly dressed men got out. When the peasant saw them, he realized they were the very same men he had fed but a few days earlier.

"I don't understand," said the peasant. "Why are you so richly dressed? And why do you arrive in this handsome carriage?"

"We oversee all our landlord's interests to the east, to the west, and to the north," said the first traveler.

"Our landlord had acquired land to the south as well, for which he needed an overseer. Each day he asked one of us to stop and share in your celebration," explained the second traveler.

"But I had nothing to celebrate," said the peasant.

"Oh, but you did," said the third traveler. "You see, our landlord had arranged for you to oversee the land he had acquired to the south. Had you shared with any of us the cake he gave to you on your birthday, you would have discovered inside a written promotion to be overseer of all the land to the south."

"But how was I to know what was inside the cake?" asked the peasant.

"Our landlord does not believe a truly happy and generous person shares only when expecting something in return," said the men.

How often do you share, even when you don't expect something in return?

Share something this week. Think about how it makes you feel.

210

I Won?

Do you not know that in a race all the runners run, but only one gets the prize? Run in such a way as to get the prize. Everyone who competes in the games goes into strict training. They do it to get a crown that will not last; but we do it to get a crown that will last forever. 1 Corinthians 9:24, 25, NIV.

Her name was Julie, and in the fifth grade she was the fastest runner in school. She creamed me in the 50-yard dash, the 100-yard dash, the long jump, and the broad jump. Since it was my first year in that school, I consoled myself with the fact that I had come in second—every time. At least I was consistent.

I'll beat her next year, I thought. And I spent all year racing anything that moved. Sometimes I ran with my dad. But his legs had muscles in places I didn't even have legs.

The next year, during the elementary school races, I was ready. Finally they announced the 100-yard dash. I slunk over to the starting line and joined the other girls. As Julie surveyed the group of us she smiled with a look on her face that seemed to say *This is gonna be a piece of cake.* I gritted my teeth, afraid I would start running before they said go.

At last Mr. Babbe raised his hand and said, "Ready, set, *go!*" and we were off. The wind caught my hair. My legs pumped furiously beneath me. I ran so fast my glasses had to be surgically removed from my face after the race. Julie, who had been winning since the beginning of time, wasn't the only one who was surprised when I flew across the finish line way ahead of her.

I won three more races that day, but the last memory I have is not the feeling of victory or the surprise of my friends. My last memory is that of Julie bawling her head off at the finish line.

🙂 **Which is more important, winning a race or doing your best? How do you feel about competitive sports?**

🙂 **The next time you play your favorite game, change the rules so that whoever "wins" is actually the "loser," but the one who "loses" is actually the "winner." Does that change how you play?**

211

Stand True to the Lord

We stand true to the Lord whether others honor us or despise us, whether they criticize us or commend us. We are honest, but they call us liars. 2 Corinthians 6:8, TLB.

t's going to be fun," Roger promised. "Just wait and see."

"I don't know if I want to go," Jasper said.

"I don't like to hang out with your friends. I feel uncomfortable."

"Ah, that's because you're not used to them. If you'd spend more time with them you wouldn't feel that way."

"I—I just don't know," Jasper stammered. She really didn't want to go to Roger's birthday party. But if she didn't, Roger wouldn't like her. He would probably spread it around that she thought she was too good for him and his friends, then no one would like her. Jasper's stomach felt tight.

Roger put on his most perfect puppy-dog smile. "Lots of cool music, any kind of pizza you like, and whatever you want to drink."

What he didn't say was there would also be lots of foul language and probably some alcohol, too.

Jasper thought about Roger's invitation. Then she remembered reading 2 Corinthians 6:8 at evening worship with her family. "We stand true to the Lord whether others honor us or despise us, whether they criticize us or commend us. We are honest, but they call us liars."

With words like those, who needs friends like Roger? Paul, who was writing to the Corinthians, didn't care what anyone else thought about him as long as he remained faithful to the Lord. Paul knew that Jesus cared for him, and as long as Jesus cared for him it didn't matter what anyone else thought.

Jasper decided it was more important to remain faithful to Jesus than to compromise and go to the party with Roger.

Have you ever been put in a situation in which you felt a lot of peer pressure to do something you really didn't want to do? How did you react?

To keep from giving in to peer pressure follow Paul's example of staying true to the Lord.

Awesome Fort!

The city was laid out like a square, as long as it was wide. He measured the city with the rod and found it to be 12,000 stadia in length, and as wide and high as it is long. He measured its wall and it was 144 cubits thick, by man's measurement, which the angel was using. Revelation 21:16, 17, NIV.

I sneaked out of my backyard, down the alley, and into the backyard of the home two lots down. Then I disappeared into the box fort the neighbor kid had built. It wasn't just any old fort made of a few so-so cardboard boxes. It was a mansion made out of huge freezer and refrigerator boxes with wood framing to keep it sturdy. I was impressed. I was excited. But I hadn't been invited, so I felt like a criminal, too.

I crawled inside onto the first floor. (It wasn't a regular fort—it was three stories high.) I climbed up to the second floor. (No one knew I was there.) I got onto the third floor. And then—I just sat there.

Soon I realized I wasn't having any fun by myself. Worse still, I hardly knew the neighbor boy who had built it. In fact, I didn't know him at all. He was quite a bit older than I was. And let's face it, I was trespassing.

Remember that city of mansions in heaven, the New Jerusalem? Wow! Now, that's some fort, huh! (A fort with the gates wide open!) I want to walk down every street. I want to tour every mansion. And after I've toured for a while, I want to play some games of hide-and-seek with my friends.

I'm glad I've been invited to the New Jerusalem. I can just walk in as Jesus' honored guest. But best of all, I know that Jesus *wants* to share His awesome fort with me.

Did you ever build a fort? How big was it? Why is it fun to build forts and treehouses?

Do some research to find out how big the New Jerusalem is.

God's Part

"Bring the whole tithe into the storehouse, that there may be food in my house. Test me in this," says the Lord Almighty, "and see if I will not throw open the floodgates of heaven and pour out so much blessing that you will not have room enough for it." Malachi 3:10, NIV.

Samantha Reese pushed open the door of the clubhouse to see Dillon dancing around the room, a wad of bills clutched in his hand.

"Mr. Weinbrener just paid me for mowing his lawn last week."

Sam eyed the fistful of bills. "How much did he pay you?"

"Ten dollars," Dillon said, flushed with happiness.

Sam stared at him blankly. "Ten bucks? That's it? Ten bucks?"

Dillon's face fell a little. "Well, it was a small lawn. But money has been tight around our house since my dad lost his job. I haven't gotten an allowance in weeks, and I owe my mother $5."

"That doesn't leave you with much," Sam pointed out.

"Enough for two yogurt sundaes. Come on, I'll treat." Dillon grabbed Sam's arm and started for the door.

"Hold on, Dillon," Sam said. "Aren't you forgetting something? Sundaes are $2.50 each. That's $5."

"Yeah? So?"

"What about tithe and offering?"

Dillon chewed his lip while he thought. He laid two $1 bills on the desk. "Well, we'll just have to settle for cones."

When they got to the ice-cream parlor, Sam's mouth was watering. Before she made it to the counter, Dillon dragged her to a halt, pointing excitedly. A large sign read: "Sundae special, today only. Two for the price of one"!

🙂 **When you receive money, what is the first thing you do with it? What determines how much you will give as an offering?**

🙂 **For one month try giving a double tithe. At the end of the month ask yourself this: "Did I lack anything this month?"**

Plant a Flower

Let your conversation be always full of grace, seasoned with salt, so that you may know how to answer everyone. Colossians 4:6, NIV.

Have you ever helped your parents clean out a patch of weeds, till the earth, and plant a flower bed? It may be hard work, but the result is sure worth it.

Have you ever been insulted at school? Ever been called names by kids you hardly knew? Worse, how about having been insulted by your friends? If anyone ever resembled a weed, it was probably whoever was hurling insults at you at the moment. Right?

An elderly woman had asked President Lincoln to release her husband from the Army so he could come home and support his family. Lincoln granted her wish. The woman was so grateful that tears filled her eyes. As she told Lincoln goodbye, she said, "I shall probably never see you again till we meet in heaven."

Lincoln was very moved. Caught in the midst of the turmoil of the Civil War, President Lincoln had serious doubts that he would ever reach heaven. He replied to the woman, "That you wish me to get there is, I believe, the best wish you could make for me."

Later, as he was talking to his friend Joshua Speed, Lincoln said, "Die when I may, I want it said of me, by those who know me best, that I have always plucked a thistle and planted a flower when I thought a flower would grow."

Insults hurt. They also have a horrible tendency to light a fire in us, and we want to fire insults right back. Who cares if it only makes things worse? And it always does.

There is an art to graceful conversation, but it takes a lot of work. It also requires Jesus to be in our hearts. Wouldn't you rather plant a flower?

- Have you ever allowed yourself to fight a verbal war with anyone? How did it make you feel afterward? Did you feel as though you had planted a flower? Or more thistles?

- The next time you feel the urge to speak unkind words, remember Lincoln's wish. Pluck a thistle and plant a flower.

215

Read the Map

Enter through the narrow gate. For wide is the gate and broad is the road that leads to destruction, and many enter through it. But small is the gate and narrow the road that leads to life, and only a few find it. Matthew 7:13, 14, NIV.

My brother loves to drive, which is a good thing, because he doesn't read maps very well. And people who don't read maps very well should learn to love to drive, because they'll do a lot more of it than everyone else.

I got home from work at midnight, and then returned to work at 3:00 that same morning to meet the morning freight truck. If I had gotten any rest that night, I wasn't aware of it. The good thing was that I had been able to get off work early so my brother Philip and I could take off on our trip to the Grand Canyon.

Not far out of Boise, Idaho, I left final instructions with Philip on the route he should take. Up ahead the freeway would split. "Watch for it and take the right fork," I said. "I'm going to sleep for a while."

When I awoke three hours later, things seemed a little out of place. My biggest concern was that the sun wasn't where it was supposed to be. I questioned Philip about whether he had seen any peculiar forks in the freeway lately.

He glanced over at me. "Oh, was I supposed to turn back there?"

I couldn't believe Philip had missed the turn! It was so obvious! There were huge signs with big letters telling travelers how to get where they wanted to go! How could he miss it?

Sometimes it doesn't matter how much we want to follow God, we still end up going down the wrong road. That's because Satan never stops trying to turn us away from God.

🙂 **What are some things you have done that didn't seem wrong at the time? Why didn't they seem wrong? How can you know God's will?**

🙂 **When you have a question about what God wants you to do, get out your Bible and look up God's answers to your questions.**

Locked Out!

Here I am! I stand at the door and knock. If anyone hears my voice and opens the door, I will come in and eat with him, and he with me. Revelation 3:20, NIV.

Today started out wrong. I had a lot of things to do and very little time to do them. Then the phone rang. Again.

"I'm at the convenience store in town," my grandmother said over the phone. "I locked my keys in the car."

"Are all the windows rolled up tight?" I asked, hoping that at least one was down far enough so that I could wedge a clothes hanger inside and unlock the car.

"Yes, all the windows are rolled up. Tight."

With no idea what I could do to help, I told her I would be right down. The clerk at the store suggested someone who might be able to help, so I rounded him up. His name was Bill. He brought his tools: master keys and a slim jim. I stood back and watched Bill work.

He struggled with the master keys for several minutes. Nothing happened. He tried the slim jim and still couldn't unlock my grandmother's car. I could tell he was getting frustrated, but he didn't give up. He continued to work at it.

While Bill worked, it occurred to me that this must be what Jesus meant when He said "Here I am!" What an announcement! "I stand at the door and knock." It's a good thing Jesus keeps trying and trying to get in. "If anyone hears my voice and opens the door, I will come in and eat with him, and he with me."

A couple minutes later Bill unlocked the car door.

☺ **Do you have some friends you are trying to share Jesus with? How are they responding? Do you feel like giving up? Remember that Jesus always stands at the door and knocks.**

☺ **If you are trying to witness to a friend who doesn't seem to care about Jesus, don't give up. Keep being a Christian influence.**

Art Gallery

The heavens declare the glory of God; the skies proclaim the work of his hands. Psalm 19:1, NIV.

Think it's going to rain?" Dillon asked for the hundredth time. Sam shook her head. "No. Where should I put this one?" Dillon waved a hand toward the clothesline they had strung up to display some of the artwork for the poster contest/art gallery showing. Sam hung the painting up and stood back to eye it critically, finally deciding that it wasn't crooked.

"Zeb, stop eating the refreshments," Sam scolded, moving the plate of sandwiches out of his reach.

"I was just doing some quality control," Zeb mumbled. "They're OK, but I really need to have another one to be sure."

"They're fine," Sam assured him.

"Hello, Mrs. Rainer," Dillon was saying. "Welcome! The works on display were painted by kids from our local church. The theme is Creation. We're selling the paintings for donations to the local soup kitchen."

Before Sam realized it, people were milling all around, looking at the paintings and talking about buying them. She picked up the plate of sandwiches and began circulating, offering them to people.

A half hour later, Pastor Jones gave a small speech about Creation and how important it is to remember our Creator. Then the panel of judges awarded prizes for various categories. By the time everyone left, every poster had been sold.

"Look at this!" Sam said excitedly as she counted the money in the donation can. "We made $70 for the soup kitchen. Isn't that great?"

🙂 **Everyone is creative in his or her own way. Why do you think that is? How are we, by creating things, honoring how God created us?**

🙂 **Have your own art gallery in someone's backyard. Display your art and have judges. Offer to sell the art and donate the proceeds to a local charity. Make special sandwiches by cutting them out with cookie cutters and serve them with punch or juice.**

Fool's Gold

Then the Almighty will be your gold, the choicest silver for you. Surely then you will find delight in the Almighty and will lift up your face to God. You will pray to him, and he will hear you, and you will fulfill your vows. What you decide on will be done, and light will shine on your ways. Job 22:25-28, NIV.

Rob and I were on vacation in Tennessee. As we drove there from Vermont, it was like watching spring in fast-forward. The cold, drab landscape was replaced by lush vegetation, trees with real leaves, and flowers.

While we were sightseeing, we came across a place where you could pan for rubies and other precious stones. Sluice boxes had been set up, and there was a jewelry store out back that would polish and mount your stones in whatever setting you wanted, or you could just take them home.

We were hooked. Plunking down a couple bucks for a bag of dirt, we found a sluice box and started sifting through it. The dirt quickly washed away in the water, but lots of stones were left in the bottom of the box. An attendant poked through our findings, telling us what each stone was and if it was worth anything.

Even though we couldn't tell by looking, we'd found some pretty nice stones. With a little time and work, they could be made into modestly priced, beautiful stones worth much more than we had invested in them.

Reading the Bible can be like searching for precious stones. Sometimes it looks like a jumble of stones. It's hard to see the value of the verses if you read them hastily or neglect to pray first. In order to receive the biggest blessing from reading the Bible you need to spend time and do a little work. Soon you'll be rewarded with something worth far more than what you invested.

Is there anything that is more important to you than God? What determines how much value something has?

The next time you go for a walk keep your eyes peeled for fool's gold. You will probably find flecks—or chunks—of it embedded in other rocks. It's not worth anything, but it sure is pretty, isn't it?

"Do I Have to Go?"

But even though my sickness was revolting to you, you didn't reject me and turn me away. No, you took me in and cared for me as though I were an angel from God, or even Jesus Christ himself. Galatians 4:14, TLB.

Daniel was looking forward to riding his mountain bike on the hills at the south edge of town. All he had left to do after tuning up his bike was to put the tools away. And then Dad came outside.

"Put your bike away, Dan," he said. "We're going to the hospital."

Daniel felt his whole body let down with disappointment. "Why do *I* have to go to the hospital? I had plans. Can't I just stay here? I'll even stay at home instead of going bike riding."

"Mike Johnson is in the hospital. I'm sure you can spare a few minutes to go and help us show our support."

As Dad went back inside the house, Daniel shook his head in disgust. "I don't know why I have to go," he muttered. "I hate hospitals."

Before leaving, Daniel grabbed his Gameboy and a couple games. He decided he would make the best of a rotten situation. Maybe he could sit in the lobby and play games while his parents visited Mr. Johnson.

Dad agreed to let Daniel play with his Gameboy in the waiting room, as long as he said hi to Mr. Johnson first. So Daniel followed his parents inside the hospital room. "Hi, Mr. Johnson. How do you feel?" he asked, forcing a smile.

Mr. Johnson smiled back. "Bored," he said. "I've read the paper a dozen times, every magazine in the hospital, and I've watched more TV than I can stand. You wouldn't happen to have any other ideas, would you?"

Daniel fingered his Gameboy. Then he grinned. "As a matter of fact, I might. Do you like video games?"

- Why do you and your family visit people in the hospital? Do you always like to visit sick people? Why is it good to visit the sick?

- The next time someone from your church is in the hospital, ask your parents if you can go visit them.

220

Glasses to See With

The eye is the lamp of the body. If your eyes are good, your whole body will be full of light. But if your eyes are bad, your whole body will be full of darkness. Matthew 6:22, 23, NIV.

Tears blurred Zeb's vision as he stumbled across the street. "I'm not ever going to wear those new glasses," he muttered stubbornly to himself. "I'll just learn to get by without them." He stumbled across the grassy park and sat down next to a boy who had a big yellow suitcase beside him.

"Something the matter?" the boy asked.

Zeb noticed that the boy was wearing sunglasses. At least sunglasses were *cool* glasses. Zeb shrugged. "I'm upset."

"Oh," said the boy. And then, "Do you want to talk about it?"

"It's just that my parents made me go to the eye doctor, and now I have to wear glasses. They look horrible. And what's worse is that it's hard to play sports with them."

The boy nodded sympathetically. "That's too bad." After a pause he added, "I always wanted to play sports."

"You don't know what you're missing," Zeb sighed.

"At least you can still play," the boy pointed out. "Don't they make some kind of strap that would help your glasses stay on while you play?"

"Well . . . yeah," Zeb agreed grudgingly.

The boy smiled. "You'll get used to your glasses soon and won't even notice you have them on." He stood up. "I have to get back home. It's time for my piano lesson. Come on, Reno."

Zeb watched in astonishment as the yellow suitcase obediently stood up. "Forward," the boy commanded the dog.

Zeb stood up and slowly made his own way home. Maybe glasses weren't so bad after all.

🙂 **Have you ever been upset because you had to wear glasses or special shoes or a hearing aid or some other device to help you?**

🙂 **Check out a book from the library on sign language. Learn the alphabet.**

221

Hedgehog Haven

In his hand is the life of every creature and the breath of all mankind. Job 12:10, NIV.

I n England they're as common as chipmunks or squirrels are in the United States. Although they've gotten a bad rap as garden pillagers or garbage raiders, the people of England claim the rumors aren't true. So what's all the fuss over a snuffly little pincushion called a hedgehog?

Instead of fighting, if hedgehogs sense danger, they curl up into a ball so that their prickly spines stick up. But spines aren't very good protection against cars or garden rakes. Thousands of hedgehogs are injured every year.

That's where St. Tiggywinkles comes in. St. Tiggywinkles is a wild animal hospital that cares for hedgehogs and other wild animals that have been injured. Hedgehogs have their own section at St. Tiggywinkles, and it's the busiest one in the hospital. Many of them travel to the hospital by train. British Rail carries them to the Aylesbury Station in specially labeled boxes. People volunteer their time to work at the hospital, taking care of the animals.

I know a hospital that desperately needs volunteers. It's very busy. Every day its patients are injured by words, actions, or circumstances. It's the Christian hospital of your local life. Have you seen any injured Christians lately?

You never know where you'll find the next patients. Sometimes they're in school, where people poke fun at them for what they believe. Sometimes they're in church, where they are excluded from activities because someone doesn't like something about them. Sometimes they're in your own family.

Will you help? Your duties would include encouraging them, being their friend, believing in them, and reminding them that Jesus loves them. Your Boss is Jesus, and He'd like to meet with you about your job each day. What do you say?

- What kinds of animals live near you that are similar to hedgehogs? Does anyone care for them if they get hurt?

- Make a visit to the nearest institute of natural science to see how you can help protect wildlife.

Keeping Memories Alive

Celebrate the Feast of Unleavened Bread, because it was on this very day that I brought your divisions out of Egypt. Celebrate this day as a lasting ordinance for the generations to come. Exodus 12:17, NIV.

I t started the day Cain killed Abel and has only gotten worse since. Mass killings. Countries at war. People slaughtered because they believe one thing or another. It will all end one day, but until then, what can we do? How much are we responsible for?

Last year people around the state of Vermont got involved in the Terezín Project. Terezín was a "model" concentration camp the Nazis used to show the world that Jews were receiving wonderful care from them. Many Jewish musicians, artists, composers, and intellectuals were sent first to Terezín before being sent on to another concentration camp to be put to death.

"Terezín: a Remembrance" is a collection of poems, writings, and music created by the children and adults of Terezín and area students. Not long ago the Holocaust Memorial Museum was opened in Washington, D.C.

"What's that got to do with us?" you might say.

The museum points out that we are all bound together. What affects one of us affects all of us. We can't hide from the pain of others or condemn them because they believe differently than we do. They have the same rights that we do.

Elie Wiesel, who is an author, scholar, and survivor of the Holocaust, said, "Let us not forget that there is always a moment when the moral choice is made. Often because of one story or one book or one person, we are able to make a choice, a choice for humanity, for life."

- What do you know about the Holocaust? Are there any events in the news today that are similar to it? What can you do about it? Define human rights.

- What would it have been like to be in a concentration camp during the Holocaust? Write a poem, letter, or essay about how you feel.

6

Singing Star

Sing to the Lord, you saints of his; praise his holy name. Psalm 30:4, NIV.

You could be a star! You could be famous! You could be rich! You could sell millions of albums! Your voice could be heard on radio stations across the country! Your voice is that good!" What would you think if you heard those words?

Ann ("Scotty") Moray de Ceballos was a young Scottish girl whose voice was so beautiful she could have easily had all those things happen to her. But Scotty decided to do something far more glorious with her lovely voice.

Scotty first came to the attention of the United States Army at a rally in Madison Square Garden. The singer who was supposed to sing "The Star-Spangled Banner" failed to show up. A plea was made for anyone in the audience who could sing the anthem to come forward. Scotty went up. As soon as she started singing, the crowd became silent. Her soft soprano voice was hauntingly beautiful.

A U.S. Army general heard Scotty that day and asked her if she would sing for the troops. She sang at Army posts and hospitals in America, the Caribbean, and Italy. Psychiatric wards often held the most difficult and hopeless cases, but Scotty's soothing voice seemed to have the most amazing positive effect on the patients.

One night Scotty was admitted to a locked psychiatric ward. She didn't know that one of the men she was singing to sleep had lost his memory on an Italian hillside during a heavy German artillery bombardment. During the bombardment he had been listening to her on a portable radio. As Scotty sang that night in the ward, she heard a soldier crawling toward her. The shape stopped a couple feet away, and Scotty quit singing.

"You're Scotty Moray!" he said. "You were singing the night of the barrage."

Scotty's beautiful voice had helped the soldier remember.

Ann Moray de Ceballos not only gave her time and voice to help many soldiers, but also helped her husband, Dr. Juan de Ceballos, with his work in a leper colony.

☺ **Why would Scotty give so much in return for so little? What was she really getting back?**

☺ **Volunteer for special music this week.**

224

Act Like a Christian

But the fruit of the Spirit is love, joy, peace, patience, kindness, goodness, faithfulness, gentleness and self-control. Galatians 5:22, 23, NIV.

When I was in high school, several of my classmates and I took a science trip to California. One of our stops included a tour of the University of California at Berkeley. As we entered the administration building of the prestigious school, a few of us noticed a man walking in circles in front of the elevators.

None of us had anything kind to say about him. He was dressed in stale-smelling clothes and wore a ratty green Army jacket. His shoulder-length blond hair was unwashed and stringy. He had obviously abused his mind with drugs. We had no sympathy at all for him.

Some of us stood by and snickered as he continued to wear a circular path in the floor. Some of us made fun of him by imitating him. But his expression never changed. He never seemed to notice we were there.

A group of Christian youth invaded Berkeley that day. But if you were to look at how much of a Christian impression we made in front of the elevators, you might have questioned whether or not we were really Christians at all.

You and I are called Christians because we follow Christ and want to be like Christ. If we have Christ in us, we have the fruit of the Spirit. "The fruit of the Spirit is love, joy, peace, patience, kindness, goodness, faithfulness, gentleness and self-control."

I wish I could remember feeling compassion for the man in front of the elevator. The next time I am in a situation like that, however, I will ask myself what Christ would do, and then I will follow His example.

- Have you ever tried to avoid someone because he or she was just too strange? What did you say about them to your friends? Did you show compassion? Were you kind?

- Replay in your mind everything you did today. Did you act the way Jesus would have acted?

Damaged Goods

But he said to me, "My grace is sufficient for you, for my power is made perfect in weakness." Therefore I will boast all the more gladly about my weaknesses, so that Christ's power may rest on me. That is why, for Christ's sake, I delight in weaknesses, in insults, in hardships, in persecutions, in difficulties. For when I am weak, then I am strong. 2 Corinthians 12:9, 10, NIV.

José was a potter. He had been molding clay from the time he could stand up beside his father with his hands positioned over the wet clay and his father's hands over his, guiding him. His first attempts, though praised by his father, were clumsy, graceless containers now collecting dust. Mostly he kept them to remind him of how far he'd come.

Now his pieces were highly prized by collectors all over the world, selling for hundreds of dollars. Although many were bought simply to decorate homes, José made sure that each one was functional and not just an art piece. With the proper care they could last for many lifetimes. Today he would take his latest creations out of the kiln. Carefully he removed each one and inspected it. Only the last one made him frown.

"What is it, my son?" his father asked, looking over his shoulder.

"It has a crack," José said.

"It happens," his father shrugged. "When they are tested in the fire, sometimes they cannot withstand the heat."

José sighed. "Another one for the dump heap."

"Oh, no!" his father exclaimed. "Just because it is damaged does not mean it is not useful." Shuffling to the corner, the old man reclaimed three more cracked pieces José had placed there. Setting them on end, he placed an old door on top of them. "See? A table. The value of the creation is in the mind of the creator, my son. Remember that."

Even though we may be damaged or bruised, we are of infinite value to God, who created us. He doesn't see us as damaged goods, but as redeemable goods.

😊 **Have you ever made something that turned out less than perfect? How did you feel?**

😊 **Try making something out of clay.**

226

In My Father's House

We had to celebrate and be glad, because this brother of yours was dead and is alive again; he was lost and is found. Luke 15:32, NIV.

The young man had nothing left but the rags on his back. The servants stared, not only once, but twice. And the elder brother couldn't believe what *he* was seeing! But there the younger brother stood in the middle of a beautiful estate, probably smothered in one mighty bear hug after another from his father. The prodigal son knew he didn't deserve to call his father's home *his* home anymore, but Dad insisted, much to the older brother's disgust.

It was on a stormy winter day that a poor farmer went to see President William Henry Harrison, the ninth president of the United States. But the president was at dinner, so the servant told the farmer he would have to wait, and showed him into a chilly room where there was no fire.

Later President Harrison scolded the servant. "Why did you not show the man into the drawing room, where it is warm and comfortable?" he asked.

The servant replied meekly that the farmer would have tracked dirt on the floor.

"Never mind the carpet," Harrison said sternly. "The man is one of the people, and the carpet and the house, too, belong to the people."

Jesus makes a similar claim in the parable of the prodigal son. He welcomes us, no matter what we have done. If you feel dirty and unforgivable because of the sins you have committed, take heart. Jesus is more than willing to forgive us and invite us into His home. Just remember that Jesus welcomes you and me with open arms. He has gone to prepare a home for us. I get the impression He wants us there. Don't you?

- What happens when you track mud through the house? Do your parents still let you live there?

- Surprise your parents by mopping the floor for them this Friday.

227

Dead Sea

For the Scriptures declare that rivers of living water shall flow from the inmost being of anyone who believes in me. John 7:38, TLB.

There is so much salt in the Dead Sea that no animal or plant life can survive in it. In fact, when the Jordan River empties into the Dead Sea, all the fish from the Jordan soon die and become food for the birds.

The Dead Sea is a huge body of water. It is 48 miles long and 3 to 11 miles wide. It is also at the lowest elevation of any body of water in the world, and none of the water that flows into it ever drains back out. The only way water is carried out of the Dead Sea is through evaporation. But when the water evaporates, it leaves behind large concentrations of salt, potash, magnesium, chloride, and bromine. That makes a very, very salty sea.

The Dead Sea is just that—dead! Since there are no outlets, all the minerals are trapped in the remaining water. No fish or plants have a chance in all that salt. In fact, so much salt is trapped in the Dead Sea that a man can float in it with his head and shoulders above the water.

Many people are like the Dead Sea. They go to church every week and enjoy being with Christian friends. They listen to the sermon and study about God. But when church is over on Sabbath, that's it—all that remains during the rest of the week is a Dead Sea Christian!

Christians who are excited about God want to share what they have found seven days a week, 52 weeks a year, year after year after year. Not only do they want to learn as much as they can about God; they have many outlets through which to share God with other people.

What are some of your outlets for sharing God with others?

At least once a day for the next seven days, talk to a friend about what God means to you.

228

Broken Candlestick

You may be sure that your sin will find you out. Numbers 32:23, NIV.

"Honey, would you mind dusting for me before you take off?"

Sam groaned. Dusting was her least favorite chore. "Sure, Mom."

With one eye on the blue sky outside and one on the duster in her hand, Sam wasn't really paying attention. A muffled crash brought her back to what she was doing. With a sick feeling in her stomach, she looked at the shattered candlestick at her feet.

It was one of a set. Her mother lit them every Friday night as Sabbath began. She was going to be furious! Hastily Sam scooped up the fragments of the candlestick and the candle, shoving them in the space behind the bookcase.

"Did I hear something break?" her mother asked.

"No, nope, nothing," Sam assured her, panic and dread mixing with the fear in her stomach. She finished the dusting and went skating. If she tried hard enough, she could almost forget about the candlestick. Almost.

That night as the sun sank below the mountaintops her mother grabbed a box of matches and went to the mantel to light the candles. A perplexed look crossed her face.

"Sam, do you know what happened to the other candlestick? Did you see it when you were dusting?"

Sam squirmed in her chair. "Yes."

Her mother pinned her with an intense stare. "And where is it?"

Sam dragged her feet as she went to the bookcase and pointed behind it. "I'm sorry, Mom. I knocked it over when I was dusting, and it broke."

"Oh, Sam! Why didn't you just tell me? You must have known I'd find out eventually."

"I'm sorry, Mom. I thought if I could hide it . . . Well, it was a silly thought. I'm sorry."

- Have you ever tried to hide a sin? What happened when it was found out? What would have been a better way to handle it?

- Offer to dust for your mom. But be ready to catch her when she faints from shock!

Prayer Warrior

For this reason, since the day we heard about you, we have not stopped praying for you and asking God to fill you with the knowledge of his will through all spiritual wisdom and understanding. Colossians 1:9, NIV.

When I think of a warrior, I think of flashing armor, clashing swords, and charging horses. Or I think of powerful Indians with war paint painted on their faces, fighting fierce battles against their enemies. The warriors I envision live fast, fight fiercely, and die hard.

The story is told of a young girl who was very sick. Although I don't know what she had, apparently it was serious enough that she was not expected to live. But the girl loved Jesus very much. In fact, she loved Him so much that she felt bad that there was not more she could have done for Him during her short life.

Her pastor, seeing that she was troubled, suggested making a prayer list of people in her small town who needed God in their lives and to pray for them. The girl did exactly that. She made a list and prayed for each person, not just once, but several times.

Soon the girl began to hear about changes in the town that only God could be causing. He was beginning to work! When the girl heard what was happening, she prayed even harder.

After the girl died, her prayer list of names was discovered beneath her pillow. Of the 56 names on her list, all had become Christians.

Here on earth movies are made and stories written of brave men and women—warriors who fought heroic battles. History records their heroism, and their courage is inspiring. Their stories send chills down our spines and make many of us wish to be heroes ourselves.

And then there is the dying girl who became a prayer warrior for God. I'm sure all heaven is talking about *her*. Aren't you?

How was the girl able to make such a difference in her small town? What kind of faith did she have?

As you finish your worship with prayer each evening, pray for a specific individual who needs God in his or her life. Continue to pray each evening. Don't give up.

Shelter in a Storm

For he will command his angels concerning you to guard you in all your ways; they will lift you up in their hands, so that you will not strike your foot against a stone. Psalm 91:11, 12, NIV.

My brother and I piled in Grandma's car to go to the mountains for the weekend. Mom, Dad, and our two sisters were already at the camping spot and setting up camp when we arrived. But what had started out as a nice day down in the valley was beginning to turn ugly in the mountains. Clouds blew in and covered the sky. Angry winds began to blow.

While Dad and Grandma fixed supper, my brother, Philip, and I picked up wood for the fire and played tag around the trees. We stopped occasionally to stare up at the tops of the tall pine trees, making ourselves dizzy as they swayed in the wind.

As evening approached, the storm grew worse. The clouds became darker.

Teresa was only 2 years old then, so Mom put her in the playpen while she took care of Carmen, my baby sister. But when the storm got worse, she was impressed to take Teresa out of the playpen and get her ready for bed.

A few seconds later my brother and I heard a crack as the wind blew the top out of a nearby tree. Grandma tried to run, but she tripped and fell, and the treetop fell on her, breaking her pelvis.

A couple miracles happened that night. Although Grandma was injured, she could have easily been killed if she had not tripped and been lying flat on the ground when the tree fell on her. The second miracle was evident when we saw that the tree had also crushed the playpen Teresa had been in only a few minutes earlier. Certainly our guardian angels stood by that night in the mountains.

- **What are some experiences you or your family have had in which your guardian angels protected you?**

- **Ask your parents to share an experience during which they believe guardian angels protected your family.**

On the Move—Again

The Lord had said to Abram, "Leave your country, your people and your father's household and go to the land I will show you." Genesis 12:1, NIV.

Moving is tough. I know. I was never in the same school for more than two years in a row. Just as I would make some friends, it would be time to switch schools. Every time I moved I thought nothing would ever be the same again.

Boy, was I wrong!

The food at each new school was just as bad as it had been in the school before it.

A few things were hard to get used to. For instance, one school I went to didn't have "periods." They had something called a "mod." A mod is 20 minutes long. I had one mod for lunch. It took me five minutes to get to my locker and ditch my books, 10 minutes to go through the lunch line, and five minutes to go back to my locker to get my books. I never did figure out when I was supposed to actually eat my lunch. But as I said, the cafeteria food wasn't really worth eating anyway.

Making all those changes was really hard sometimes. There were times I just wanted to move back to my old school where everything had finally gotten comfortable. One thing I learned, however, is that even though everything around us can change, there is One who remains the same. God.

The Bible says He does not change. I can always count on Him to be there for me, no matter what school I'm in or where I live.

I like to think that making these changes is helping me to prepare for all the other changes I'll be making as I get older—going to college, getting a job, getting a better job, getting married, having kids, being nominated for a Pulitzer prize . . . Let's face it—change is going to happen. It's unavoidable. And I guess I'm glad. I'd hate for life to stay the same forever.

🙂 **Have you ever had to move? What was it like? What did you miss most? What did you miss the least?**

🙂 **The next time you or someone you know has to move, resolve to keep in touch. Send your friend cards to let them know you miss them.**

"Surprise, You're Caught!"

If you do what is right, will you not be accepted? But if you do not do what is right, sin is crouching at your door; it desires to have you, but you must master it. Genesis 4:7, NIV.

C asey and a couple of his buddies skipped school and drove 10 miles away to another town, where they parked in a grocery store parking lot. After they had waited a few minutes, they saw two men pull into the parking lot.

"Do you suppose they'll buy us beer?" Casey asked.

Casey's friends nodded. "Sure. Let's ask them."

So Casey approached the two men. He gave them money to pay for the beer, plus a few extra dollars for their trouble.

What Casey didn't realize was that the manager of the store was watching the whole transaction. While Casey and his friends were waiting for the men to return with their beer, the manager came out to talk to them. As soon as they realized their plan had been discovered, they raced off, leaving their money behind.

Casey's problems didn't end there, however. When the police officer showed up a few minutes later, the manager began to give him a complete description of the kids. As the manager described Casey, the police officer's eyes suddenly narrowed and his face became stern. "I know the boy who gave the men money to buy beer with," he said. "He's my stepson. It doesn't look like this is going to be his lucky day."

Casey thought he had escaped trouble at the store by taking off before he got caught. But imagine his surprise when his stepfather came home that evening. Doing what is right leaves a person free from guilt and the fear of being found out, a lesson Casey hopefully learned.

- Have you ever thought you escaped getting caught when you did something wrong, only to discover later that someone had known all along? How did you feel even when no one had seen you? How much is a clear conscience worth to you?

- Make a list of all the temptations you avoided today. Ask yourself why you avoided each.

233

Sailplane

But O my soul, don't be discouraged. Don't be upset. Expect God to act! For I know that I shall again have plenty of reason to praise him for all that he will do. He is my help! He is my God! Psalm 42:11, TLB.

One summer while on vacation, Dad and I decided to experience flying in a sailplane. We paid our fee, signed releases, and climbed in the three-seater craft to be towed into the air by a prop plane. When the tow plane had pulled us to the proper altitude, our pilot released the tow rope and immediately turned us toward the cliffs.

I remember the silence as we soared like a bird. It was peaceful. For half an hour we sailed along the face of the cliff and then out over the beach before we returned to the cliffs again. On more than one occasion I thought we were flying much closer to the cliffs than seemed like a good idea. Sailplanes have a much wider wingspan than regular prop planes have, so as the wing tips reached out toward the jagged cliffs, my teeth automatically clinched together. My idea would have been to stay away from the cliffs altogether and just hang out over the beach, like the seagulls were doing.

But I guess it was a good thing I wasn't the pilot. Before I would have figured out where to go for rising air currents to lift the plane up, I would have had to land. And those cliffs were what was giving us enough lift to stay in the air.

Sailplane pilots know where to go for lift so they can keep flying. Just as pilots need to know where the rising air currents are, Christians need to know where to go when they need a lift too. Everyone has times when they feel depressed, tired, or lonely—even Christians. During those times it's important to know where to go for help. Focus on God. Trust Him to make you smile again.

What do you do when you feel depressed? Do you pray for God to help lift you up? Do you put your hope in Him?

When you feel depressed and discouraged, read Psalm 42.

Litterbug

The earth is the Lord's, and everything in it, the world, and all who live in it; for he founded it upon the seas and established it upon the waters. Psalm 24:1, 2, NIV.

She was my friend, but she drove me nuts. She thought nothing of making the outdoors into her own personal garbage can. She tossed used tissues, gum wrappers, candy wrappers, and soda cans along the side of the road.

"I'm just a litterbug," she'd say.

One day while eating at her house I decided to turn the tables. Grabbing a juice box out of the refrigerator, I slurped it down and tossed the empty box onto the floor. She stared at it for a minute before pointing out that the garbage can was still where it had always been.

"I know," I said cheerfully. "I'm just a litterbug."

My napkin joined the juice box on the floor. So did the empty bread wrapper and my empty yogurt container.

"What do you think you're doing?" my friend sputtered. "My house isn't a dump. Throw your stuff in the garbage."

I popped a piece of gum into my mouth and tossed the wrapper on the floor. "What's the difference between your house and God's house?"

She glared at the gum wrapper before answering. "Nothing, I guess. What's that got to do with anything?"

I chewed slowly. "Well, God created the earth, and you think it's OK to litter outside. This is your house, so why can't I litter here?"

Then she smiled. "All right. You made your point. I won't litter anymore. Now help me pick up this mess."

☺ **How do you think it makes God feel when we litter? What can you do about litter? How can you help other people become aware of litter?**

☺ **Make garbage bags for your parents' cars. Take a brown paper lunch bag and draw a scene of Creation on it with today's verse. Make a hole to hang it from, or attach a piece of Velcro to the bag and stick one to the back seat of the car. *But ask your parents' permission first!***

I'm Not Leaving

I will never leave thee, nor forsake thee. Hebrews 13:5.

The two dogs looked ridiculous together. One was a big mixed breed named Scotty, and the other was a dachshund we named Snoopy because of her black-and-white markings and because she liked to sit on top of her doghouse. Though an odd pair, Scotty and Snoopy had become fast friends. One would not go anywhere without the other.

Between the two of them they mastered the art of escape. If Scotty couldn't tear the fence apart, Snoopy would dig beneath it. They could escape from about any type of fence I built.

One day some teenagers tossed firecrackers into the dog pen. From then on Scotty would become highly upset whenever he heard firecrackers or gunshots and would often try to run away. Every year as the Fourth of July approached, he would become frantic. And during the part of the summer when people started lighting fireworks until they quit after the Fourth, it was nearly impossible to keep Scotty from running away. Just to be safe, we adopted extreme measures and chained him up inside the fence.

Even so, one year Scotty managed to pull the stake he was chained to out of the ground, and he and Snoopy escaped from the backyard. They were gone all day long on one of the hottest days of the year while my wife and I were at work.

When we discovered Scotty and Snoopy were missing, we went out to look for them. An hour later we came across the two dogs in a field. Scotty was nearly dead from exhaustion and dehydration because his chain had gotten tangled in some wire, trapping him in the hot sun. Snoopy was in nearly as bad shape, even though she was free to go to the nearby creek for water. But Snoopy never left Scotty's side, not even for water. She would have stayed until the end.

- Do you have friends who stick by your side even when you're going through some rotten times? Why would your friends stick around during the bad times?

- Write a promise to one of your friends who is going through some bad times that you will neither leave nor forsake him or her.

Pretty Little Butterfly

And God said, "Let the land produce living creatures according to their kinds: livestock, creatures that move along the ground, and wild animals, each according to its kind." And it was so. Genesis 1:24, NIV.

Sam crowded beside Dillon, nose up to the netting, and squinted at the interior of the whatever-it-was. "What is this?" she asked finally.

"A butterfly hatchery," Dillon pointed at the milkweed plants that were standing upright in the middle of the hatchery. A circular tube of netting stretched from the floor to the ceiling.

After staring at the inside of the netting until her eyes hurt, she stood up. "I don't see anything."

Zeb's voice came from the other end of the clubhouse. "I couldn't see them at first either. They're green cocoons with little gold dots in a ring around the top."

Sam looked again. "I see one!" she finally exclaimed.

"Look! Look!" Dillon shouted. "This one is hatching."

The walls of the cocoon had become so transparent that they could see the butterfly's wings through them. The cocoon shook and spun until suddenly it popped open and the butterfly's wings unfurled. Delicate black legs clung to the remains of the cocoon. The butterfly's wings drooped like wilted flower petals.

"What's the matter with it?" Sam asked worriedly.

"Nothing," Dillon explained. "Its wings will stiffen up in a minute. Watch."

A few minutes later the butterfly began to fly around the hatchery.

"That was awesome!" Sam said.

"Awesome," Dillon and Zeb agreed.

- Have you ever spent any time really looking at some of the beautiful things God created? What did they make you think of?

- Many different kinds of caterpillars can be brought inside where they will spin a cocoon and hatch out as butterflies. Find out which ones in your area are best and catch a few. Make them an area surrounded by netting. Be sure to let them go after they hatch.

Sweet Dreams

On my bed I remember you; I think of you through the watches of the night. Because you are my help, I sing in the shadow of your wings. My soul clings to you; your right hand upholds me. Psalm 63:6-8, NIV.

How often do you think of God during the day? Do you ever imagine Him going through the day with you, or sitting with you when you talk to your friends, or playing a game with you?

I read about a woman who when she would have her devotional time in the morning would save a seat for God and imagine Him sitting there listening to her and talking to her. At the end of her devotional time, instead of leaving God sitting there, she would invite Him to go with her through the rest of her day.

Isn't that a great idea?

Through the Holy Spirit, God can be with us wherever we are and in whatever we are doing. But the most important thing is that we take God with us in our hearts through the day. It can be very hard to imagine that the Creator of the entire universe is interested in the silly little things that we do each day, but He is!

God cares about everything you go through. He wants to be there for you every second of the day. And that is possible if you rely on Him. David says, "My soul clings to you; your right hand upholds me." How about you? Is God just a crutch you use in times of need? Or is He a friend you lean on every second of the day?

God created us to talk to Him, to share ourselves with Him, to be His companions. In exchange He offers us Himself. It is the greatest gift He could give us. Won't you accept it?

🙂 **Do you think it's possible to think about God all day and all night? What do you think David was talking about?**

🙂 **Obtain an old pillowcase. Using fabric paint, write out your favorite Bible text on the edge of the pillowcase. Sweet dreams!**

If You're a Sunny-side Up Christian, You . . .

Sing to the Lord, for he has done glorious things; let this be known to all the world. Isaiah 12:5, NIV.

Are you a sunny-side up Christian? If so, you might:
- make smiling a habit.
- laugh at least 15 times a day.
- love to watch the sun rise.
- be looking forward to today.
- tell some good jokes.
- love the wind in your hair.
- sing with your favorite Christian music artist.
- like to walk barefoot in the grass.
- stop and smell the flowers.
- take a long nap under a huge shade tree.
- climb a mountain because it's there.
- gallop on a horse.
- give cuts in line.
- offer to do someone a favor.
- be a friend.
- share Jesus with someone.
- make a kitten purr.
- play with your dog.
- share a sunset.
- read the Bible because you like to.
- talk to Jesus as to a friend.
- trust God in all things.

Being joyful in all things may take some practice. Let's face it—if you are walking to your lunch table and someone knocks over your lunch tray, it's going to take some effort to respond in joy! Spend time each day with Jesus. It will become easier and easier. He promised.

Are you a sunny-side up Christian? How do you reflect that to the people around you? How can you tell if someone is filled with the joy of the Lord?

Today do five things out of the above list.

If You Serve Others

For even the Son of Man did not come to be served, but to serve, and to give his life as a ransom for many. Mark 10:45, NIV.

Sunny-side up Christians have a habit of serving others. Have you noticed that Christians are happiest when they are doing something for someone else? I'm sure that whenever Jesus helped someone He didn't think to Himself, *Boy, this is a real drag. I wish I were doing something else today—anything else but having to deal with all these sick people.*

No way! Jesus never missed an opportunity to serve. He was always on the lookout for a chance to make someone's life better in this sinful world.

Jesus didn't cause sin, but because He loves us He committed Himself to saving us from it, a commitment that would one day require Him to sacrifice His life. Until that time came He spent His time doing what He could to help people and to teach them about the kingdom of God.

For a long time the disciples misunderstood Jesus because they couldn't comprehend that His mission was to save everyone from sin, not free them from Roman oppression. They had visions of greatness in a kingdom they believed Jesus would set up here on earth. Jesus' example of service hardly made an impression on them. Instead, they thought it was a big publicity stunt to gather the thousands of followers He would need to overthrow the Romans.

People may misunderstand your motives too. They may think you are trying to be popular or get on their good side because you want a favor or for some other personal, selfish reason. Don't let that stop you from doing good. Jesus didn't let it stop Him.

It hurts when people misunderstand us. Tell Jesus about it. He knows what that feels like, and He'll help you through it. In the end the only thing that really matters is your motives—and He knows just what those are.

- Were the disciples always willing to help people? Do you act more often like Jesus or the disciples?

- Find a way to serve someone today. Try to surprise that person with your actions and your attitude.

Secret Club

Every day they continued to meet together in the temple courts. They broke bread in their homes and ate together with glad and sincere hearts, praising God and enjoying the favor of all the people. Acts 2:46, 47, NIV.

People wanted to kill the early Christians for believing in Jesus. Paul and Peter were stoned and thrown in prison. Stephen was killed. Being a Christian wasn't easy. But Paul never said, "This is too much. I never realized being a Christian could be hazardous to my health. I'm getting out. Forget this!"

Paul found joy in every circumstance, even prison. He learned to be happy when he was hungry or when he was well fed, when he was in want or when he had plenty.

Of course, early Christians did what they could to avoid persecution. They changed their meeting places frequently and met in secret. They used the symbol of a fish to tell others that they were Christians. The Greek word for fish is *ixoyc,* and the letters stand for the Greek words that mean "Jesus Christ, God's Son, Saviour." You've probably seen these letters inside the fish symbols sold in Christian bookstores.

In the United States we are fortunate to be able to worship the way we choose to. We've never known what it is like to have to hide behind closed doors, worshiping quietly, listening unconsciously for the footsteps outside that mean the secret police have found us. We don't know what it's like to be afraid each time we leave for church, knowing it will possibly be the last time.

Today, remember to thank God that we are free to worship as we please. Ask Him to protect those who still must worship secretly. Someday soon we'll all worship together just as loudly as we please.

- 😊 **How would you feel if you lived in a country in which you could be put in prison—or even killed—for talking about Jesus? What do you think you'd do if you lived in a place like that?**

- 😊 **Start your own secret club at school or in your neighborhood. Change the meeting place each time to make the meetings more secret. Begin by studying the book of Acts.**

241

I Want

Whoever wants to become great among you must be your servant, and whoever wants to be first must be slave of all. Mark 10:43, 44, NIV.

James and John took Jesus aside one day. "Listen," they said, "we have a request.

"Let's say You let one of us sit at Your right hand and the other at Your left. We want to have the two highest places in Your kingdom, next to You, of course."

Jesus said it wasn't up to Him to make that decision. It was up to His Father. But that didn't end the power play among the disciples; it only added more fuel to the flame. James and John had secretly made their move, and when the rest of the disciples heard about it, they got a little hot under the collar. "How dare *they* secretly try to grab the top positions!" They all wanted the top positions. Sound familiar?

Ted wants to be the quarterback. Allen wants to play pitcher. Jennifer wants to be the striker on her soccer team. At home Cory thinks his parents favor his sisters over him.

Imagine! Jesus has recently told His 12 disciples that He will be condemned to death. He will be crucified. *Zoom!* Jesus' words go right over their heads as they concentrate on who will be the greatest. When James and John made their play for the top positions, the rest of the disciples got angry. Jesus called them all together.

"You know, you are different from earthly kings and rulers," He told them. "You shouldn't be so concerned with greatness, but instead should focus on serving others. Service is more important than being served."

There are many examples in the Bible of God choosing people who weren't popular, famous, wealthy, or even especially good-looking to do a special work for Him. They weren't at the top. They weren't even near the top. That's one of the reasons He chose them. Do you know why?

😊 **What does it mean to be a slave of all? Are people more happy when they follow Jesus' example and think of others first?**

😊 **Read Mark 10:35-45. Instead of thinking of yourself first, try to think of ways to be of service every day.**

Who Needs Glasses?

And pray in the Spirit on all occasions with all kinds of prayers and requests. Ephesians 6:18, NIV.

There are few things more joyful than answered prayer in a moment of crisis. What a sense of peace to know that God is with you and me when we need Him. It makes me wonder—who needs glasses when they have God?

The last time I ever walked in my sleep came after a long, tiring day of backpacking in the Sawtooth Mountains. I was past tired; I was *zonked*. And whenever I got that tired, I ran the risk of taking a midnight stroll.

After supper I crawled into my sleeping bag and immediately fell into a deep sleep, only to wake up a couple hours later in the middle of the forest. I had remembered to bring my sleeping bag—it was wadded up under my arm. But I had forgotten my glasses. I was standing in the middle of a fuzzy forest with no idea which way to go. But before I took one step, I prayed.

"Jesus, I can't do this by myself. I can't see even 10 yards in front of me. You're going to have to help me find my way back."

Out of all the directions I could have walked, I chose to turn to my right, praying every second and with every step. When I stumbled through a stream, I immediately sent a thank-You prayer up to God. I remembered the stream! God had sent me in the right direction! Later I stumbled over some tents in our camp, nearly scaring some of my companions to death. But at least I found my way back.

I'm convinced that God answers prayers. He may not answer right away. He may not always answer the way we want Him to. But that night when I woke up from a deep sleep to find myself standing in the middle of the forest, I was happy to know that God was listening to and taking care of me.

- **Does praying make you feel better? Why does praying bring us comfort?**

- **I wouldn't suggest sleepwalking to see if prayer really works, but you can use prayer every day in every situation. Give it a try today.**

243

Prayer Chain

Therefore confess your sins to each other and pray for each other so that you may be healed. The prayer of a righteous man is powerful and effective. James 5:16, NIV.

Will you pray for me?"

"Remember me in your prayers."

"Would you pray for my sick grandmother?"

"Thanks for keeping me in your prayers."

Have you heard statements like these? Has anyone ever asked you to pray for him or her? Have you ever . . . forgotten?

I read a story once about a woman who was asked to pray for someone. She said yes, then totally forgot about it. When the person later thanked her for her prayers, she felt horrible! She'd forgotten to pray! After that she made a list of people she was praying for so she wouldn't forget anyone.

Do you have a prayer list?

Praying for people is important for many reasons. Praying for someone else's needs takes our minds off ourselves. It helps to develop in us a loving attitude toward others. It is also important because everyone has a choice to make between God and Satan. If someone chooses to follow the world and Satan, God isn't going to force that person to change his or her mind. But if you pray, the Holy Spirit can approach that person and try to bring him or her back to God. Praying for others and watching God answer your prayers also build your faith.

So what are you waiting for? Start praying!

🙂 **Whom do you think prayer is meant for most? God or us? Why do you think God likes us to pray if He already knows everything we're going to say?**

🙂 **Make strips of paper along the short end of a piece of construction paper. Make the strips about one inch wide. Write one prayer request on each strip. Overlap one end over the other to make a ring. Connect them as you go to make a chain. See how long you can make the chain. Can you circle your room with it? Hang it along the ceiling like a garland.**

Fast Food

Don't recite the same prayer over and over as the heathen do, who think prayers are answered only by repeating them again and again. Remember, your Father knows exactly what you need even before you ask him! Matthew 6:7, 8, TLB.

Does your family like to use the drive-up window at a fast-food restaurant? This is often convenient when everyone is rushed and Mom and Dad don't feel up to cooking supper. Think about what happens. As soon as your family pulls up to the speaker, someone you can't see says, "May I take your order?"

All of you quickly put in an order for your favorite food.

"May I get you anything else?" the voice asks.

"No, thank you."

"Your total is . . ."

Unfortunately, many Christians use the same "drive-up window" approach when they pray to God. I used to plop down on my knees at bedtime and spout off exactly the same prayer night after night. Do you do that? Have you ever been tempted to recycle the same bedtime prayer again and again?

But God isn't a fast-food restaurant. Prayer isn't like ordering your favorite milk shake. Through prayer we learn to know God better by the ways He answers us.

"How?" you might ask. "At least at the drive-up window someone is talking back. I get what I ask for. When I pray, it's a one-way conversation. God never talks back to me when I pray."

But God gives answers as long as we are sincere about wanting a close relationship with Him. A person who prays sincerely will be expecting God to answer. A person who prays boldly has faith God will talk back. And God will answer the person who expects his or her prayers to be answered.

🙂 **When was the last time you prayed boldly? Why can't people expect God to answer recycled prayers?**

🙂 **Talk to God as if He were physically right beside you. Remember, He is all-powerful, and He wants the very best for you. Tell Him whatever is on your mind. He will answer.**

245

Only the Real McCoy Will Do

Test everything. Hold on to the good. 1 Thessalonians 5:21, NIV.

For every genuine article there seems to be a fake. For every quality product, there seems to be a counterfeit. Genuine quality products often cost far more to purchase than their cheaper counterparts, yet such a large investment makes buying a cheaper counterfeit look very appealing to many people.

Being a genuine Christian often takes a lot of work. It's a big investment of time spent with Christ to live a joyful Christian life. Yet many people who call themselves Christians are not serious about getting to know their Saviour. Their lives become mere counterfeits.

Elijah McCoy knew the value of quality products. Elijah was born in 1843, the son of people who had been slaves before escaping to Canada. He studied mechanical engineering in Scotland and later moved to Michigan, where he worked with the railroads. One of Elijah's earlier successes was a lubrication system he developed for use on locomotives and other heavy machinery. Although he patented more than 50 inventions, what he may be best remembered for is the term that came about because of his strict standards for quality. After people got used to getting high-quality parts from Elijah McCoy, they wanted the genuine product every time, so they asked for the real McCoy.

Real McCoy Christians are happy followers of Christ. Their attitudes lift others up instead of causing discouragement. Real Christians have a unique opportunity to show people a better way of life through Christ. Their hands are gentle, their words are kind, and their joy contagious. These are the signs of the real McCoy.

How can people tell you are the real McCoy when it comes to your Christianity?

Always be honest and sincere, choosing to lift people up, just as Jesus did when He was here on earth.

Where Is Grandpa Going?

For the living know that they will die, but the dead know nothing. Ecclesiastes 9:5, NIV.

Samantha's stomach dropped into her sneakers. Her mother stood in the doorway to her bedroom, eyes puffy and red. Something was wrong. Really wrong.

Mom made her way across the room and sat on the edge of Sam's bed. "Honey, we've had some bad news."

"What is it?" she asked, afraid to find out.

"Grandpa had a heart attack. He's at the hospital right now, but the doctors don't expect him to live through the night."

"Grandpa's going to die?" Sam asked in a small miserable voice. "He can't die."

Mom put her arm around Sam's shoulders. "I know it's hard to believe. It's not like you can prepare for this kind of thing. It just happens." Mom shook too, and Sam knew she was crying. All of a sudden Sam realized that Mom was losing her father.

"Mom," she asked, "where is Grandpa going? I mean, is he going to heaven?"

Mom wiped her nose and eyes with the fistful of tissues she was holding. "He's not really going anywhere," she explained. "When he dies, it will be just as if he's taking a long nap until Jesus comes back. It won't seem to him like he's gone anywhere.

"When God created us, He made us from dust and His breath. While we're alive, we are living souls. When we die, our body—the dust—goes back to dust, and our breath goes back to God."

"So it will be like Grandpa is sleeping until Jesus comes?"

Mom nodded. "Yes, but right now he's still here. Get ready, and we'll go to the hospital to say goodbye."

- What is the difference between the breath and the soul? What two things does God combine to make man a "living soul"? Where does the breath go when a person dies? Where does the body go?

- Although it seems like people will live forever, life is very uncertain. Spend time with your family and appreciate them for who they are while they are here.

247

How Can I Help?

He welcomed them and spoke to them about the kingdom of God,
and healed those who needed healing. Luke 9:11, NIV.

'm sorry, Sam," Dillon said.

"Thanks, Dillon." Sam tried to stifle a sob. "Thanks for coming by. I'm glad you suggested we take a walk."

"Well, I didn't really know what to do. I'm not very good at this sort of thing. All I know for sure is that I know how much you hurt inside. My grandmother died a couple years ago from cancer. All I could think about was all the fun things I got to do with her and how much she loved me."

"How long did it take for the sick, empty feeling to go away?" Sam asked.

"I guess the empty feeling is still there when I think about her. But it doesn't hurt as much as it used to," he said.

"Yeah, well, I doubt *my* heart will ever stop hurting," Sam said.

Dillon wanted to be able to make her feel better right away, but he knew it would take time. Then he thought of a story his dad had told him. "Remember the story of Jesus feeding the crowd of 5,000 people with just five loaves of bread and two fish?"

Sam frowned. "Yeah. What's that got to do with Grandpa dying?"

"Well, Jesus had just heard that His cousin, John the Baptist, had been killed. The Bible says He wanted to be alone, but the crowds followed Him. Nobody seemed to care how *He* was feeling. But Jesus didn't send them away. He healed the sick and talked to them about God. Even though He was sad, He wanted to make other people feel better. I think it helped Him feel better too."

Sam walked a little farther without saying anything. "You know something? I think I know exactly how Jesus felt. I think Grandpa would rather I remembered him by helping other people too, just as Jesus did."

- Have you lost a family member or a close friend? How did it make you feel? What did you do to help yourself feel better?

- Ask your pastor what you can do to help support a family in your church who has lost a loved one.

AUGUST 31

Going Home

And the ransomed of the Lord will return. They will enter Zion with singing; everlasting joy will crown their heads. Gladness and joy will over-take them, and sorrow and sighing will flee away. Isaiah 35:10, NIV.

Everyone has seen pictures of missing children. You and I have seen their names and faces on milk cartons, in newspapers, and on posters. Some children have been missing for months; some have been missing for years. Many may never be found again.

But on a recent trip my wife and I had the privilege of flying with a child who had been a kidnapping victim. Before the flight ended in Fresno, California, the captain announced that the 10-year-old girl was on the last leg of her journey home. The whole plane erupted in a round of applause.

A huge crowd awaited her arrival at the airport. Family and friends couldn't wait to hug her, and the news crews eagerly awaited a chance to report the good news. What a joyful occasion! One less picture on a milk carton! This child was going home!

But there is more good news. You may not have realized it, but we've all been kidnapped. How? Satan did it. He wedged himself between us and God. Now we're stuck on a sinful planet, sep-arated physically from our heavenly Father. Often Satan puts his arm around us, whispers in our ear, and leads us away from God.

The girl who was going home wasn't going home alone. The two people who rescued her were flying with her that day. It re-minds me of a trip you and I are going to take someday. On that day our Rescuer is coming with a host of angels to take us home with Him. That will be a joyful occasion too.

I don't know if there are milk cartons in heaven, but I'm sure Jesus has each one of us etched in His heart.

- **What are some of the ways you have been kidnapped lately?**

- **Ask your parents if the police station in your town or city offers a safety course for kids. Many offer finger-printing and other means of identification.**

249

Trust

Trust in the Lord with all your heart and lean not on your own understanding; in all your ways acknowledge him, and he will make your paths straight. Proverbs 3:5, 6, NIV.

I had backpacked several times in the Sawtooth Mountains and climbed mountains using hundreds of tedious switchbacks. Once on top, I stared down numerous steep shale mountainsides—my feet securely planted, of course. But when I began riding horses on the same trails, I had to put my faith in an animal instead of in myself. That was sometimes very hard to do.

You see, Magic had bucked on numerous occasions for no apparent reason. But up the side of a mountain, on trails so narrow that Magic's head and neck were hanging out over empty space coming down a switchback, I had to learn to trust him.

In the back of my mind I remembered all the instances something had spooked our horses in the past. I imagined all sorts of horrifying scenarios of rearing horses, slashing hooves, and tumbling bodies. But there was only one thing I could do if I ever wanted to stand on top of the mountain and look across at awesome granite peaks and rich green forests far below. I had to learn to trust Magic to get me there safely. I had to believe that Magic didn't want to fall down the side of the mountain any more than I did.

It wasn't too difficult to trust Magic when I knew he didn't want to get hurt any more than I did. But how do we trust God when we can't see Him? How do we know He's there? Most of all, how do we know He really cares?

My dictionary says trust is the "assured reliance on the character, strength, or truth of someone or something." The key to trusting God is to know His character.

😊 **Do you trust God to guide and protect you? How does someone get to know God's character?**

😊 **Test God's character. Using the Bible for reference and an experience from each person in your worship group, finish these statements: I know God is fair because . . . I know He is honest because . . . I know He loves me because . . .**

Care and Feeding of Poor Me's

When you fast, do not look somber as the hypocrites do, for they disfigure their faces to show men they are fasting. I tell you the truth, they have received their reward in full. But when you fast, put oil on your head and wash your face, so that it will not be obvious to men that you are fasting, but only to your Father, who is unseen; and your Father, who sees what is done in secret, will reward you. Matthew 6:16–18, NIV.

Bonnie sighed and slumped her head into her arms. I looked at her, not sure if I ought to ask or not. Finally, I did. "Something wrong?"

She looked up. There were dark circles under her eyes, and her face looked pale. "It seems like everything has been going wrong lately. My sister is mad at me because I borrowed a sweater from her and got a stain on it. My father said that if I don't clean my rabbit's cage I can't go to the concert this weekend. But I have so much homework I just don't know how I'm going to manage it. And my mother wants me to help her make dinner for the local halfway house this week."

I shook my head sympathetically. "Wow, you sure have it rough, all right," I agreed. "Your parents ought to be more understanding."

Bonnie held her hands up. "Please don't feed my poor me's."

I blinked at her. "Poor me's?"

"Poor me, I've got too much to do. Poor me, no one treats me right. Poor me, no one understands me. . . . I'm trying to think about the positive things. I don't have time to feel sorry for poor me."

Well, I felt pretty silly. Instead of helping her with her problems, all I was helping her do was to feel sorry for herself.

"Say, Bonnie, I could clean your rabbit's cage," I suggested.

What do you do when you feel sorry for yourself? Why shouldn't we encourage ourselves, or others, to have pity parties?

Every time you feel sorry for yourself, write down 10 things to be thankful for. You can be sure you won't feel sorry for long. Review the list every now and then.

251

Courage

Be strong and courageous. Do not be terrified; do not be discouraged, for the Lord your God will be with you wherever you go. Joshua 1:9, NIV.

A fire in a Brooklyn building nearly cost a cat and her five kittens their lives. Instead, it became a story that proves courage is not limited to the strongest or the most powerful.

As the building burned, the mother cat (who was later named Scarlet) raced back inside time after time to rescue her five kittens. Scarlet's courage did not come without cost, however. By the time she had made five trips into the burning building, her eyes were blistered shut and her paws were burned. Yet after she rescued her last kitten, she continued to worry over her small family. She gently touched each of them with her nose to make sure all were safe, and then began to move them across the street.

Scarlet wouldn't give up until she had moved all her kittens to safety. She wasn't concerned about the flames and the heat, only about saving her family.

Often the biggest step toward overcoming a challenge is the first one. There are so many huge obstacles in the way that it seems impossible to imagine the goal at the end of the struggle. While consequences do have to be considered, we shouldn't let them keep us from achieving our goals.

Joshua had just taken over the command of the children of Israel after Moses had died. God told Joshua to follow Him, and he would be successful. God also told Joshua not to be afraid, because He would be watching out for him wherever he went. God is watching out for you and me, too.

- Are strength and power more important than faith and love and doing what God wants?

- Make a bar graph. Put a mark every 10 points from 0 to 100 on the left side. Underneath, list the challenges you think are the most overwhelming. Draw a bar representing how much effort you would put into overcoming each challenge by yourself. Then beside your best effort, draw a bar representing how much more you can do, knowing God is with you.

You Serve Others By . . .

But I am among you as one who serves. Luke 22:27, NIV.

Jesus especially wanted His disciples to understand that in His kingdom those who serve are far greater than any king or ruler in this world. You can serve others by:

- visiting the elderly.
- going to see a shut-in.
- mowing a neighbor's lawn.
- taking care of your neighbors' pets during a vacation.
- doing your chores happily.
- surprising your parents by doing extra duties.
- cooking a meal for a family who is having a crisis.
- singing in a retirement home.
- telling people you appreciate them.
- encouraging the talents of others.
- lifting people up instead of putting them down.
- helping schoolmates understand their schoolwork.
- planning a family picnic.
- being honest.
- being a good role model for young children.
- taking a stand against drugs.
- taking a stand for Jesus.

Being of service to someone doesn't always mean you have to *plan* to do something such as mowing the lawn or visiting someone who is sick. One of the best ways to be of service is to be cheerful. Just being in a good mood will help to give people a much-needed boost.

> What things have you done during the past two days to help someone? How did it make you feel? What are some things you can do during the next two days to help others?

> Take several small pieces of paper. Write one of the above suggestions on each slip of paper. Think of other things to write also. Then make a commitment to serve and choose things to do each day or week. Then just do it!

253

Broken Arrows

If you love those who love you, what reward will you get? Are not even the tax collectors doing that? And if you greet only your brothers, what are you doing more than others? Do not even pagans do that? Be perfect, therefore, as your heavenly Father is perfect. Matthew 5:46–48, NIV.

you know, you say some pretty dumb things, but that's got to be one of the dumbest," Colleen scoffed. "When are you going to grow up, anyway? What a baby."

Tears stung my eyes as I watched Colleen and some of my other friends walk away. I felt just as though she had taken an arrow and shot it into me. Her unkind words continued to sting me as they replayed over and over in my mind.

The more I thought about it, the madder I got. Just then someone sat down at the table next to me. It was Jienette. She was not popular, but for some reason she'd taken a liking to me and hung around with me whenever she could.

"Is something the matter?" Jienette asked.

It was on the tip of my tongue to tell her that any idiot could see that yes, something was wrong, and maybe I did just lose my best friend, but it certainly wasn't her.

Is that a nice thing to say? a voice in my head asked.

I squirmed uncomfortably. Jienette hadn't done anything wrong. She was just worried about me. If I were mean to her it would be just like taking the arrow Colleen had shot into me, taking aim at Jienette, and shooting it at her instead!

I came here to break arrows, the voice in my head continued. *You don't have to let evil continue. Give Me the arrow. I'll break it and it will end here.*

Yes, it would end here. I smiled and turned to Jienette. "Thanks for asking. I'll be OK."

😊 **What do you do when someone shoots an arrow of hurt into you? Why do you think it's important not to string it up and shoot it into someone else?**

😊 **Gather some craft materials and make your own arrow. Hang it on a wall in your room to remind you of today's devotional.**

Ultimate Service

For whoever exalts himself will be humbled, and whoever humbles himself will be exalted. Matthew 23:12, NIV.

Being sick is no fun. In fact, it can be very, very miserable. And people who are sick are usually not fun people to be around, either. When my wife gets sick, I do what I can to make her feel better. When she wants something, I get it. When she calls me, I come running to see what she wants. I've discovered that taking care of someone who is sick can be very demanding with very few rewards.

But I also realize that when I am sick, sometimes I want to know someone loves me enough to take care of me. I always felt better when Mom took care of me whenever I got sick. And I always feel better knowing that my wife loves me enough to take care of me when I get sick now.

Saint Bernardino of Siena did more than just take care of a few sick people. He and several other young men risked their lives to take care of hundreds of people stricken with the plague. In the Middle Ages the plague, or the Black Death, as it was called, was raging through Europe. When it came to Siena in 1400, these men helped nurse people who contracted the dreaded plague. As many as 20 people died each day in the hospital, and several of the young men died too. But Bernardino and his companions continued to nurse the sick.

Sometimes taking care of those who are sick can be a real drag. In the case of Bernardino of Siena and his companions, it was even a life-threatening risk. But can you imagine what it meant to those people who were dying to know that other people cared enough to risk their lives for them?

💬 **How do you like to be cared for when you are sick? What do you do for someone else when he or she is sick?**

💬 **When someone in your family is sick, think about how it makes you feel to have someone care for you when you are sick. Does it inspire you to want to help them even more?**

Face Your Fear

There is no fear in love. But perfect love drives out fear, because fear has to do with punishment. 1 John 4:18, NIV.

I t's the first day of school. You're going to wear the beige sweater. . . . No, the aqua sweater. . . . No, the white shirt. You've got roughly a thousand freshly sharpened pencils stuffed into your backpack and enough notebook paper to write *War and Peace* in longhand. You've checked and rechecked your outfit a hundred times and called everyone you know to see what they're wearing.

Now as you wait for the school bus to pick you up, they start in. Those butterflies. Fluttering around in your stomach like it's warm-up for the butterfly Olympics in there. There's the bus. Steady now. Count to 10. It's stopping, and you put one foot on the first step. You can do it. You can . . .

What happens next? Do you slink down the aisle and throw yourself into an unoccupied seat, glad you didn't have to talk to anyone? Do you look for a familiar face and sit with that person, starting up a conversation where you left off last year?

You can't get away from fear. But if you want to overcome it, you have to meet it head-on. You can't just hope that it will go away.

President Theodore Roosevelt once said, "I have often been afraid, but I wouldn't give in to it. I made myself act as though I was not afraid, and gradually my fear disappeared."

Fear of doing something new is normal. But if you act with confidence and faith, your fears will vanish. When they do, you will experience a sense of satisfaction from trying something new and succeeding. Feeling nervous on the first day of school is normal, and if you accept your feelings as normal, you can deal with them.

> **What is your first reaction when you are afraid? What positive things can you do to face your fears?**

> **The next time you are confronted by a new situation, ask yourself why you are afraid. Then say a prayer for God to help you, and try to act as if you are not afraid.**

Brandon's Fingertips

Hear this, you kings! Listen, you rulers! I will sing to the Lord, I will sing; I will make music to the Lord, the God of Israel. Judges 5:3, NIV.

Mark slumped at the organ and listened to the sounds of his friends playing tag outside. He wished he could be out there instead of inside practicing his organ lesson.

"I don't hear any music, Mark," his mother called.

Mark heaved a sigh and began to play the scales. Then, just for fun, he did them with a little pizzazz, making his fingers jump up and down on the keys. While he was playing, Brandon, a little hearing-impaired boy his mother took care of during the day, crawled over and put his hand on the speaker. As Mark's fingers jumped up and down the scale, Brandon, who never made any noise at all, squealed with delight.

Mark poked one finger on the key. Brandon squealed again. Brandon was "hearing" the vibration of the sound through his fingertips on the speaker.

He flipped to a fast song by Beethoven. Brandon smiled and cooed while Mark played. Mark played song after song. He didn't realize until he stopped that he was having fun.

"Well, you certainly got inspired," his mother commented as she came into the room and picked Brandon up.

"Mom, he was 'listening' to the music with his fingers," Mark explained, showing his mother what he meant.

"Isn't that amazing?" his mother said. "You see, Mark? Now aren't you glad you shared your gift of music with others?"

Mom took Brandon into the bedroom to change his diaper, and Mark flipped to the next song. He realized that playing tag outside right this moment wasn't as important as he had thought it was. He could play later. Right now he was making music.

> 😊 **What is more important, the music or the heart of the person who makes it? Why is music important to God? Why is it important to us? What kind of music do you like best? Why? How does it bring you closer to God?**

> 😊 **Make up your own song. Offer to play it for special music for church.**

Not Quite Wise Enough

If you are wise, your wisdom will reward you. Proverbs 9:12, NIV.

Ever heard someone use the expression "Better safe than sorry"? It means there is much more joy in being cautious than in having to suffer the consequences of not being careful in the first place.

One summer my brother, Philip, and I were making repairs in the girls' dorm at the academy where we went to school. One of our projects was to replace the broken floor tiles in several of the rooms. To remove the broken tiles we used a torch to heat up the tar holding the tiles enough so that we could pull the tiles up.

After an old tile had been heated for several minutes, whoever was handling the chisels and screwdrivers wedged it out of its place. Once the old tiles were removed, we spread contact cement (very flammable contact cement) on the subfloor in preparation for the new tiles.

In order to speed up the process, I convinced Philip that one of us could be spreading the contact cement while the other finished removing the old tiles. When Philip agreed that it was a good idea, we were in deep trouble.

As I remember, our scheme worked very well until Philip and his contact cement caught up with me and my torch. That's when the fire started. After a few moments of sheer panic over our own small chemical fire, Philip and I graduated to firefighting. We raced for the fire extinguisher and were able to put the fire out.

My brother and I were very lucky. The only damage we had done was to one wall that had to be repainted, although I still have visions of the dorm being completely gutted by fire.

It's far better to think things through before you do them than to suffer the consequences of a thoughtless action afterward. Choose your friends wisely. Make your decisions carefully. Think about the possible consequences first. And always include God in prayer.

😊 **Do you always make wise decisions? What were some of the consequences of some of your poor decisions?**

😊 **The wisest and easiest first step to take in making a decision is to talk to God first. Try it.**

258

Why Bad Things Happen

When the woman saw that the fruit of the tree was good for food and pleasing to the eye, and also desirable for gaining wisdom, she took some and ate it. She also gave some to her husband, who was with her, and he ate it. Genesis 3:6, NIV.

God made this happen to teach me a lesson."

"God's trying to show me something; that's why these bad things keep happening."

"God is mad at me. I've got to do something good to make Him happy so He will let me alone."

Have you ever heard anyone say things like this? Have you ever (gulp!) said things like this yourself? It can be easy to blame God when bad things happen to us. After all, He's God, and nothing happens without God's knowing about it. If God knows how many hairs are on your head, He certainly knows what's happening to you. But does God cause bad things to happen to us?

Stop. Wait. Slow down. Back up. Remember this scene?

It was a beautiful garden. Not a sin in sight. Everything was perfect. Then a wily snake slunk up to a wandering woman and convinced her that she couldn't live without eating the fruit of the only tree she was supposed to avoid. She chowed down and gave some of it to her husband, and he chowed down too.

And that's how sin happened.

Lots of bad things were the result of that sin. The woman and her husband got kicked out of the garden. The ground was cursed. They couldn't live forever. Things around them died.

But these bad things didn't happen because God wanted them to happen. They happened because the man and woman in the garden sinned. Because of sin lots of bad things happen.

What God does is help us through the bad things that happen as a result of sin. He's such a wonderful Creator that He can even make good things come from bad things, if we let Him help us.

Why do you think bad things happen? Have you ever felt that God made something bad happen to you to teach you a lesson? Why did you feel that way? Is it the truth?

Write a story about what you think heaven will be like.

Mr. Smythe Takes a Trip

Again, it will be like a man going on a journey, who called his servants and entrusted his property to them. Matthew 25:14, NIV.

By all accounts Mr. Smythe was a very shrewd businessperson, although very fair. When he decided to take a trip to Florida, he didn't want his property to languish idly while he was away.

He decided he would distribute his holdings among his employees, giving to each what they were best suited to have. He turned his investment portfolio over to his stockbroker. To the chef he entrusted the use of the kitchen, with all its provisions. And he lent his limo to the chauffeur. Satisfied that he had placed his valuable possessions in the hands of those best qualified to use them to their utmost advantage, Mr. Smythe departed.

When he returned, he was eager to see what exciting things had been done in his absence. He immediately called a staff meeting. The stockbroker brought charts, graphs, and a stack of *Wall Street Journals*. Carefully she demonstrated that she had doubled the investment portfolio she had been left with, in addition to paying a faithful tithe and supporting the work of various ministries in which Mr. Smythe had an interest.

"That's wonderful!" exclaimed Mr. Smythe. "Well done! I'd like you to manage the accounts of several of my new enterprises."

The chef hastily added that during his employer's absence, he had begun a humble line of baked goods that had expanded into a rather substantial bakery order from surrounding restaurants. Nothing had been wasted, he assured Mr. Smythe, as even the day-old bread was donated to the local soup kitchen. He modestly handed over his record books that indicated he also had doubled the monetary value left to him, as well as providing for the needs of those in the community who were less fortunate.

"How exciting!" cried Mr. Smythe. "Well done! I'm so pleased. If your business continues to expand, I will see about getting you your very own bakery and staff."

🙂 **What are your talents? What are you doing with them?**

🙂 **If you aren't sure what your talents are, ask someone who can help you, such as your parents or your pastor.**

The Fate of the Chauffeur

For everyone who has will be given more, and he will have an abundance. Whoever does not have, even what he has will be taken from him. Matthew 25:29, NIV.

The chauffeur shuffled his feet nervously, avoiding the eyes of his employer. He cleared his throat a few times before he spoke. "I knew you were a very shrewd businessperson and kept track of every penny, so I was afraid to drive your limousine. After all, what would happen if something broke? I can't afford to fix it. And I don't have money for gasoline or oil changes and routine maintenance, either. So I decided that the best thing to do was to park the limo in the garage. You can go out and see it, if you like. There's not a scratch on it. And," he continued a little proudly, "the odometer reading is exactly the same as it was on the day you left."

Mr. Smythe was so dumbfounded that it was difficult for him to speak. "Do you mean to tell me that my limousine hasn't been driven since the day I left? The least you could have done was to hire it out for weddings and proms so that at least it would be driven enough to keep the engine in tune. I'll probably have to take it to the dealer to have it serviced just because it's been sitting around for so long. And all this time it's been depreciating. This is unbelievable. You're fired!"

Disgruntled, the chastised employee found work as a taxi driver in the city. The job didn't pay well, though, and he was forced to take up residence inside an abandoned Chrysler. Though he often thought of returning to his old employer, he was too proud to consider it seriously.

One brutal November day, when he wished he hadn't found his pride so hard to swallow, he got the news that Mr. Smythe was taking all his faithful employees on an all-expense-paid vacation to the Bahamas.

Why did Mr. Smythe fire the chauffeur? Do you think he should have? Why is it important for us to use the talents we have been given?

Plan some way to use at least one of your talents this week.

Do What You Do Best

To one he gave five talents of money, to another two talents, and to another one talent, each according to his ability. Matthew 25:15, NIV.

I can't do any of those things," Dillon whined.

"Surely you can do something," Sam argued.

Dillon reddened. "All right, I'll make the invitations."

Sam stared at him. "You sure you can do that? I mean, that's kind of a hard one. I didn't even know you could draw."

I can't, Dillon thought to himself. "No," he insisted aloud. "I'll make the invitations."

"OK," Sam agreed. "I'll need them by the end of the week."

"No problem," Dillon said.

But later, after Sam had gone home, he drew one invitation design after another. All of them contained stick figures that looked like, well, stick figures. There was no way they could send out invitations that looked like that.

Late Thursday night Dillon called Sam. "Um, Sam, I'm having a problem with those invitations."

"Oh, no! You mean you need some more time?" Sam wailed.

"No, not quite. You see, it's just that I can't draw the design. I've tried and tried, but I just can't draw."

There was a long pause, and Dillon was afraid that Sam had hung up on him. Or fainted. "Listen, Dillon, I wish you had just told me that straight out, but it's too late now. Can't you design them on the computer?"

Dillon almost dropped the phone. "Of course! I don't know why I didn't think of that! I sure can, and they'll look great."

Sam giggled. "OK, just so I have them tomorrow."

"No problem!" Dillon assured her. "I'll be working on a computer. That's what I do best."

🙂 **Do some people have more important gifts than other people? Why aren't all gifts exactly the same? How can you decrease the value of a gift? How can you increase it?**

🙂 **Make a list of all your gifts and how you can use them. Then just do it!**

Make It Important

Know also that wisdom is sweet to your soul; if you find it, there is a future hope for you, and your hope will not be cut off. Proverbs 24:14, NIV.

Hi, Zeb," Samantha said, as she sat down beside Zeb in the library.

"Hi, Sam," Zeb replied with a deep sigh.

Sam looked at Zeb's backpack with books spilling out onto the table. "Whatcha doin'?"

Zeb frowned. "I'm trying to study. But I can't seem to remember anything. There's got to be an easier way to remember stuff."

Sam's eyes lit up. "Maybe I can help. Last week Baxter scared me while I was trying to cram for a history test just before class. I forgot everything I had tried to memorize and bombed the test. After class I asked Baxter how *he* studies for tests. He had some great ideas."

"So do they work?" Zeb asked eagerly. "What are they?"

Sam set her backpack on the floor. "Well, I've had only a week to try them, but I think they work. First of all, if you have to read a chapter in history, the first time you read it, just skim over it and see what it's about. Are you with me so far?"

Zeb nodded.

"After you skim over the chapter, then go back and try to make up questions, using the headings of each section. Like, if a heading says 'The Inventions of Thomas Edison,' you can ask yourself, 'What were some of Thomas Edison's inventions?' Then when you read about Thomas Edison, you look for the answers to your question. It makes it easier to remember what you read."

"Wow!" Zeb said as he sat back in his chair. "It sounds real simple, too. I think I'll try it. Do you have any more ideas?"

Sam smiled. "Sure I do. But right now I have to go home and study. I'll tell you some more later."

🙂 **What are some of the ways you study for tests? In what ways do we bring glory to God as we do our schoolwork? Were you better prepared for tests this week?**

🙂 **Try using Sam's study technique the next time you have a reading assignment.**

The Prayer

Simon, Simon, Satan has asked to sift you as wheat. But I have prayed for you, Simon, that your faith may not fail. And when you have turned back, strengthen your brothers. Luke 22:31, 32, NIV.

This is one of my all-time favorite Bible verses.

Have you ever done something you felt was so wrong you couldn't mention it to anyone? And even if you could tell someone, it was still so bad they probably wouldn't forgive you for it? Have you ever felt that Jesus couldn't forgive you, either? Everyone has probably felt that way, or *will* feel that way, at some time in their life. Maybe that's why this verse is in the Bible. If anyone needed to know that he was forgiven, it was the man called Peter after the rooster crowed.

Let's face it. Peter had set himself up to take a big fall before Jesus was crucified. Peter loved Jesus so much that it was impossible for him even to consider he might deny his Lord. *What an absurd idea!* he thought. And he told Jesus exactly how he felt. "Lord, I am ready to go with you to prison and to death" (Luke 22:33).

There's no doubt Peter loved Jesus. He wanted to be a faithful follower. But Peter was so self-confident that he thought he could avoid any temptation to deny Jesus by his own power. But then that fateful moment came when he realized he *had* let Jesus down. That is why Jesus told Peter ahead of time, "But I have prayed for you, Simon, that your faith may not fail. And when you have turned back, strengthen your brothers" (Luke 22:32). He wanted Peter to remember that he was forgiven ahead of time.

It doesn't matter what the sin is; Jesus has already prayed for you and me, just as He did for Peter. All we have to know is that Jesus wants us to turn back to Him. Is there anything more awesome than Jesus praying for you and me?

🙂 **Have you ever denied that you were a Christian because you thought your friends didn't think it was cool? How did you feel afterward?**

🙂 **If you have ever rejected Jesus because of peer pressure, you probably felt terrible about it afterward. Take a few minutes to talk with Jesus and accept His forgiveness.**

Forgiveness, Jesus Style

But go, tell his disciples and Peter, "He is going ahead of you into Galilee. There you will see him, just as he told you." Mark 16:7, NIV.

Sometimes it's hard to forgive—almost impossible, it seems. But Jesus forgave Peter, so quickly, in fact, that Peter was forgiven even before he denied Jesus. Now, *that's* forgiveness. But Jesus even went a step farther to let Peter know that He still loved him. The incident reminds me of a story of a father's forgiveness toward his daughter.

Janie raced to the hospital to see her father, fearing he might pass away before she arrived. Almost a year before, she had stormed out of his life after a bitter argument. Her final words to him had been "I hate you!" Unfortunately, her father went into cardiac arrest. Despite the most valiant efforts of the hospital staff to revive him, he died before Janie arrived.

Janie was devastated. She had missed her only opportunity to tell her father that she loved him. She still wanted to see him, however, so the nurse led her to the room where he lay. As Janie stood in silence beside her father's body, the nurse discovered a note written on a piece of paper.

My dearest Janie, I forgive you. I pray you will also forgive me. I know that you love me. I love you too. Daddy.

At the empty tomb the angel had the same kind of message for Peter, when he told the women, "But go, tell his disciples and Peter, 'He is going ahead of you into Galilee.'" Jesus especially wanted Peter to know He was not upset and that all was forgiven.

Now, that's awesome love! But do you know something even more wonderful? Jesus does the same for us. When we ask for forgiveness, He casts the sin away. It is no more. And then He wants you and me to know that He will not disown us. He loves us way too much.

☺ **Why is Jesus so willing to forgive? How does it make you feel to know Jesus loves you so much?**

☺ **Do you know someone who needs to know that Jesus loves him or her, no matter what? If so, please tell that person.**

Forgiveness, Part 1

The good man brings good things out of the good stored up in his heart, and the evil man brings evil things out of the evil stored up in his heart. Luke 6:45, NIV.

Harry had a nice home and a lovely wife and daughter. But Harry always wanted more . . . or just something different. He also had a habit of getting involved with the wrong people, too, and that's just where Harry went wrong the most. He let people talk him into doing things he knew weren't right.

Harry squandered the money he and his wife had saved. When things got tense at home because he was out spending money instead of spending time with his wife and daughter, Harry decided he wanted a different life. One day he left for good.

Harry became involved in labor disputes between the labor union and mine owners. The more involved he became, the more the Federation leaders trusted him. When they found out Harry was willing to kill people for their cause, they began to hire him to assassinate those who opposed them.

Harry planted several bombs that killed or disabled many people. He had become so coldhearted that he felt no remorse for the murders he committed.

On Sabbath afternoon, December 30, 1905, Harry planted a bomb at the front gate of the home of Frank Steunenberg, the former governor of Idaho, who had once opposed the Western Federation of Miners. Harry's bomb killed Steunenberg, but Harry was quickly captured, found guilty, and sentenced to die.

Harry Orchard often realized he was becoming involved in activities that were leading down a path toward destruction, yet he never made a stand against what he knew was wrong. Harry admitted he wasn't happy with the evil life he had led. Was there any hope for Harry, a man condemned to death? Well, through Jesus, amazing things are possible.

😊 **Can Jesus forgive a man like Harry Orchard?**

😊 **If someone has hurt you, can you forgive him or her? Read tomorrow's conclusion.**

Forgiveness, Part 2

And now, through Christ, all the kindness of God has been poured out upon us undeserving sinners. Romans 1:5, TLB.

Harry Orchard had caused so many people so much pain and suffering. How could anything good come out of his wrecked life?

With God all things are possible.

Mrs. Steunenberg, the wife of the murdered former governor, was a Seventh-day Adventist. Every morning she held family worship, though her husband, Frank, rarely attended. Frank had not yet given his heart to Jesus. But on Sabbath morning, December 30, he was restless as his wife again asked him to give his heart to Jesus. Later that day Frank told friends and associates he was claiming Saturday as his day of rest. Though he was killed later that day, he had already surrendered his life to God.

One day, after Harry Orchard's trial, Julian Steunenberg, Frank's son, arrived at the prison with a package and asked to see Harry. Although the warden felt Julian wanted to kill the man who had taken his father's life, Harry decided to meet with Julian anyway. Julian put out his hand to Harry. Shamefully Harry wondered how he could shake hands with the son of the man he had killed. But there were no harsh words, only words of kindness. Then Julian gave Harry the religious literature his mother had sent in the package. Harry was so deeply moved by Mrs. Steunenberg's attitude of forgiveness that he believed her to be a "true Christian."

Mrs. Steunenberg visited Harry four times. Never once did she pass judgment on him. She was concerned only that Harry give his heart to Jesus. And Harry Orchard did, fully and completely.

Harry's death sentence was commuted to life in prison, where he spent the rest of his life, giving Bible studies and helping to lead many other men to Christ.

Why was it possible for Mrs. Steunenberg to forgive the man who had killed her husband?

If there is someone you think you should forgive, ask Jesus to help you.

Love Shines Through

Bless those who curse you, pray for those who mistreat you. If someone strikes you on one cheek, turn to him the other also. Luke 6:28, 29, NIV.

I just read a story recently about an army that was forced to hike through the most horrible weather. It was dark, wet, and cold. When the troops finally reached their resting place, they immediately fell into bed exhausted. Except for one soldier, who collapsed to his knees to pray before he went to bed.

His sergeant took one look at him and totally lost his temper. Taking one of his heavy, soggy boots, he hurled it at the soldier's head, hitting him on the side of his face. Still the soldier continued to pray. Fuming, the sergeant picked up his other boot and hurled it at the other side of the soldier's head, hitting him on the other side of his face.

With his face stinging and aching, the soldier finished his prayers and climbed into bed. The sergeant went to bed and fell asleep. And that's when the soldier paid him back. When the sergeant woke up the next morning, the first thing he saw was his boots, sitting at the foot of his bed, cleaned and polished.

It is very hard to respond in love to people who treat us badly. If we try to do it by ourselves, we will fail. Humanly it's impossible. It's only when we let Jesus love people through us that we are strong enough to pay people back with kindness when they mistreat us.

Have you ever heard the story of the boy who kicked the cat? It all started with the boss who yelled at his secretary, who snapped at the receptionist, who went home and chewed out her son, who turned around and kicked the cat. Bad things are easy to pass along. Stop the cycle at the beginning and pet the cat instead. You'll be glad you did.

- Has anyone ever done something really mean to you? How did you react? Do you wish you had reacted differently?

- After reading this story, rewrite the ending of your own story to reflect a more loving way you could have reacted to the situation.

One Good Turn Deserves a Kick in the Pants

Be merciful, just as your Father is merciful. Luke 6:36, NIV.

Mrs. Preston seems so lonely," my mother observed.

"Picklepuss?" I asked, accidentally using the nickname we kids had for her.

Mom gave me one of her "now-is-that-nice?" looks. "I think it would be a very nice gesture if you brought her some of the snapdragons from the garden."

I heaved myself up and went out to pick them.

Later, as I stood on Picklepuss's doorstep, I wished I could be anywhere else.

She jerked the door open. "I ain't buying any," she snapped, and slammed the door in my face.

Mom sent me back with freshly baked banana bread.

Picklepuss answered right away, as if she'd been waiting for me. "I told you, I'm not buying any of your junk." *Slam!*

Mom turned me around and sent me back over with an invitation to dinner. This time I didn't even have to knock.

"You *are* a persistent one," Picklepuss said with a hint of admiration in her voice.

"I'm here to invite you to dinner," I forced myself to say.

"Why?" she demanded.

"Because, uh, because my mom made me," I confessed.

She chuckled. "All right, I'll come," she said abruptly.

She came. She even dressed up.

"Mrs. Preston, I'm so glad you could come," Mom beamed.

"I could hardly refuse," she replied. "Your daughter was so persistent and well-mannered." She winked at me.

I blushed, thinking of all the horrible things I had wanted to do to her because she had been so mean. I thought about it all summer, whenever I sat in Mrs. Preston's kitchen eating fresh-baked cookies. What would have happened if I had lost my temper and been mean to Mrs. Preston?

- **How do you feel when you do something nice for someone and they act mean to you?**

- **Choose someone in your neighborhood and do something nice for them.**

Stand Firm

And Moses said to the people, "Do not be afraid. Stand still, and see the salvation of the Lord." Exodus 14:13, NKJV.

There are many things to be afraid of. If you don't come across one thing today that you are afraid of, then you probably didn't get out of bed at all. As crazy as it sounds, fear itself isn't something to be afraid of. I know that sounds silly, but really, think about it. Maybe there are some good reasons for fear.

Fear makes us stop and think about what we are about to do. It makes us pause a moment and make sure we are not about to do something crazy that might hurt us. Fear is sort of like our sense of touch around a hot stove. If we couldn't feel the heat, we would end up getting some nasty burns. But once we learn the stove is hot, we can learn to fix some fabulous meals on it.

Fear shouldn't paralyze us. It shouldn't keep us from living happy, fulfilling lives. People who claim they are not afraid of anything have not discovered that fear is a useful tool.

Has fear gotten the best of you lately? Don't worry. Take the time to understand why you are afraid. Once we understand what is causing our fear, we are better able to make a stand against it, instead of running away from it.

Take time to listen to God. The best way to overcome our fears is to listen for God's guidance. Hand your fears over to Him. Isn't it wonderful to have God in our corner when we are afraid?

Move. Once our fear is acknowledged, we should move. No, not run away from fear! But defeat it!

No one is immune to fear. But we do have a God who defeats all fear. He will help us confront our fears. One day we will stand firm and unafraid as we look upon Jesus in the clouds when He comes to take us home. Aren't you eager for that day? I am!

☺ **What fears did you have last week? How did you overcome them? Did you ask for God's help?**

☺ **Starting school again always brings new fears. Hand your fears over to God. Begin your morning by asking for strength to face your fears.**

Time Out

Who then is the faithful and wise manager, whom the master puts in charge of his servants to give them their food allowance at the proper time? It will be good for that servant whom the master finds doing so when he returns. Luke 12:42, 43, NIV.

Zebulun, have you studied your lesson today?" his mother asked as she passed by the living room doorway.

Zeb shifted positions on the couch. "No time."

Mom's footsteps halted, and she retraced her steps.

"What?" Zeb asked.

"You haven't had time?" his mother repeated. "You had soccer practice after school. When you got home, you played video games with Bryan, and now you're watching television."

"Yup," Zeb agreed. "See? It's like I said, I didn't have time."

Mom sat down next to Zeb on the couch and picked up the remote control. She switched off the TV and put one hand on Zeb's knee. "You know, Zeb, everyone is given 24 hours every day to do the things they need to do. We can't waste our time and expect God to bless it."

"But, Mom, I didn't waste my time! I was doing stuff."

"Then maybe you should take a look at the 'stuff' you're doing. Is it all necessary?"

Zeb thought for a minute, then shook his head. "No, I guess not. I didn't really need to play video games or watch TV."

"Sometimes if we aren't careful our time can get away from us, and we end up squandering it on things that aren't important. But God holds us accountable for our time, and we need to use it wisely."

Zeb nodded. "You're right. And right now I need to use my time to study my lesson."

😊 **Why is it important how we spend our time? How much of our time should be spent with God?**

😊 **On a piece of paper write the numbers 1 through 24. Now list what you do for each of the 24 hours in a day. What do you think? Do you need to adjust how much time you spend for some things?**

Camp No Fear, Part 1

Even though I walk through the valley of the shadow of death,
I will fear no evil, for you are with me; your rod and your
staff, they comfort me. Psalm 23:4, NIV.

It was my first solo camping trip. My only hiking partner was a slobbery black Lab named Indiana Jones. We stayed at a place called Twin Brooks Tenting Area, but to me it was—and always will be—Camp No Fear, because it was there I conquered my fear of being alone.

We were two miles away from any other campers in either direction. It did occur to me, trying to sleep that first night, that a tent was flimsy protection from whatever walked the woods at night. But we woke up the next morning unharmed. My first thought was that this wasn't so hard, after all.

The next night was different.

It was a long time before I fell into a very light sleep, during which I kept hearing things outside the tent. The rustling of the leaves drove me crazy, waking me up every time it sounded regular, like the footsteps of an animal. My imagination was working so hard I could almost hear it whir.

The breaking branches, as they gave under the weight of a very large animal, was not in my imagination. It was outside the tent, in the direction of the trail.

Bear!

I bolted upright in the tent, heart beating wildly, ear pressed to the screen window of the tent, trying to figure out if it was coming in my direction or going away from me. The more I listened to it, the more I was convinced it had to be a bear. (Although for a little while I did try to convince myself that it might just be a large, friendly deer.) The cracking of branches grew fainter, and I decided that whatever it was, it was moving off.

🙂 **Have you ever seen a bear? What would you do if you saw one while you were hiking?**

🙂 **Find out where you can take a course about hiking safety in your town.**

Camp No Fear, Part 2

You prepare a table before me in the presence of my enemies. Psalm 23:5, NIV.

Somehow I managed to fall into a light sleep—until I heard it again. Louder this time, and coming from the direction of the tree I had hung our packs from. Branches were snapping like twigs under *its* weight, and I could picture *it* reaching out long claws to snag the packs. And then I couldn't hear *it* anymore.

As soon as it was light enough, we broke camp hurriedly and headed back down the trail to the parking lot three miles away. Reaching the parking lot, I had one thought in my mind: to get in the car. I threw all the gear in the trunk, jumped in, and slammed the door behind me.

Safe!

As I sat there, I thought back over the experience. After the first night I had thought my fear was conquered. I had done what I had set out to do—spend a night alone in the woods. But by being afraid of the bear, I wondered if the entire experience was worthless. And then it hit me.

I didn't set out to conquer a fear of bears! And maybe a little fear was a good thing. As long as fear didn't control my life, it had a beneficial quality, like pain, by making me aware of danger. The next time I entered the woods with only the thin filmy material of a tent between me and possible harm, I would be better prepared to defend myself.

I had set out to conquer fear, but instead I had gained a new respect for it. There would always be things to be afraid of, but in facing them I would learn to confront the fear and make friends with it. In that way it could not control me.

With those thoughts in mind, I drove home, Indy's muzzle resting contentedly on my hand, and the flattened face of Mount Mansfield receding in my rearview mirror.

- **When is fear a good thing? When is it a bad thing? What are you most afraid of? Why? How can you work on this fear?**

- **Discuss your fear with your parents and get their ideas on how it can help you, and what you can do to overcome or control it.**

273

Never Give Up

But Christ, God's faithful Son, is in complete charge of God's house. And we Christians are God's house—he lives in us!—if we keep up our courage firm to the end, and our joy and our trust in the Lord. Hebrews 3:6, TLB.

Depression, loneliness, and failure. If you've ever felt like quitting, you were probably feeling one, two, or even all three of these emotions. It didn't help if you got up this morning and poured sour milk into your cereal bowl. Or your younger brother or sister misplaced your library book. Or you have not one test today, but two or three. And to top it all off, you just know you are going to blow all of them because you didn't study hard enough.

What if your parents are fighting, the house is a disaster, and your best friend is moving away or is spending more time with other friends? Feel like giving up yet?

During the fourteenth century, Tamerlane ruled a vast empire. He was a fierce warrior who led his warriors to conquer territory from Russia to Arabia, and from Turkey to India. But on one occasion, instead of chasing his enemies, he was running from them. Discouraged, he took refuge in an old house and hid for several days.

While Tamerlane was hiding out, he noticed an ant carrying a large object trying to climb a wall. Each time the ant tried to climb the wall, it fell back down. Tamerlane watched the persistent little ant make 69 attempts, followed by 69 failures. Finally, on the seventieth attempt, the ant climbed the wall. Tamerlane was inspired by the ant's persistence, and his own discouragement disappeared. He left his hideout and went on to conquer Asia.

- Have you ever been so discouraged you felt like giving up? When was the time you felt discouraged?

- If you are discouraged, take a moment right now to relax and pray to Jesus for strength. When you let Jesus share your problems, things won't seem nearly so bad.

Say I Love You

My command is this: Love each other as I have loved you. John 15:12, NIV.

When was the last time you told your parents that you love them? Here are some unique suggestions:

- **Be your own baby-sitter:** Give your parents the night off. Offer to take care of younger brothers and sisters for the evening. Tell your parents to spend some time together.
- **Make a valentine:** Even though it's not Valentine's Day, make a huge valentine for your parents and put it on the breakfast table.
- **Servant for a day:** Offer to do any and all chores uncomplainingly for a whole day.
- **Buy or pick some flowers:** Put flowers in a vase on the dinner table with a note, telling your parents that you love them.
- **Write a love note:** Put it in their lunch bags.
- **Memo:** Write "I love you" on a page in their daily calendars.
- **Habit forming:** What do your parents nag you to do? Pick up your room? Don't fight with your siblings? Whatever it is, tell them that for one day, you will (or won't) do it.
- **Personal verse:** Choose a verse from the Bible that you want to give your parents. Leave them a note in their Bible about why you chose that verse for them.
- **Maid for love:** Make your parents' bed and leave a chocolate on each of their pillows.
- **On tape:** Record a message on tape, telling your parents how special they are to you, and why. Pop the cassette into their car stereo, where they will hear it on the way to work.
- **Shaded by love:** Make a car windshield shade declaring how much you love your parents. Put it in the car when they aren't looking.

Why is it important to tell the people we love that we love them? Don't they know it without being told? How do you feel when someone tells you that they love you?

Do one of the above suggestions every day until you've done them all. Then think about how you feel.

275

Sometimes You Just Gotta Prove It

In everything set them an example by doing what is good. In your teaching show integrity, seriousness and soundness of speech that cannot be condemned, so that those who oppose you may be ashamed because they have nothing bad to say about us. Titus 2:7, 8, NIV.

Sometimes people just won't take you seriously unless you prove your point. Or, in the case of Roberta "Bobbi" Gibb, run the race.

Hidden in the bushes in Rockport, Massachusetts, 26-year-old Roberta Gibb anxiously awaited the crack of the pistol that would start the Boston Marathon. She was wearing her brother's Bermuda shorts and a sweatshirt with a hood she had pulled up over her blond ponytail. When she heard the gun, she quietly emerged from the bushes and fell into step among the 500 men who were running the race.

Though she had to do it secretly, Roberta was the first woman ever to run the famous race. She was denied an application because organizers thought women were not built to run the distance. Not until six years after her run were women "officially" recognized runners of the Boston Marathon. Only then were they given numbers and the chance to receive medals.

Roberta could have told everyone she knew that she *could* run the Boston Marathon. But would anyone have been convinced? Not unless she actually did it. Then they would *have* to believe her.

Christians often have the same trouble convincing people that Jesus' way is better. Sure, it's easy to tell friends and neighbors that we are Christians. But will they really believe us unless we act as though Christ is inside us? People need to see to believe, just as they needed to see Roberta cross the finish line of the Boston Marathon to believe that she, a woman, could run it.

- **What is it about being a Christian that makes you the happiest? Do you show others how happy you are?**

- **Ask five Christian friends what they like best about being a Christian. Do they all have the same answer?**

Shy?

The Lord said to him, "Who gave man his mouth? Who makes him deaf or mute? Who gives him sight or makes him blind? Is it not I, the Lord? Now go; I will help you speak and will teach you what to say." Exodus 4:11, 12, NIV.

've always been a shy person. Maybe you're shy too. I don't know if you've noticed, but being shy is sometimes inconvenient. For instance, I couldn't just walk up to a group of unfamiliar kids and strike up a conversation. No way! Oh, and girls? Imagine how afraid I was to talk to girls! It's a wonder anyone even knew I existed! Do you know how I felt? Maybe you are a shy person yourself.

Being shy means to be timid or afraid. So when you're shy, you unfortunately also have a lot of fears to confront and overcome. The great news is that the more fears you overcome, the stronger you become. No joke! Overcoming one fear leads to conquering another fear. Then another. And another.

For example, I just knew before I started speech class in high school that I was going to fail, because I was too shy to get up in front and make a speech. It looked as though I was going to get an F—F for fear!

Then I decided that the only way I could go was up. I decided that if I took the time to prepare a good speech, I would feel more comfortable in front of class. And sure enough, that's what happened! Because I prepared to confront my fear, I discovered I wasn't as shy about talking in front of people as I thought I would be. Every time I gave a speech, it got easier. I not only received an A in speech class; I also got to play one of the best parts in our school play! Quite a leap for a shy kid, huh?

Do you have some fears this school year? What can you do to overcome them? Have you prayed for God's help in overcoming your fears?

Besides asking for God to help you overcome your fears, take time to prepare yourself to overcome them. If a particular class in school is worrying you, spend more time preparing for that class. Preparation builds confidence.

277

Bumper Cars

We are happy to tell other churches about your patience and complete faith in God, in spite of all the crushing troubles and hardships you are going through. 2 Thessalonians 1:4, TLB.

When Bill got up on Wednesday morning, he had no idea how his day was going to turn out. If he had, he might have decided to stay in bed. His first major roadblock to a good day was discovering two new pimples on his face.

To make the morning worse, Bill's shower was cut short when the hot water ran out. Since he had gotten up 20 minutes later than usual, the water heater had not yet recovered from the showers his brother and sister had taken.

When the teacher handed back the history tests, Bill saw a miserable D written in the top right-hand corner.

Bill played baseball, hoping to get his mind off the depressed, sluggish feeling he had in the pit of his stomach. But baseball didn't help much either, because he struck out twice and dropped an easy fly ball. He felt worse than ever.

It's hard enough to get over just one disappointment at a time. But when they come one right after another, what can we do? How can we be positive and happy when it seems as if we can't do anything right?

Many times when difficult problems and depressing situations arise, they act a lot like bumper cars at an amusement park. You're stuck in the middle, and everyone keeps ramming you. Sometimes it seems as if you will never get free. When problems keep piling up like bumper cars, it's easy to become discouraged. When that happens, stop for a minute and listen for God.

- **Have you ever been stuck in the middle while driving a bumper car for most of the time limit? How did you feel? Is life sometimes like that?**

- **When it seems as though way too many problems are getting you down, stop and take time out. Ask God to help you get control.**

Celeste's First Law of Pyrotechnics

Enable your servants to speak your word with great boldness. Stretch out your hand to heal and perform miraculous signs and wonders through the name of your holy servant Jesus. Acts 4:29, 30, NIV.

Have you ever heard of Murphy's Law? It goes something like this: Whatever can go wrong will go wrong, and at the worst possible moment.

There are lots of laws like that one. Here are a few more:

Gillette's Law of Telephone Dynamics: The phone call you have been waiting for will come the minute you're out the door.

Anthony's Law of Force: Don't force it; get a larger hammer.

First Law of Bicycling: No matter which way you ride, it's up-hill and against the wind.

Shedenhelm's Law of Backpacking: All trails have more uphill sections than they have level or downhill sections.

Have you noticed that all of the laws are negative? I decided to write my own law, one that is positive. Ready?

Light something on fire, and it will be too hot to hold.

Do you know what really scares Satan? A Christian who is on fire for God. Someone who is really happy about being a Christian and is not afraid to show it. Someone who reflects his or her close personal relationship with Jesus by everything he or she does. Someone who enjoys serving others.

See, when we are on fire for God, Satan can't touch us. We're too hot to handle. You wouldn't reach into a roaring fire and try to take out one of the burning logs, would you? Of course not. If you wanted a log, you'd take one that hadn't been in the fire yet. Well, Satan is no dummy. He's not going to stick his hand in the fire either. He'd rather go after all those Christians who aren't doing anything but sitting around, stacked up like cordwood.

So get out of the woodpile and into the fire!

What happens when we think about a negative outcome all the time? Why is it important to think positively? What do you consider to be "on fire" for God?

Write your own law, like the ones above, but make it positive.

The Doll Maker, Part 1

Have we not all one Father? Did not one God create us? Malachi 2:10, NIV.

nce upon a time long, long ago and far, far away, there lived a kind and gentle old man. He was a doll maker by trade and had a small studio in the front of his home in which he displayed his creations. He made the most beautiful dolls in the world. People came from all over the world just to buy his dolls.

Each of his dolls was special. With his own hands he cut the bleached muslin cloth and stitched their bodies. He fashioned their hair from the finest yellow cotton, just like spun sunshine, his customers said. He painted each of the faces on the dolls, and they were identical. Each face had big, blue eyes, like the ocean, and scarlet lips, like the nodding poppies in the flower box by his window. But one day the doll maker grew tired of making all the dolls the same.

"I want to make some of my dolls different from the rest," he told his friends.

"You shouldn't do it," they warned. "Everyone likes your dolls because they are all the same. They will not like them if they are different."

Just the same, the doll maker decided to make some of his dolls different. Late at night, after he finished making his blond, blue-eyed dolls, he sat up making other dolls. He worked by the light of a single candle and always hid his work before opening his shop the next morning.

☺ **Why do you think God made us each different? What do you think the world would be like if we all looked exactly the same?**

☺ **Set a timer for one minute. Then list as many different nationalities as you can in that one minute. For a real challenge, gather some of your friends together and see who can come up with the most nationalities in the time allotted.**

280

The Doll Maker, Part 2

For we are God's workmanship, created in Christ Jesus to do good works, which God prepared in advance for us to do. Ephesians 2:10, NIV.

The doll maker tried many different things. For one doll he took the crisp white muslin and dyed it in black walnut shells until it turned a nutty brown. Another dye was made with nutshells and the roots of certain herbs. The cloth dyed in this mixture came out reddish brown. Others he dyed an earthy ocher, and still others had olive undertones, or yellow castings. He gave some of the dolls brown eyes, some green, some black, and some blue. He made the eyes all different—large, small, narrow, and wide. Each doll had a unique face.

When the doll maker finished, he had many dolls, and each one looked distinctly different. He sat back on his bench and surveyed his work. He knew that some people would be upset about the dolls just because they were different. But these dolls would demonstrate tolerance for all people. The next day when he opened his shop, he put the dolls right up in the window beside the others.

When the doll maker's customers came to the shop, they were very surprised indeed. Never had they seen such dolls. Some of them became very angry and left the shop saying they would never come back. But others could see that the differences of the dolls made them special. Before the end of the week every doll had been sold.

The doll maker smiled happily as he looked around his empty shop. He knew that these dolls, his creations, would become ambassadors to show the world that looking different isn't bad. Looking different is what makes us individuals.

🙂 **How do you feel about people who look different than you do? How much do you know about other nationalities? Does the color of a person's skin determine how you treat them?**

🙂 **Find a book in the library that tells about different nationalities. Learn about their cultures and what makes them unique.**

281

Slot Car Racing

The thief comes only to steal and kill and destroy; I have come that they may have life, and have it to the full. John 10:10, NIV.

Ever have one of those days that starts out *great* and keeps on going great until you crawled into bed? You couldn't miss all day long—not once.

It's sort of like racing slot cars and winning by several laps. You have your timing down to a science. You instinctively feel when to release the power trigger so your car will race around the corner just slow enough to avoid flying off the track. With each lap your car seems to go a little faster and a little faster until it's almost a blur.

Perfect days don't come along very often. It may seem the rotten days show up far more frequently—unless we come up with some plan to make the day positive from the beginning.

Just as beginning with a well-built, square foundation makes building a solid house easier, and studying makes taking a test less stressful, beginning the day with Jesus helps the day go much smoother.

Like the thief in today's text, who is waiting to kill and destroy, the devil is always waiting for a chance to ruin our day. He is most content when we feel hopeless and depressed. He is satisfied when we have terrible days and end up lashing out at family members and friends. He undoubtedly has a smug expression on his face when we blame Jesus for our problems. And I'm sure he updates his scoreboard whenever someone ends up forgetting about Jesus altogether.

Wise people know they have limitations. But they also know where to find help to make up for their limitations. Wise Christians know that their greatest source of strength and power comes from Jesus. How about you?

- **Have you noticed a difference in your day when you begin it with Jesus, compared to days when you don't begin by asking Jesus to be with you? What difference does Jesus make in your day?**

- **Each morning this week, earnestly ask Jesus to be with you in every aspect of your life.**

A Fishy Story

Do not forget to do good and to help one another, because these are the sacrifices that please God. Hebrews 13:16, TEV.

There is a story about a fish. He was the most beautiful fish in the whole ocean because of his beautiful, sparkling scales. All the other fish really admired those scales. And I mean *really*. But Rainbow Fish, as they called him, just drifted through the ocean being admired. He was pretty happy about that. A little lonely, maybe, but happy.

Then one day a little fish asked him if he would share just one little sparkling scale with him. Rainbow Fish was shocked. Him? Share a scale? Yeah, right! He told that little fish in no uncertain terms that he'd better just keep on swimming.

When all the other fish heard what he had done, they ignored him. That really bothered Rainbow Fish. After all, they were *his* scales. He could share them or not, right? He talked to the starfish about it, and the starfish suggested that he speak to the wise old octopus.

The wise old octopus told him that he should share his sparkling scales with the other fish. He wouldn't be the most beautiful fish in the ocean anymore, but he would be happy. Rainbow Fish couldn't believe his ears. Him? Share his scales? Right!

Later the little fish was back, asking for just one tiny, small, little scale. Reluctantly Rainbow Fish finally gave it to him. Pretty soon the other fish, who saw the little fish darting around with his new scale, all wanted a sparkling scale of their own! Rainbow Fish began handing out his scales left and right, until he had only one left. And do you know what? It made him feel happy.

Of course, this is only a story, but it makes an important point. Do you know what it is?

🙂 **Why is it important to share the things that we have? Why do you think some people have so much, while others have so little? What should people do about that?**

🙂 **Go through your closet and see if you have anything that you can donate to Community Services for those who don't have as much as you do.**

283

Knowledge and Strength

A wise man is strong, yes, a man of knowledge increases strength. Proverbs 24:5, NKJV.

"Look at this," Jovan said proudly. He picked up a barbell and did some curls. "Pretty strong, huh, Dave?"

Dave nodded. Jovan was strong. His arms were really beginning to get some muscle definition.

"If you came over and worked out with me more than once or twice a week, you could build your muscles up just like I have."

"I know, Jovan. But during the school year I really should concentrate on studying more too."

"Uh, yeah, sure," Jovan said with a snicker. "If you say so. I plan to be a bodybuilder or football player."

"Even bodybuilders and football players have to get an education. Some have their own businesses. And some are even lawyers."

"Are you sure?" Jovan asked suspiciously.

Dave nodded. "Yeah, I'm sure. And my dad gave me a great illustration to show me how important studying was. He told me it's good to want to be healthy and strong. But we are also a lot like different kinds of metals. Iron is metal, but by itself it's pretty weak. But if some manganese and phosphorus are added to it while it's molten, the result is known as steel. Steel is a very strong metal alloy. An alloy is made by mixing different metals together. Dad says that if you add knowledge to your strong, healthy body, you are really making yourself into a stronger alloy, just like steel."

Dave lifted the barbell and did a set of curls. When he was finished, he looked at Jovan. "You know, I think God wants us to have strong, healthy bodies and strong, healthy minds. Don't you?"

Why do you think knowledge makes people stronger? Is it as important to strengthen our minds as it is our bodies?

As you look forward to studying this year, think of ways you can apply the things you learn each day to your life to make you strong.

Asking Jesus for a Lift

I know that you can do all things; no plan of yours can be thwarted. Job 42:2, NIV.

Starting out each morning by spending time with Jesus doesn't guarantee a perfect day. Oh, it's not Jesus' fault. He wishes He could give each one of us a perfect day every day. He wishes for a Garden of Eden kind of day that He can spend with us.

But there is something that, at least in this world, is the next best thing. And that is making Jesus the friend we talk to in prayer. We can learn from Him by listening to His answers to our prayers and by studying the Bible. It's sort of like putting ourselves in a position where Jesus can help lift us up and over obstacles and times of depression.

Along the Panama Canal there is a series of locks to raise and lower ships as they pass from the Atlantic Ocean to the Pacific Ocean. As a ship passes through the canal from the Atlantic to the Pacific, it must be raised 85 feet to the level of Gatun Lake through a series of three locks.

When a ship enters a lock, water from Gatun Lake is released into the lock, lifting the ship to the next highest water level. These locks are so massive that the largest ships in the world can be easily lifted from one level to another.

The flotation power of water is an amazing thing, isn't it? Can you imagine the love of Jesus having the same effect in your life when you feel upset or depressed? Turn your problems over to Jesus and let Him help you with them. I think you will feel the same kind of lift coming from Jesus as ships do when they pass through the locks of the Panama Canal.

- **When was the last time you sincerely prayed for Jesus to comfort you and lift you up when you felt down in the dumps?**

- **When Jesus is working in someone's life, it might take only a kind word or a few moments of helpfulness from a Christian friend to lift that person up. Look for opportunities to help and encourage someone today.**

285

Second Chance

Forget the former things; do not dwell on the past. See, I am doing a new thing! Isaiah 43:18, 19, NIV.

All of us have made some monumental mistakes from time to time. Some mistakes affect other people. Spreading rumors, lying, cheating, and physically or emotionally hurting someone else are just a few of the kinds of mistakes that can have terrible consequences for everyone involved. But one, even two or more, mistakes do not mean failure forever. Happily, God gives us the chance to make better choices next time.

A young man named Steve was driving a wagon as a means of paying his way west on the Oregon Trail. There was a young, pretty girl on the wagon train. One day a band of Indians rode into camp, and one of the Indians indicated that he wanted to trade for the girl. No matter how persistently he asked to trade, however, the members of the wagon train flatly refused. Steve, on the other hand, thought it might be funny to make a joke, so he said, "All right, you can have her for six ponies."

The next day the brave returned with six ponies. Of course, the people sent the Indian away, but they were very angry with Steve, because he might have put the whole wagon train in danger. Consequently he was banished from the train.

For several days Steve hid during the day and traveled at night out of fear of being attacked by Indians. Finally he came across another wagon train. Unfortunately, everyone in this wagon train was sick with dysentery. Steve stayed and nursed them back to health, and they returned his kindness by taking him with them.

Though Steve had made a monumental mistake, he had the opportunity to help the people in the second wagon train. And he did. I imagine he felt pretty good about his second chance.

- **How do you think Steve felt after his joke backfired and caused so much trouble? If you were him, would you be grateful for a second chance?**

- **If you have hurt someone with a joke, make it a point to apologize to that person.**

Potter and Clay

Yet, O Lord, you are our Father. We are the clay, you are the potter; we are all the work of your hand. Isaiah 64:8, NIV.

Have you ever played with clay? When I was small, we bought a log cabin in the country. My three sisters and I explored all 10 acres that surrounded the cabin. One of the most interesting things we found was pockets of clay in the dirt. We made dishes and cups for our dolls and plates and bowls to keep in our secret hideaway. Because it was never "fired," the clay would break easily after it had dried.

Many years later my husband and I found a beach made entirely of clay. It was called Button Bay, because a long time ago natural forces caused the clay to harden into circular shapes that resembled buttons. One of our dogs, a Cairn terrier named Brodie, was with us. By the time we left he was entirely coated with clay!

My latest experience with clay was when my 2½-year-old son, Joshua, wanted me to make clay snakes. He likes the snakes to be *loooooong.* And they have to have tongues sticking out. When I first started to shape the clay, I thought it was hopeless. The clay was hard and barely moved in my hands as I pressed and squeezed it. Some pieces even crumbled off. Finally, after I had worked with the clay for a long time, it softened with the heat of my hands and I could make whatever I wanted with it.

In many ways we are like clay in God's hands. At first, no matter what He does with us, it doesn't seem as though we'll ever change. Then as the Holy Spirit works with us, we become softer and more willing to change.

God is an expert potter. He can make any shape you can imagine and probably some that you can't imagine. His work is precious and priceless. He wouldn't sell one of His creations for millions of dollars. Each one is unique.

- **How are we like clay in God's hands? How are we different from clay?**

- **Go to a craft store and buy some clay. Notice that it is hard and crumbly until it warms up. "Create" something.**

287

Dennis Brown's New Sight

I consider that our present sufferings are not worth comparing with the glory that will be revealed in us. Romans 8:18, NIV.

One day while he was training a demolition class in the army, the plastic explosives Dennis Brown was working with exploded. The blast destroyed his eyesight and his hands. It nearly ruined his hearing, and left him with a lot of facial damage. Dennis's wife didn't want to live with a disabled person, so she left him. There was no way he could do his job anymore, so his career was gone too.

Then the doctors told Dennis that he had been taken off the waiting list for a cornea transplant. That's when he felt he was as low as he could get.

"All I wanted to do was kill myself," he says, "but I couldn't cut my wrists—I didn't have any. There was no way I could hold a gun, and I couldn't get to drugs."

After 19 months in several hospitals, Dennis finally decided to ask God to help him. There was no one else.

The next morning the doctors told Dennis that the day before they had put him back on the list for a cornea transplant. The really amazing part was that that very same night they had gotten a match. It wasn't long after the cornea transplant that Dennis moved into his own apartment and started taking care of himself.

Because of sin, life on this earth will have lots of sadness mixed in with all the happy times. Maybe your parents are divorcing. Maybe a friend or loved one has cancer. Maybe, like Dennis Brown, you have a disability.

But listen to what happened to Dennis: He is married now and has children. He works as a technical support person for a company that writes computer software. The most important thing he discovered was to focus on God above everything else. And guess what? He *is* happy.

- Why do you think knowing and loving God makes people happy? Why is it important to you to know God?

- Whenever you are discouraged, take some time to memorize a favorite Bible promise.

Big Duhs

You shall not murder. Exodus 20:13, NIV.

H ave you ever seen a stupid warning? How about the one on your blow dryer? *Warning: Danger of death by electrical shock if dropped into open water.* And there's a picture of the blow dryer and the bathtub with a line through them. Like we're stupid! "Hey, Mom, I'm going to take a bath. Would you toss me the blow dryer?" *Duh!*

Or how about *Remove cover before using product.* Wouldn't it be hard to use the product *before* removing the cover? *Duh!*

Or how about this one on insect repellent: *Do not spray in eyes or mouth.* Excuse me?

Or: *Do not purchase if wrapping has been tampered with.* "Mom, let's get this one that looks like someone opened it." I think not!

I sometimes wondered why manufacturers think they have to warn us against such stupid behavior. And then I found out. People look for ways to sue them, so they have to make sure everything is explained. Otherwise someone could say, "But the label didn't *say* not to spray the insect repellent in my eyes!"

There are some things in the Bible I think are a little overstated. For instance: "You shall not murder." Or "You shall not steal." Or "You shall not lie." Isn't that a little obvious?

Yes, it is obvious. God never meant for us to wake up each morning and remind ourselves, "OK, now, today I can't kill anyone, and I can't lie, and I can't steal." He gave us the Ten Commandments and other principles to teach us more about Him.

What God is saying when He says "You shall not murder" is "Love life, respect life, because I created you, and I created all life, and I love you all very much." By looking past the command itself to what the command is really saying, we can learn a lot about God.

- **What do you think when someone warns you against something that's obvious? What happens when we are warned too much about something? Why do you think manufacturers warn us against so many silly things?**

- **Write out each of the Ten Commandments and study each to see what they tell us about God. *Warning: Remove the cap from your pen before you attempt to write!***

Assign Me Godliness and Integrity

Assign me Godliness and Integrity as my bodyguards, for I expect you to protect me. Psalm 25:21, TLB.

"Sure, I'll stay with you, Grandma," Andrew said.

Grandma smiled. "Thank you, Andrew. I'm glad. With my back giving me so much trouble, I won't be able to move around very much. If you could help with the meals and wash the dishes, you would be a big help to me."

Grandma always let him come over to her house after school, and she always did special things with him. He loved her very much. He would stay overnight on Friday and Saturday nights.

Friday after school Dad dropped Andrew off at Grandma's house. On Sabbath morning he came by and picked him up for church.

During Sabbath school Andrew's friend Carl said, "Do you want to come over to my house tonight?"

"Sure," Andrew replied quickly. "I'll ask my dad."

When Sabbath school was over, Andrew found his dad in the hallway. "Can I spend the night with Carl?" he asked.

Dad gave Andrew a serious look. "Are you sure?"

"Yeah, I'm sure. Why not?"

"Didn't you promise to stay with Grandma tonight?"

He nodded.

"Andrew," Dad continued, "I can't really tell you what to do. You are old enough to make this kind of decision on your own. You have to decide what is more important and what you feel right about doing. I hope you give the matter some serious thought."

You have probably been confronted with a conflict of interest in your life just as Andrew was, so you know how he felt. You may also be happy to know that Andrew *did* spend the night with his grandmother, just as he had promised.

- **Are you happiest when you stick to your commitments? Why?**

- **Look up the definition of "integrity." Think about how you can apply the principles of integrity to your life every day.**

Working It Out

And Jonathan made a covenant with David because he loved him as himself. 1 Samuel 18:3, NIV.

Close friends are not always easy to find. But it can happen almost instantly. It happened with David and Jonathan. The Bible says they became so close they were one in spirit. They even made a deal to stay friends, and when times were tough, they helped each other rely on God (1 Samuel 23:16).

Alexander Pope said, "In every friend we lose a part of ourselves, and the best part." Have you given the best part of yourself to your friend? That's easy to do when you find a close friend who thinks as you think, likes the same things you like, and believes the same way you believe. Those friendships are very deep and special. But sometimes those special friendships also take the most work. Even though Jonathan made a covenant with David to stay friends, that didn't mean their friendship wouldn't take work. It meant that they were committed to keeping their friendship strong. If you and a friend are having a misunderstanding, try some of these helpful ideas to work it out:

1. Agree to talk about the specific problem.

2. Try to see the problem from your friend's point of view.

3. Agree that once you have resolved the problem between you, you'll both forget about it.

4. Decide to treat your friend better than you have done in the past. Friendships take constant work. If you concentrate only on making your friendship better in the future, then what happened in the past won't matter. It should never come up again.

Little arguments and hurts in a friendship may not seem like a problem at first, but they add up to big problems after a while. Eventually your friendship could be ruined unless you do something to prevent it from happening. Before problems get too big, remind yourself why your friend is special to you.

😊 **Have you ever had a disagreement with a close friend? How did you resolve it? Are you still friends?**

😊 **Take a moment right now to remind yourself why your friends are important to you.**

291

A Mile in Your Nikes

The entire law is summed up in a single command: "Love your neighbor as yourself." Galatians 5:14, NIV.

You're nuts, do you know that?" Sam hollered. "You're ruining everything!" She stormed around the clubhouse.

"I'm sorry, but I can't go," Zeb replied.

"You're spoiling it for the rest of us!" Sam declared, pinning Zeb with a glare.

"I'm sorry, but I can't," Zeb said quietly.

"This is all your fault!" Sam cried. "You're just being selfish!"

"I can hear you guys clear in my room," Dillon said, pushing his glasses up on his nose. "What on earth is going on in here?"

Sam glared at Zeb, and he glared back.

"You know the trip I set up to go to the baseball game?" Sam asked. "We can go only if I can get six kids together so we can get the discount. And Zeb won't go with us, so now none of us can go."

"I can't go," Zeb sputtered angrily. "I promised that I would mow Mr. Lawrence's lawn, and that's the only night I can do it."

"Sam, what would you do if you were in Zeb's place?" Dillon asked.

"I'd go anyway," Sam growled.

"Would you really?" Dillon said. "I seem to remember a similar situation last year when you promised Mrs. Libby that you would help her make cookies for Billy's birthday party, and you missed out on a volleyball game."

Sam squirmed.

"Seems to me you two need to look at the situation from both sides."

😊 **What's the hardest part about trying to see where someone else is coming from? What do you need to do before you can see someone else's point of view successfully?**

😊 **Borrow a friend's shoes. Make sure they don't wear the same size you do! Walk around in them. Do they pinch? Or are your feet swimming in them? Would it be harder than you thought to walk a mile in them?**

Character Analysis

Let your gentleness be evident to all. The Lord is near. Philippians 4:5, NIV.

Jeffrey had made a name for himself. He was obnoxious, belligerent, loud, and, worst of all, mean. When Jeffrey was around, it was as if he did whatever he could to make everyone else miserable. And he was usually successful. So successful, in fact, that he didn't keep friends for very long.

Jeffrey seemed to go through friends as if he had an endless supply. But, of course, he didn't. Pretty soon he discovered he didn't have any friends at all.

In the animal world, the shrew claims the title as the smallest mammal. But the two-inch shrew might also claim the distinction of having the worst attitude, too. The shrew eats twice its weight in food every day. It will also fight—and win—against an animal that is three times its own size. And if it's hungry enough? Well, a shrew might even eat another shrew!

The shrew has a mouthful of poison and razor-sharp teeth. Its poisonous saliva can kill a mouse within three minutes. The gland that produces the poison can even produce enough venom to kill 200 mice!

Are you concerned about making a gentle, Christlike impression? Obviously, the shrew isn't concerned with making a gentle impression. But that is all right for the tiny shrew. For the shrew to survive, it *has* to be aggressive, even downright mean.

But as Christian human beings, how should we act?

As Jeffrey proved, you attract more flies with honey than with vinegar. If we want to attract friends and have a positive influence on people for Jesus, then our words need to be gentle and uplifting. Our actions should mirror Jesus' actions. And we should spend our time leading people to Jesus instead of turning them off.

- **When was the last time you made a negative impression on someone? Why did it happen? How did you feel afterward? How can people see Jesus in you?**

- **Go out of your way to be courteous today. Open doors for people, offer to help whenever there is an opportunity, and remember to smile at everyone.**

293

Word Gets Around

Pride goes before destruction, and a haughty spirit before a fall. Proverbs 16:18, NKJV.

Sometimes my brother and I were asked to animal-sit for our vacationing neighbors. We were happy to be considered reliable enough to care for someone else's pets. The word got around. Our neighbors could say, "Now, there are responsible young men. You don't see many like them these days."

One evening my brother and I finished feeding our neighbor's farm animals about the time dusk turned into full-fledged darkness. In a hurry to finish up and head for home, we checked the animals one last time and closed up the barn.

I knew that an electric fence was strung in the backyard (although I had never been able to figure out why it was strung at forehead level), because I had been warned: "Remember the hot wire. You're too tall to miss it."

Maybe you have noticed that the times when you feel the most prideful are also the times when embarrassing things are liable to happen. Embarrassing moments usually come when I am so full of pride that I forget about God and other people and think mainly about how important I am. Sometimes no one has to know but God and me. And sometimes I may do something so embarrassing that a lot of people know about it.

Anyway, that hot wire sat me down on the ground. I felt as if I'd been hit with a snappy right jab out of nowhere. Taking the fall wasn't necessarily the worst of it. I had plenty of opportunities to explain the long thin mark across my forehead. Remember? Word gets around.

I'm glad God gives us a breaker switch to remind us to be humble.

- **When was the last time you were humbled by an embarrassing experience?**

- **Ask each person in Sabbath school class to share an embarrassing moment that reminded them they are not superior to everyone else.**

Christina and the Long Walk Home

I was afraid that in some way the tempter might have tempted you and our efforts might have been useless. 1 Thessalonians 3:5, NIV.

"Hey, Christina, would you like to play a game of one-on-one before you go home tonight?" Keisha asked. "A bunch of us are going to stay after and play. We've got some good teams together."

"Sorry," Christina replied, "but I have to baby-sit my little brother at 4:30."

"Four-thirty?" Keisha exclaimed. "We're not going to play that long—just a few games. You'll be home in plenty of time."

"No, I won't," Christina replied. "I have to go all the way over to the park and backtrack up Lincoln Street to get home."

Keisha's forehead wrinkled. "Why? You're taking a really long way home. Just go straight up West Street and it will save you heaps of time. Then you can play with us."

Christina shook her head. "I can't. There are some drug dealers who hang out on West Street, and I don't want to go past them. That's why I take the long way home every afternoon."

In life there are many places where we find temptation. It can be hanging out just about anywhere. The first question, of course, is what do we do about it? Hopefully we ignore it or resist it. But what about next time? Once we know where we'll be tempted, do we go back there again and again? Or do we, like Christina, take the long way home to avoid temptation?

Be strong enough in the Lord to confront temptation when you see it. But the best way to avoid temptation is just to avoid it. Take the long way home if you have to.

- 😊 **What is the best way to avoid temptation? Can you think of any instances we need to face temptation and stand fast, rather than try to avoid it?**

- 😊 **Time yourself. Take a route you usually walk and time yourself. Then go to the same place, only take a long detour to get there. Does it take a lot more time? Which is more important, reaching the destination, or the amount of time it takes to get there?**

"My Spirit Is Generous," Part 1

Though they have been going through much trouble and hard times, they have mixed their wonderful joy with their deep poverty, and the result has been an overflow of giving to others. 2 Corinthians 8:2, TLB.

There once was a land of four kings whose kingdoms lay in each of the four corners of the land. Early one morning the king of the Western Kingdom rose early to climb the highest mountain in the land. From the top of this mountain he could see a great distance into each of the four kingdoms.

While the king gazed upon the beauty of all that surrounded the mountain, a terrible plague of locusts fell upon the Northern Kingdom and destroyed all that grew in its fields.

"Send to the Northern Kingdom all that I have in my food stores," the king ordered his aide.

"But Your Majesty," protested the aide, "you will not have enough for your own kingdom should disaster befall *it*."

"Do as I say, for my spirit is generous and my faith is full."

So the aide went away and sent wagons of wheat and corn to the Northern Kingdom.

Once again the king gazed upon the beauty of all that surrounded the mountain. And while he gazed at all the lands, great hurricanes and violent tornadoes fell upon the Southern Kingdom. Soon the king's aide arrived to give a full report of the Southern Kingdom's fate.

"Send my workers with my remaining wagons to help rebuild the Southern Kingdom," ordered the king.

"But Your Majesty," replied the aide, "should you send so much? Who will defend your kingdom?"

"Do as I say, for my spirit is generous and my faith is full."

So the aide went away and sent the workers with wagons to help rebuild the Southern Kingdom.

 Is it always easy to share? When was the last time you shared something without expecting anything in return?

 Look for an opportunity to share. Share knowledge with classmates by helping them understand schoolwork. Share your time by helping someone accomplish a task.

"My Spirit Is Generous," Part 2

Freely you have received, freely give. Matthew 10:8, NIV.

The king of the Western Kingdom again gazed upon the beauty of all that surrounded the mountain. He could see, far to the north, the many wagons of food that he had sent. He could see the many subjects he had sent to help in the southern regions.

Then, while he stood upon the mountain, a great and dreadful disease fell upon the Eastern Kingdom.

"There is a disease in the Eastern Kingdom," reported his aide. "Many, many people are dying."

"Send all my doctors to the Eastern Kingdom."

"But would it not be wisest to let them perish?" asked the aide. "If they die you will have no reason to fear them."

"How good would it be to let so many perish? Would we not be worse than the disease? Go now, for my spirit is generous and my faith is full."

So the aide sent all the doctors to the Eastern Kingdom. When he returned, he was very worried, and the king saw this.

"Why are you worried and afraid?" asked the king.

The aide replied, "Oh, king, if your kingdom were to suffer from famine, we would all certainly perish, for the warehouses are empty. If your kingdom comes under attack, there is no one to defend it. Oh, king, if sickness comes upon your people, would not all surely die? You have sent away your food, your subjects, and your doctors."

As the aide spoke, a great and tremendous earthquake struck the king's own kingdom. It was so powerful that the king and his aide felt it even as they stood upon the mountain.

"Oh, king, it is fortunate there is no one left in your kingdom, for all would surely have been killed," said the aide.

- Have you ever shared without expecting a reward, and then received an unexpected reward anyway?

- If there is someone at school whom you have had trouble with, why not take your favorite dessert to share with him or her?

Never Do Homework Alone

Give me wisdom and knowledge. 2 Chronicles 1:10, NIV.

Another week of schoolwork. How much homework this week? You want the knowledge, but don't you wish there were an easier way to get all that information into your head?

You have parents and teachers who give you wonderful support. You may have friends you study with in groups. You probably have access to a library full of information. You may even have access to the Internet. But you have probably noticed that when it comes down to getting the most out of all that information, studying is a lonesome task.

Keith closed the door to his room and unloaded his schoolbooks. He knew that if he started his reading assignments that very day, he would be on top of his studying all week.

Ten minutes later, however, the schoolbooks were still stacked right where Keith had left them. Five or six wads of notebook paper littered the floor around his Snoopy trash can, and one was sailing through the air. "Two points," Keith muttered.

Have you ever felt like Keith? The task of studying seems so boring and sometimes difficult that it's hard to get started.

Look at it this way. There's only one you. There is only one *now*. How are you going to make the most of the situation? What do you want to do with your opportunity to learn? What are your goals, and where do you have to begin to reach them? What can you do to increase your wisdom?

Oh, and the most important key to successful study? Prayer. When you invite God to your homework session, you are never studying alone.

How is knowledge pleasant to the soul? Are you happy with the knowledge you have, or are you constantly eager for more? Where will you be in 10 years if you don't make the best of your opportunities now?

Write neatly or use a word processor with a fancy font to make a copy of today's verse; then frame it and hang it where you will see it while you are doing your homework.

Puzzling It Out

Some people keep on doing good, and seek glory, honor, and immortal life; to them God will give eternal life. Other people are selfish and reject what is right, in order to follow what is wrong; on them God will pour out his anger and fury. Romans 2:7, 8, TEV.

S am sighed deeply. "I give up. I can't do it."

Dillon's eyebrows shot up in surprise. "Already? You just started that puzzle. Where's your persistence? Like when you're studying the Bible and can't figure something out, you don't just give up."

"*I* do," Sam said, a little embarrassed. "I don't understand some of the words, and sometimes what the text says doesn't make any sense."

Dillon grabbed a Bible and flipped to the concordance/dictionary section. "If your Bible has one of these, you can look up the words you don't understand. It will also list other places the word appears so you can compare the texts to see exactly what they mean. Also, if your folks have something like *Strong's Exhaustive Concordance of the Bible* you can look up words and find out what they mean in the original Hebrew or Greek."

"Study Bibles explain a lot of things," Dillon continued. "But if you don't have one, find the verse that confuses you in the listing in the middle of the page. It will list other verses that are similar. Look them all up, and they will help you understand the text you are reading."

"That sounds a lot like work," Sam said.

"It can be," Dillon agreed. "But think of it as searching for buried treasure!"

- What are some things you can do to help yourself get past a rough spot when you feel like you're stuck?

- Set up a card table in your room and empty a challenging jigsaw puzzle onto it. See how many days it takes you to complete it. How do you feel about having finished it?

21

Courage to Go On!

I have told you these things, so that in me you may have peace.
In this world you will have trouble. But take heart! I have
overcome the world. John 16:33, NIV.

In an instant, tragedy struck. Ben Hogan, one of the greatest golfers ever to play the game, was driving home with his wife after playing in a tournament when a bus skidded out of control. Ben couldn't miss the bus, but he did try to save his wife by throwing himself in front of her body to try to protect her.

Valerie Hogan survived the collision with only a few injuries. Ben, however, was hurt badly. He had taken most of the impact and suffered several broken bones and internal injuries. Valerie thought for a brief moment that Ben was dead, he looked so pale and lifeless.

When the doctors arrived, they too must have thought he was dead, because they covered him with a sheet. But Valerie heard a faint groan from Ben, and he was quickly rushed to the hospital, where doctors worked continuously on him for two days.

The doctors were convinced that Ben would surely never play golf again. It would take a lot of work for him even to walk, and he would probably never walk normally. Ben's body was pretty beat up.

However, Ben wasn't the type of person to give up. He wanted to play golf. He began to walk—only a little at first, then a little more, until finally he began to exercise, even though it was painful to do so. He worked hard to get back into the game after the doctors had said he would never play again. Two years later he won the U.S. Open, the Masters Tournament, and the British Open.

Courage to make a comeback like Ben Hogan's doesn't just benefit the person who is making the comeback. It helps other people have courage too.

☺ **Think of a time in your life when the courage you showed helped someone else have courage too. Is courage contagious?**

☺ **With your Sabbath school class, design and make medals for the members in your church who are showing courage in dealing with difficult problems.**

300

Right and Wrong

May the favor of the Lord our God rest upon us; establish the work of our hands for us—yes, establish the work of our hands. Psalm 90:17, NIV.

Christian youth are honest, kind, and happy, and most of all, they love God. Christian youth are called Christians because they love and follow Christ. True Christians present themselves as examples of Christ. They are His ambassadors.

Two boys thought they had come up with a foolproof idea to get some quick cash. Maybe they reasoned it wouldn't exactly be robbery if they didn't use a weapon. In fact, maybe it wasn't really the money they were after in the first place. It could have been that they thought their plan was more of a game, so it wouldn't actually be stealing. Whatever their reasoning, what they planned to do *was* against the law.

The success of their plan rested most of all on whether or not anyone believed they were who they pretended to be. So the boys decided that their plan had to be carried out at night, when it would be easier to fool their unsuspecting victims. Then they bought the equipment they needed.

On the night they had chosen, the boys prowled the streets until they found a promising victim. They followed the car and turned on the blue flashing light they had bought. Soon the woman who was driving the car pulled off the road, thinking she was being pulled over by a police officer.

After the boys pulled up behind the woman, one of them got out of the car and walked up to her window, just as a police officer would do. The woman didn't realize until it was too late that she had been fooled. She hadn't been stopped by the police at all! Quickly the boy snatched away the woman's purse and ran back to the car, where his partner waited to make a fast getaway.

- Have you ever tried to fool yourself into thinking wrong was right? What happened? How do we know the difference between right and wrong?

- Look at a traffic light. The red, green, and yellow lights are always in the same order. Similarly, wrong is always wrong, and right always right. Make a traffic light poster for your room. Put today's Bible verse on it.

No Fishing

You will be merciful to us once again. You will trample our sins underfoot and send them to the bottom of the sea! Micah 7:19, TEV.

Kerrie heard a *thunk!* She pulled over and glanced into the rearview mirror. Something small and furry was lying in the road. She'd hit somebody's cat. Scooping up the lifeless animal, she went to the closest house and knocked on the door. A man answered.

"I'm so sorry," Kerrie wept. "I ran over your cat."

The man took the cat from her arms. "I'm sure you didn't mean it. I forgive you. Don't worry about it."

That night she couldn't sleep, so she drove back over to the man's house. There was a little grave out back where he'd buried the cat. She dug it up and carried the cat to the door.

"I'm so sorry about your cat!" she wailed when he sleepily answered the door.

"It's OK. I forgive you," the man said, taking the cat again.

The next night Kerrie still couldn't sleep, she was so upset about the cat. So she drove back to the man's house, dug up the cat, and woke him up again.

"I'm so sorry about your cat," she wept.

"Look, I told you it's OK. I forgive you. Now go home!"

Kind of a silly story, isn't it? But we do the same thing with our sins sometimes. It's hard for us to realize that God has forgiven us. Sometimes it's hard to forgive ourselves.

Corrie ten Boom likes to think of it this way. "God throws our sins into the depths of the sea and, though the Bible doesn't say this, I believe He also puts up a sign: No Fishing!"

The next time you sin, confess it, ask for forgiveness, and then think of it as being at the bottom of a bottomless sea. God forgives you. Forgive yourself.

🙂 **How deep is the sea? How deep can humans go in the sea? What does that tell you about the depth of God's love and forgiveness?**

🙂 **Rent a National Geographic video about the sea and sea life.**

Huckleberry Eater

So the last will be first, and first will be last. Matthew 20:16, NIV.

Every year my family planned a camping trip to Lost Valley Reservoir around the time huckleberries were at their best for picking.

I always put more huckleberries into my mouth than into the bucket. At the end of the day my bucket of huckleberries would look very pitiful compared to everyone else's.

But I had developed a good plan. After every hour or so of picking, I dumped my few huckleberries into Mom or Dad's bucket. That way no one could ever tell how many I had eaten and how few I had contributed to the family's supply.

I never fooled anyone, though. Mom and Dad knew that I ate more huckleberries than I ever put into the bucket. But it didn't matter. When Mom made huckleberry pie, I received an equal share, no matter how few berries I saved.

Jesus tells a story about a generous landowner who hired workers early in the morning to work in his vineyard. He hired more workers three hours later, then some more six hours later. Finally, 11 hours later, people were still standing around in the marketplace, so the landowner hired them, too.

When it came time to pay all the workers, the landowner paid each of the workers he had hired last a denarius. He also gave each worker he had hired in the middle of the day a denarius. The workers who had worked faithfully all day long were upset they had received the very same pay. It was totally unfair, they reasoned.

By telling that story, Jesus wanted to show that it didn't matter how important people were or how long they had been Christians. He would save anyone who accepted Him. Isn't that great news?

- 😊 **Think of a time you were upset because you thought you deserved a bigger reward than someone else. How do you feel about it now?**

- 😊 **Make it a point to treat everyone equally, instead of basing your attitude toward them on how much they do for you.**

"I Ain't Gonna Leave a Friend"

Be full of love for others, following the example of Christ who loved you and gave himself to God as a sacrifice to take away your sins. Ephesians 5:2, TLB.

Wouldn't it have been something to spend time with Jesus when He was on earth? Think about it. Who could have been a better friend than Jesus was? He helped anyone who wanted His help. But that isn't even the best part. Jesus was the most loyal friend anyone could ever have had. He still is, even today, for every one of us.

A young man named George Hunt was traveling with several companions on the way back from mining in California. As they traveled through the Siskiyou Mountains, George came down with a fever that made him too sick to keep going. To make matters a lot worse, the men were afraid Indians might attack at any moment and kill them all.

"He's too sick to travel," one of the men said. "If we wait for him to die, the Indians will get us for sure. We've got no choice. Got to go on."

Another suggested dividing up George's gold among them. But a man by the name of Sappington spoke up. "I ain't a-gonna leave a friend when he needs me most." And he volunteered to stay. He asked if there was anyone else willing to stay with them.

Another man, named Bush, stepped forward. Sappington and Bush stayed with young George all day. Late in the evening, however, the Indians were gathering to mount an attack, so Sappington and Bush built a travois (a makeshift bed on two poles) for George. They loaded him up and in the night escaped over the Siskiyou Mountains. After many miles they finally reached the settlement of Eugene. Sappington and Bush found George's father and handed over George and his $4,000 worth of gold dust.

🙂 **Do you think Jesus is your most loyal friend? How can you be a loyal friend?**

🙂 **The only sure way to be a loyal friend is to put your friend's needs first, just as Jesus put other people's needs first.**

304

Perseverance

The man said, "Your name will no longer be Jacob, but Israel, because you have struggled with God and with men and have overcome." Genesis 32:28, NIV.

Mandy Wilson's dream was to go to the U.S. Air Force Academy. But would she ever be able to turn her dream into a reality? Her first setback came when she took her Scholastic Aptitude Test and scored 10 points below academy standards. She took the test a second, then a third time. She took the test a fourth and fifth time, too, and raised her scores 230 points.

However, in 1995 the Air Force Academy declined to admit Mandy, so she attended a preparatory school for four months to increase her knowledge of calculus, chemistry, and English. She also kept herself in physical shape by faithfully working out.

On March 19, 1996, Mandy's dream finally became a reality when the Department of Defense appointed her to the academy.

Does perseverance pay off? For Mandy it did. She committed a lot of hard work toward reaching her goal. Every time she retook her SATs, she kept her eyes focused on her goal. Even when the Air Force Academy wouldn't admit her, she continued to persevere.

Christians rely on God. Perseverance through tough times builds character and strength. It builds faith in God, as well as faith in ourselves. Mandy has four tough years ahead of her at Air Force Academy, but she can look back at what she overcame to get into the academy when only 15 percent of all applicants are accepted.

Another person persevered to gain a blessing from the Lord. His name was Jacob; his spiritual life needed a boost. When Jacob learned he was wrestling with God, he knew there was no possible way he could win. But that wasn't the point. Jacob knew that with his faith and persistence he could expect God to bless him. And so God did.

- How can you plan to achieve the goals you have set for yourself?

- Begin discussing with your parents what you would like to do when you are older. Ask them to help you begin taking steps toward achieving your goals.

Oh, No, Not Sabbath!

He blessed the seventh day and set it apart as a special day,
because by that day he had completed his creation and
stopped working. Genesis 2:3, TEV.

Although God meant for Sabbath to be a blessing, we often think of it as a list of "can't do's." But what would happen if we thought of the Sabbath as a list of *"can* do's"?

For example:

On Sabbath I *can* rest. I don't have to do schoolwork or chores or go to a job. And I don't have to feel guilty about it!

On Sabbath I *can* spend time with my family, friends, and God.

On Sabbath I *can* go on nature hikes, canoe trips, or rock climbing to see the beauty God created.

On Sabbath I *can* take some time to show God how much I love Him.

There are so many opportunities to have fun on the Sabbath. Try thinking of all the things we *can* do. One girl I heard about enjoyed drawing, so on Sabbath she used her talent to draw pictures from the Bible. When a neighbor boy wanted to know what she was doing, she was able to share the Bible with him. Some kids enjoy playing instruments and get together for sing-alongs on Sabbath. Many people go for nature hikes, canoe trips, and bike rides on Sabbath so they can enjoy what God created.

If you're obeying the Sabbath command just to obey it, you won't receive the blessing that you could if you obeyed it because you were glad to. Check it out. Does your Sabbath attitude need adjustment? Think positive!

Why is Sabbath so important? In what ways do we break the Sabbath, even though technically we are keeping it? Which matters most to God, that we keep the Sabbath and enjoy it, or that we simply keep it?

Start your very own Sabbath tradition. Buy a candle to light at sunset or chose a special song to sing to welcome Sabbath, and open Sabbath by reading a chapter of the Bible.

Thrown Off the Horse

Let us rid ourselves of everything that gets in the way, and of the sin which holds on to us so tightly, and let us run with determination the race that lies before us. Hebrews 12:1, TEV.

I 'll never forget the first time I got thrown off a horse. Her name was Velvet, and she was my first horse. She was young and not broken properly. The only horses I had ridden before I got her were at the fair. Those horses didn't buck. Velvet did.

One moment I was riding in the pasture. The next moment I was on my back on the ground. It never occurred to me that I could get bucked off. After Velvet tried to throw my mother, we traded her for an older horse named Blueboy.

Blueboy was normally quiet, except in spring. Then he would buck and rear and try to shake me off. He never succeeded, although a few times I fell off. Once I was riding bareback, and he turned suddenly for our race back to the gate. When the rein in my hand snapped, Blueboy went one way and my momentum carried me the other. Another time I had on a bareback saddle and it slipped around so that it was under his belly. Off I went.

I don't like falling off of horses or getting thrown. But when you ride horses, there is always the chance that you will end up on the ground. The only way you can be sure you never fall off another horse is never to ride again.

Some things take more effort than others. But if we don't keep trying, we won't ever succeed. It can be hard, but we have the best coach available. Jesus will help us with any problems we have, and He will stick with us until we succeed. Aren't you glad He's on our side?

🙂 **Why do you think persistence is so important? What would happen if we gave up as soon as anything got hard? What does persistence teach us?**

🙂 **Try writing your name with the hand that you don't usually use to write with. Don't give up until you can write it so other people can read it!**

Desiring God's Strength

I desire to do your will, O my God; your law is within my heart. Psalm 40:8, NIV.

The compass has been around for many hundreds of years. It has been spoken of in both Asian and European writings that date back to around 1200. But not until 1345 was a compass reportedly used on a specific ship. That was the British ship *George,* and even 200 years afterward sailors were still not happy with its poor accuracy, a condition that stemmed from its primitive construction. The needles were often carelessly magnetized, which meant that it could never really be trusted. It was easy to see why. Sometimes while in the middle of a voyage the poorly magnetized needles lost their magnetism and would spin like a top. Not much help to a sailor.

Though many scientists pondered the compass's power and how to make it better, few really understood it well enough to improve it. Then came a man by the name of Dr. Gowin Knight. He had figured out how to improve the magnetic strength of the compass. He impressed people by taking a weak needle into a room by himself, and then returning with a much stronger magnetized needle. Although we know now that Dr. Knight simply placed the weak needle between a pair of huge compound magnets to transfer their power to the needle, no one then knew how he did it. And Dr. Knight never told, either. He died with his secret.

Today the compass is not such a mystery. We know how it works and why. We know that Dr. Knight improved the magnetic strength of a needle by exposing it to the power of two much larger magnets.

For you and me, being a Christian is like being the magnetized needle in a compass. The closer we come to God's power through study, prayer, and godly actions, the stronger our faith becomes, and the easier it is to lead others to Christ.

How do you keep your faith strong? What do you do when you feel you need to recharge your Christian life?

Take a few minutes every day to read a passage from the Bible to help give yourself a recharge.

Hidden Blessing

I will bless them and let them live around my sacred hill. There I will bless them with showers of rain when they need it. Ezekiel 34:26, TEV.

Has anybody ever told you to count your blessings? That's pretty easy, right? When you're counting them, do you ever list things like health, food, shelter, or clean water? Consider a place like Somalia. In one area of this African country the people have to walk four hours to get water, and then four hours to get back home. Camels and cattle compete with people at drinking sources, fighting one another for water.

Have you ever been sick? I have. I've been so sick that I didn't even feel like praying. When you're so sick that all you can think of is having the pain end, good health seems like the ultimate blessing.

In some cities and towns (maybe even yours) people live in cars, under bridges, on park benches, and in shacks and shelters made of cardboard or other materials they find. Can you imagine living in a place that is so temporary, so inadequate? A hermit I heard of lived in a woodpile. When he needed wood for his fire, he simply pulled out another log surrounding him. Does your home seem like a palace compared to that?

In some places in the world children are left to fend for themselves. If they are to eat anything, they must find it or catch it all by themselves. A woman who grew up on the streets of China talked about how the children would all head for the fields and catch mice and insects to eat. No matter what you had for dinner, it must have been better than that.

We are all blessed, more than we realize sometimes. Take a few minutes to thank God for all your "hidden" blessings.

🙂 **Why is health so important? When our health is bad, what else suffers? Are there other "hidden" blessings that God gives us but we rarely recognize?**

🙂 **List as many "hidden" blessings as you can.**

Whaddaya Know?

I was determined to learn the difference between knowledge and foolishness, wisdom and madness. But I found out that I might as well be chasing the wind. Ecclesiastes 1:17, TEV.

I don't get to see it very often, but I like to play *Jeopardy*. It's the only game show I like, because it challenges how much I know. I learn a lot by watching that show, because it is all information.

Information is important. In fact, experts believe that in the future, information will be the most important thing there is. Wars will be fought over information. It will be worth millions of dollars. You've probably heard the buzzword "Information Superhighway" to describe the Internet, a place full of information.

Not only do we have newspapers (and sometimes there is more than one in a city), news magazines, and news magazine TV shows, but we have access to up-to-the-minute, cutting-edge information through online services like the Internet. There isn't enough time in the day to absorb all the information we are exposed to.

Yes, information is important. Knowledge is important. But it must be balanced with other things as well. You can't spend your whole day reading everything you can get your hands on. You need to get outside and breathe fresh air. You need to exercise your body. You need to talk to your friends. You need to do some kind of work.

If all we did was absorb information all day, we wouldn't be very well-rounded people. And we would never get to put into practice what we learned. Reading the Bible can be like that. We can't be satisfied simply to read what the Bible says. We have to *do* what it says too. That's where the real knowledge comes in.

- **Which is more important, how much you know or how much you understand? Is there anything more important than knowledge?**

- **See how many Bible verses you can find that say wisdom or knowledge is important. Then see how many you can find that say it isn't.**

Sarge

Even birds and animals have much they could teach you; ask the creatures of earth and sea for their wisdom. All of them know that the Lord's hand made them. Job 12:7-9, TEV.

"Zeb, Sarge has run off again."

"Again?" Zeb wailed. "I don't have time to look for him!"

"Zebulon Dalton, Sarge is your responsibility," his mother said. "You know he likes to run off when you put him outside. That's why we installed the dog run. But it won't work if you don't use it. Whatever you're doing will have to wait till you find the dog."

Zeb stomped down the stairs and grabbed a leash before heading out the door. This was the third time this week that Sarge had run away. Zeb knew he didn't do it to be mean or spiteful. Usually he heard kids playing at the playground down the road and headed over there to play with them.

The playground was the first place Zeb checked. No Sarge.

"Sarge! Sarge, come!" Zeb yelled. Then he noticed a horrible odor. He decided to check down by the creek. Sarge sometimes liked to go for a swim there. Zeb stood on the bank, scanning up and down the creek. No Sarge. Just then the dirt gave way beneath his feet, and he tumbled headfirst into the creek. He came up sputtering and dragged himself out of the cold water.

Deciding to go home for a fresh change of clothes, he walked into the yard, only to find Sarge on the front steps. The big dog bounded down the sidewalk to greet him.

"Stupid dog!" Zeb said, giving Sarge a kick.

The dog cowered and headed for the front door. Immediately Zeb felt sorry. He knelt down beside Sarge and hugged the dog. "I'm sorry, Sarge. I shouldn't have done that."

Sarge thumped his tail and licked Zeb's face.

Does how we treat animals reflect how we treat people? What can you tell about a person from the way he or she treats animals?

Take your dog (or your neighbor's/friend's dog) for a walk.

The Power of Confidence

But the Lord said to me, "Do not say, 'I am only a child.' You must go to everyone I send you to and say whatever I command you. Do not be afraid of them, for I am with you and will rescue you," declares the Lord. Jeremiah 1:7, 8, NIV.

Confidence is one of your greatest assets. If you have confidence in yourself, you can do things other people might never attempt. With God's help, you can accomplish things even *you* might never have believed possible.

On October 8, 1918, in the Argonne Forest of France, the weight of command of a small group of American soldiers suddenly fell squarely on the young shoulders of Corporal Alvin York. It promised to be a short-lived command, however, for the handful of soldiers York was to lead were surrounded by a much larger force of Germans.

Corporal York wasn't about to give up. Instead, he flattened himself against a tree and fought back. Several Germans fell. More Germans charged toward the Americans, yet Corporal York continued to hold his ground against them.

The Germans didn't know they had a small handful of Americans surrounded. Rather they began to believe they were themselves outnumbered, so they surrendered their weapons and gave up. York and his six men suddenly found themselves the captors of 92 prisoners, whom they dutifully began marching toward American lines.

As York and his men marched toward safety, they encountered several more German machine-gun nests. Each time the Germans failed to realize soon enough that the six Americans were not the prisoners, but the captors. By the time Corporal York reached American lines, he had captured 132 prisoners.

If Corporal York had not had confidence, could he have achieved such a victory? Why should Christians have confidence in themselves?

Ask God to give you confidence. Approach every day with an I-can-do-that attitude. Use your confident attitude as you study your schoolwork this week.

312

Ground Sludge?

Then God said, "Let us make man in our image, in our likeness, and let them rule over the fish of the sea and the birds of the air, over the livestock, over all the earth, and over all the creatures that move along the ground." Genesis 1:26, NIV.

Picture it: At your feet a pond of thick mud boils, spewing out muck every now and then. It has been like this every day for millions of years. Then one day some little pond creature "evolves" into something that can crawl out of the sludge—and "life" is born.

I don't believe it, but a lot of people do. According to scientists, we evolved from some primordial muck soup and became the complex, unique creatures we are today.

Yeah, right. We didn't evolve—we were created. How do I know? What fantastic scientific theory did I go by to come up with my analysis? Simple. I performed an easy experiment, one that you can duplicate with complete safety in the comfort of your own home, using one flower of any variety.

Follow all the steps exactly and don't miss one. Look the flower over carefully. Smell the flower. Approximately how many varieties of flowers are there? (I'll help you out here: "The largest family of flowering plants is the Compositae [Asteraceae], comprising about 1,100 genera and more than 20,000 species and characterized by many small flowers arranged in a head looking like a single flower and subtended by an involucre of bracts.")

Now, if you will gather all your data, you can clearly see that no way did we crawl out of a sludge pile. To create one flower alone, even if it didn't have a scent, would have been a glorious, magnificent accomplishment, enough to convince any skeptic that a loving God created it. But God didn't create just flowers. He created *everything*. Incredible? You bet! Unbelievable? Not hardly!

😊 **What could you tell someone who believed in evolution about why you believe in creation?**

😊 **Make some mud soup. Set it outside for a week, a month, a year. Then take a look at it. Did it change any? Read the account of creation in Genesis. Any questions?**

Hidden Pockets

And then they will come to their senses and escape from the trap of the Devil, who had caught them and made them obey his will. 2 Timothy 2:26, TEV.

*U*sually we went to a nice ski resort, such as the Von Trapp Family Lodge or Sherman Hollow, where there were nicely groomed trails, well marked as to the degree of difficulty. But this . . . Well, this was much different.

"Come and ski at my resort," Rolf had invited.

And that's what we did. One snowy Sunday afternoon my family, my friend Terry, and I went to Rolf's to ski. We found that there were no marked trails at all. We just set off into the woods at the base of Jay Peak and hoped for the best. Fortunately, Rolf was there to guide us. Our progress was slow and painful, since we had to break our own trails. It was nothing at all like skiing at our usual resorts.

As I tried to climb one particular hill I suddenly found myself waist-deep in snow, trapped by my skis, which were buried beneath me. I couldn't move! Rolf maneuvered his way back to me.

"Must have hit an air pocket," he said cheerfully. He offered me one end of his pole and pulled hard. Eventually I managed to work my way free of the snow and wedge my skis on solid snow again.

Christianity can sometimes be like that ski trip. We're used to being in "safe" areas, where we can perform well. Then we find ourselves in unchartered territory and get sucked under by a hidden trap. There is no way we can prepare for something like that except to keep our relationship with Jesus strong. Grab hold of His ski pole; He can get you out of anything.

- How can we avoid falling into the devil's traps if we can't even see them? Why is it easier to avoid the traps than to try to get out of them once we've become stuck?

- Do some research on traps. Find out what kinds there are and how they work (for example, a lobster trap, a leg trap, a humane trap, etc.). Then try to think of a trap that Satan uses that is like each of the traps you learned about.

Set Free

Remember those who are in prison, as though you were in prison with them. Hebrews 13:3, TEV.

Every month I am responsible for getting a group of people together to make food for the Dismas House in Rutland. The Dismas House is a place where convicts live when they get out of prison. While they are at the Dismas House, they try to establish themselves in the community, get jobs, attend therapy groups, and learn how to live as contributing members of society.

Cooking for the people at Dismas House is one of the few times my cooking gets praised! They even give us a round of applause. (When was the last time your mom set dinner on the table and you clapped?) But I like going there for more reasons than that.

By cooking meals for them and eating with them, we are showing them that the community cares for them and accepts them. Yes, they did something bad. Yes, they paid the price for that. Now they're ready to live in society again and need help so they don't fall into the same old bad patterns again.

Some people would rather forget that there are people in prison. They would just as soon lock the door, throw away the key, and forget all about them until their time is up. However, if inmates aren't educated and helped while they are in prison, they will return to their life of crime as soon as they leave. It's up to us to help them adjust to their new life.

The apostle Paul spent a lot of time in prison. I think he felt for the people who were in prison because he knew what it was like. I'm sure not all of the people Paul met in prison were innocent. Nevertheless, he loved them as Jesus would have and prayed for them. Shouldn't we do the same?

🙂 **Why is it important not to ignore people in prison or who are trying to learn how to live in the community after having just left prison? Are there any people in prison who are innocent?**

🙂 **Ask your parents or pastor if it would be possible for you to join them the next time they visit the prison or halfway house.**

315

Spoiled Rotten

For everyone who exalts himself will be humbled, and he who humbles himself will be exalted. Luke 18:14, NIV.

Samson blew it. Big-time. He was *supposed* to save Israel from the Philistines. That was God's plan for him. But Samson decided to do his own thing. *Why not?* he might have thought. *I'm the strongest man who ever lived.*

Samson was obviously spoiled rotten. He knew it wasn't right to marry the Philistine girl, but he was determined to do it anyway. His parents knew it wasn't right too, but they caved in to Samson's demands anyway. So Samson went ahead and did exactly what was against God's law and his parents' wishes.

And then there was Derek.

It all started when Derek was only a baby. He discovered that if he cried loud enough and long enough, he eventually got what he wanted. As Derek grew older he learned that he could get whatever he wanted if he begged long enough. Derek was smart, too, but he usually used his intelligence to find ways to get out of doing his homework rather than using it to increase his wisdom. Derek spent more time bullying his schoolmates than helping them. As he got older he ignored his parents more, too. Eventually he stopped listening to them altogether.

Derek sounds a lot like Samson; they both thought about themselves first. Everyone else was a distant second. Were Samson and Derek happy? I don't think so. People who think about themselves first are usually not very happy.

God wants to use you and me. He has given each one of us special talents and abilities. But it's up to us to use them wisely for God and for other people.

- If you'd had Samson's gifts, would you have used them for personal gain or as God wanted you to use them? How do you use *your* gifts?

- Think of a way to match your gifts with the needs of someone in your family, in your church, or in school that will help build his or her self-esteem.

Two Different Men, Two Different Talents

Whatever you did for one of the least of these brothers of mine, you did for me. Matthew 25:40, NIV.

If you had been given Samson's abilities, would you have used them to serve other people? That's what God had intended for Samson to do. Samson could have done so much good and helped so many people, but because of his selfishness he wasted his very special talents.

Johannes Brahms was one of the world's greatest composers, but had you met him, you might have had difficulty believing so. Why? Because Brahms was not a man to boast of his talents. His music brought in enough money to make him quite comfortable, yet he lived a very quiet, modest lifestyle. Instead of using his money on himself, he gave much of it to less fortunate people when he heard about *their* needs.

Although Brahms never belonged to a specific church, he studied the Scriptures and had a deep faith in God. He is quoted as saying, "People do not even know that we north Germans long for the Bible *every* day and do not let a day go by without it. In my study I can lay my hand on my Bible, even in the dark."

Perhaps the most important lessons to be learned from Brahms are his faith in God's power and his willingness to put others first.

Brahms believed that the greatest works could come only from composers who allowed themselves to be inspired by God, and he himself always began his work by praying to God. He never exalted himself. Instead, he lifted others up through praise and encouragement.

Samson could have spent his life doing what God wanted him to do. He could have used his talents to help the Israelites as God had intended, just as the composer Johannes Brahms used his talents to benefit others. Instead, Samson selfishly wasted his talents.

Why do you think Johannes Brahms was so generous with his money? Why do you think he felt comfortable putting others first? Why didn't Samson do what God wanted him to do?

Listen to a tape or CD of some of Johannes Brahms' music.

God Never Leaves

Then Samson prayed to the Lord, "O Sovereign Lord,
remember me." Judges 16:28, NIV.

For most of his life Samson had either ignored or blatantly gone against God's will. Maybe that is one of the most important reasons Samson's story is told in the Bible. God wants us to know that no matter how badly we mess up our lives, He always loves us and wants us with Him in heaven. He can use us, even if we have had many failures. I like to think that the most important reason for the story of Samson is that it shows us that God never gives up on us.

After Samson told Delilah the secret of his strength and had fallen asleep, she simply cut off his hair. Then the Philistines came, obviously prearranged by Delilah. Instantly Samson jumped to his feet to fend them off, not realizing at first that God's power had left him, just as God said would happen if his hair was cut. Suddenly Samson was as weak as any other man, unable to fight back or to even escape. At once the Philistines subdued him and gouged out his eyes. Samson was shackled and made to grind wheat for the very enemies God had planned for him to deliver Israel from.

All through his life Samson had fallen short of God's plans. He had spent so much time and energy on selfish pursuits, when he should have been saving Israel from the Philistines, that he was drawn farther and farther away from God.

But God did not separate Himself from Samson. He still loved Samson, just as He always loves us. Standing by the temple pillars in front of the mocking, jeering crowd, Samson asked God to remember him and help him one last time. And God forgave Samson and helped him. Three thousand of the Philistines' most elite and powerful rulers died in the Philistine temple on that day.

Why is it important to know that God always loves us?

The most important action we can take is simply to accept God into our lives right now. Nothing we have ever done will stand in God's way of having a relationship with us if we ask forgiveness and accept Him.

Oh, No! I Forgot!

Watch therefore, for you do not know what hour your Lord is coming.
Matthew 24:42, NKJV.

Sam sat on the floor, her back propped against the wall outside her history classroom.

Slam! Bang! Crash!

Sam's heart flipped over a couple times. Then she threw down her book and jumped up. "Baxter! Grow up!"

Baxter Burney grinned. He bent down and picked up the books he had purposely dropped on the floor beside Sam to scare her. "What's the matter?" he asked innocently.

"I was studying for our history test," Sam shot back.

"Oh, you were cramming." Baxter nodded his head knowingly.

It really irritated Sam. "And I suppose you're ready?"

Baxter nodded. "Sure am. I studied for it last week, right after Mr. Wilkens told us what chapters the test would cover. Then I studied again on Sunday. And I reviewed everything last night. I even had my mom and dad ask me some questions." Baxter grinned. "It's better than cramming just before a test. I don't know if you've noticed or not, but when you cram for a test, the information you put in your head only goes into your short-term memory. You have to study it at least a couple times to get the information to stay in your long-term memory. Sometimes what you have in your short-term memory disappears as soon as you get distracted by something else."

"Is that so?" Sam snapped. "What makes you an expert?"

"A couple months ago someone dropped a whole bunch of books right beside me while I was cramming for a test. I forgot everything I had just read." Baxter grinned again. "Who was our sixteenth president, Sam?" he asked smugly.

"The sixteenth president of the United States was . . ." Sam froze. "Oh, no! I forgot!"

🙂 **How is preparing for a test like preparing for Jesus to come again?**

🙂 **Look over Baxter's study technique. Try using some of his ideas the next time you study for a test.**

Judge Not

Do you, my friend, pass judgment on others? You have no excuse at all, whoever you are. For when you judge others and then do the same things which they do, you condemn yourself. Romans 2:1, TEV.

She stood on the side of the track, breathing effortlessly while everyone else panted and puffed, and I decided I didn't like her. Sweeping her long blond hair back over one shoulder, she walked up to my best friend, Jodie, who crouched in a gasping heap at the finish line. Jodie hated track.

Smiling, she reached down and helped Jodie to her feet. She said something to her that I couldn't hear. To my amazement, Jodie looked up and smiled—actually *smiled*—back at her. No way. What was going on here? This had to stop.

I made my way over to Jodie. "Are you ready to go, Jodie?"

"Actually, Tisha was just asking me if we wanted to go over to her house to study."

"I'm studying at my house. Are *you* coming or not?"

Jodie looked at Tisha and then at me. "You are being ridiculous, Lauren. I'm going to Tisha's house. You can do what you want."

And then they were walking away. Together! Without me!

For the next couple days I fumed. It seemed like Tisha was everywhere, helping someone with math, showing little Annie Carlson how to get a better start out of the blocks, doing extra chores for the teacher. Tisha, I decided, was a goody-goody.

"Just look at the way she's always hanging around when she's not needed," I pointed out to Jodie. "She's just trying to get on people's good side. It's not like she actually cares about them."

"You don't know that," Jodie said. "How can you judge her when you don't even know her? Why don't you like her, anyway?"

I slumped down in my chair. "I don't have to know her. I know about her. That's plenty for me."

🙂 **Why is it not a good idea to judge someone? Do you judge people? Do they judge you? How can you change that?**

🙂 **Choose someone you don't know at school or church and get to know him or her. Don't form any opinions until you know the person well.**

Jealous? Who, Me?

Anger is cruel and fury overwhelming, but who can stand before jealousy? Proverbs 27:4, NIV.

You're jealous of her," a little voice whispered.

OK, so what if I am jealous of her?

"Hey, Lauren, why don't you sit with us?" It was Tisha, swaying in the aisle of the bus.

I shook my head stubbornly. "No, thanks."

"Why not?"

"Because," I snapped irritably, "I don't want to, OK?"

"Lauren Bryce, you're jealous!" Oh, great. Now Jodie was swaying beside Tisha.

I bristled. "I can be jealous if I want to be."

"Do you like it?" Tisha asked quietly.

"What kind of question is that?" I snapped. "Of course I don't *like* it."

"Then don't do it."

I snorted. "Yeah, and how am I supposed to do that?"

"If you love people enough, you can't be jealous of them."

"You expect *me* to love you?" Yeah, right.

"The Bible says that 'perfect love casts out all fear,'" Tisha pointed out.

"But I'm not afraid of you," I sputtered.

"You're not afraid that I will steal Jodie's friendship?"

She had me there. "Well . . ."

"I don't know why we can't all be friends," Jodie said suddenly. "You'd really like Tish once you got to know her."

I flinched. It would take me a while to get used to hearing her say "Tish." The question was: Was I willing to try?

You've got nothing to lose, the little voice in my head said.

I swallowed hard. "I'm willing to try," I said finally.

Tisha smiled, and Jodie slapped me happily on the shoulder.

"I'm really a very nice person," Tisha assured me.

"Yeah, and modest, too," I grinned. Who knew? This could be the start of a beautiful friendship.

😊 **Have you ever been jealous of anyone? Why?**

😊 **When you feel jealous, try loving that person instead.**

Knowledge Before Choice

Show me your ways, O Lord, teach me your paths; guide me in your truth and teach me. Psalm 25:4, 5, NIV.

God gives every one of us the freedom to ask questions, seek answers, and make choices. Pretty cool, huh? One of Robert's pet peeves was that he felt he was being pushed into going to church with his parents every Sabbath because his parents wished that he would go with them. *How could that be freedom?* he thought.

I know how Robert felt. Maybe you do too. Maybe you have also learned, as I did, that even though it is part of our responsibility to obey our parents (including going to church with our families), it doesn't mean we *have* to become Christians. Actually, accepting or rejecting Jesus is something each person has to decide on his or her own. That is the ultimate in freedom of choice.

When parents insist on the whole family going to church together, they hope their children are taking the opportunity to learn about Jesus. Parents realize they can't force God on their kids, but they do hope that their kids will give God a fair chance. Then when their kids are older they will have the information that will help them make wise decisions about God.

I don't know if Robert still goes to church today. He may have stopped going altogether. But I hope he stopped thinking about going to church as something he *had* to do. And I hope he learned that church is a warm and joyful place where people want to go because they feel close to Jesus there.

I'm thankful my parents loaded my brother, two sisters, and me into the car every Sabbath morning whether we wanted to go to church or not. If they hadn't, I may never have learned enough about Jesus to build my own personal relationship with Him.

- Why do you look forward to Sabbath? Do you think your parents are trying to push God on you? Are you willing to give God a fair chance?

- Invite a friend to spend a Sabbath with you. Make it all day long. Try to make it as relaxing and enjoyable as possible.

Peculiar Pants

Rejoice in the Lord always. I will say it again: Rejoice! Philippians 4:4, NIV.

Ask anyone and see if they enjoy receiving a gift. I'm sure you'll find there are very few people who don't like receiving a gift now and then. Don't forget about the people who give gifts. They're happy too. Gifts are as much fun for people to give as they are to receive.

There is a story about a rich, unmarried man who died in 1880, leaving everything to his nephews and nieces—all except 71 pairs of pants. His plan for the pants was that they should be auctioned off in a public sale. Each pair, of course, would go to the highest bidder, and the proceeds of the sale were to be given to the poor. Oh, there was one final stipulation—a person could purchase only one pair of pants.

The auction took place as planned. Seventy-one pairs of pants were sold to the highest bidders. But that wasn't the end of the story about the rich man with the very strange request! You see, the buyers soon discovered that sewn inside the pocket of each pair of pants was a $1,000 bill. What a surprise discovery!

Sometimes it's difficult to find joy in what we already know. For instance, we know what Jesus did for us by coming to this earth and dying for us. But how many of us feel as excited about salvation as those people at the auction felt after reaching into their pants pocket and discovering they were suddenly $1,000 richer?

God gave His Son to die for our sins! He gave us the ultimate gift! That sounds much more exciting than $1,000 sewn inside a pair of pants, doesn't it? Jesus is our most precious gift. Rejoice!

- After careful thought, what reasons can you think of to be *extremely* excited about Jesus' gift of salvation?

- Surprise your brother or sister by putting a $5 bill in a pair of their pants (preferably a pair not headed for the laundry) at a time when they are short of money.

Reading Material

Happy is the one who reads this book, and happy are those who listen to the words of this prophetic message and obey what is written in this book! For the time is near when all these things will happen. Revelation 1:3, TEV.

What kinds of things do you like to read? You may have trouble believing this, but when I was in high school I really liked reading Stephen King books. I know, I must have been nuts. For years I was afraid of the dark. I couldn't be left at home alone without leaving all the lights on in the house. It was awful. I felt like a prisoner.

I've heard people say that it doesn't matter what we read. They say that if we read about violence or horror or other nasty stuff, it won't affect us. Well, I know better. I stopped reading Stephen King books, but it was years before I could go for a walk at night without thinking some horrible monster was going to sneak up on me and kill me.

Romance novels are also popular, but they offer a distorted view of life. If you believe them, you will be very disappointed in real life. Another kind of book that is popular is thrillers, or spy books. People get blown up, bumped off, shot, and killed at an alarming rate. Though this type of book doesn't usually condone killing, it uses it to entertain. Hitting someone doesn't seem like a big deal when you compare it to blowing them up.

Whatever we expose ourselves to will affect us in some way, whether negatively or positively. It is up to us to screen carefully what we read or watch on television. God will protect us from negative outside influences, but He can't do that if we are exposing ourselves to those influences voluntarily.

The next time you look for a book to read, ask yourself one question: Would I read it out loud to Jesus? As long as you can answer yes, you should be OK.

Does it matter what we read? What effects do the things we read have on us? What kind of reading material do you think is appropriate?

Make a list of the most recent five books you've read. Would you recommend them to Jesus?

324

No Excuse Is Good Enough

"Well, then," said his master, "go out into the country lanes and out behind the hedges and urge anyone you find to come, so that the house will be full." Luke 14:23, TLB.

Have you ever missed out on dessert because you were late for a party? Have you ever purposely taken your time, even when someone was expecting you?

An officer who was to report to General Zachary Taylor during the Seminole War decided to stop off at an inn for a couple days before continuing on to his post in Florida.

Two other people were also staying at the inn. One was a shabbily dressed man wearing a black hat. He and the young soldier talked of many things. Eventually the old man asked the soldier what excuse he might give to General Taylor upon his late arrival.

"They say Taylor is a very easy old soul," the young officer replied. "I can easily make up an excuse."

Later that evening, before retiring to bed, the young officer asked the landlord if he knew who the old man was.

"Why, don't you know General Taylor?" replied the landlord.

At midnight that same night the young officer who had once been so at peace, believing he could take as long as he wanted getting to his post, hurriedly jumped on his horse and made tracks for headquarters.

Jesus told a story (Luke 14:15-24) about a man who had invited many guests to a great feast. The guests, however, all had one excuse or another. So the man brought in the poor and the crippled instead. Everyone who wanted to come was invited, and those who had a million excuses were left completely out.

Jesus offers us the reward of being with Him in heaven. Everything is paid for. It promises to be a joyful experience. I don't want to miss it. How about you?

😊 **Read Jesus' parable in Luke 14:15-24. Why do you think Jesus told that story? What does it mean to you?**

😊 **Ask your parents if they will help you plan a friends-and-family get-together. You plan and cook the meal (with your parents' help) and send out the invitations.**

Doing Your Best in All Things

He who is faithful in what is least is faithful also in much. Luke 16:10, NKJV.

I know a rather careless student who is much more concerned about finishing his schoolwork than he is about putting an extra amount of effort into doing it as well as he can.

"At last I'm finished," he might say. "Now can I go play football?"

His attitude reminds me of a golfer who became careless in a very important game. You see, during the 1968 Masters Tournament in Augusta, Georgia, a golfer named Roberto de Vicenzo was playing so well that he might have won.

At the end of the first round (18 holes) De Vicenzo was only two strokes off the lead. He finished round 2 only three strokes from the lead. And at the end of round 3 he was still one of the leading golfers in the tournament.

Toward the end of the tournament De Vicenzo played very well, which put him close to winning. But on the seventeenth hole De Vicenzo's partner, Tommy Aaron, accidentally wrote down the number 4 when he should have written down 3 for De Vicenzo's score. (When two players are "paired" in a golf game, one player keeps score for the other.)

De Vicenzo missed a putt on the last hole and ended up tying with another player, or so he thought. He was so happy about the tie that he signed his card without taking time to add up his score.

When the officials tallied up De Vicenzo's card, it showed that he had scored a 66 instead of a 65. Because of that one wrong score Roberto de Vicenzo lost the tournament. There was simply no way he could change his score after signing his scorecard. It was the closest he ever came to winning the Masters.

Even though some details are small, that doesn't mean they are unimportant. Always begin with an attitude of faithfulness in small things, and you will not be afraid to sign your name to anything you do.

☺ **Why is it always important to do a job to the best of your ability?**

☺ **Make several cards that say "I certify that this job was done to the best of my ability," then sign your name. Put a card with each job or school assignment you do.**

Hole in One

Above all else, guard your heart, for it is the wellspring of life. Proverbs 4:23, NIV.

There is this really old tree that I can see from my bedroom window. I know it's old, because for one thing, it's big. But it is also dead. And it's been dead for a long time, because there are no branches left on it. Every year woodpeckers come and drill holes in it, and turkey vultures sit on top of it.

One year a really nice woodpecker came and drilled a hole. Not just an ordinary hole. It kept drilling until it had drilled a hole big enough to fit in. Then it got inside and drilled some more, kicking out the sawdust with its feet. The next thing we knew, there it was, sitting inside the hole where it had made a nest.

We were thrilled! We'd never seen baby woodpeckers, and the tree was close enough to the house so that we could watch them hatch and be fed and do all the other neat things baby birds do. Then one day, while the mother and father woodpecker were gone, a blackbird came to the hole looking for a nesting site. He threw out all the nesting material and the eggs of the woodpeckers. When they returned they found that their home had been vandalized and that someone else was living in it!

So they packed up and moved off. We never did get to see the baby woodpeckers, and the adults didn't bother to come back the next year.

Have you ever had that happen with your heart? You try really hard to do what you know is right, and then just for a little while you aren't paying attention. Before you know it, Satan has moved in. He just loves it when we're not paying attention! We have to be on our guard every second, or else we will find a new resident in our heart, and it will be someone we don't want around.

- **What does the Bible mean when it says to guard your heart? How can you do that? Why is it so important?**

- **Make a poster with today's verse on it and hang it in your room.**

327

Pie in the Sky

But those who want to get rich fall into temptation and are caught in the trap of many foolish and harmful desires, which pull them down to ruin and destruction. 1 Timothy 6:9, TEV.

I'm going to make a wad of money," Dillon chortled.

"What are you so happy about?" Sam asked.

"I'm going to be *rich!*" Dillon practically shouted.

"And I'm going to be president," Sam said sarcastically.

"I'm serious, Samantha," Dillon said, irritation edging his voice. "I figured out a great way to make money, and I hardly have to do anything."

Sam laid her book aside. "OK, Dillon. What do you want it for? I mean, you can spend only so much money."

"I can spend all the money I make," Dillon retorted.

"You won't spend it all," Sam pointed out.

"Well, no, there's tithe to pay," Dillon agreed. "But the rest I can spend."

"What about all the people who have nothing? Don't you feel any sense of responsibility to help them?" Sam asked.

"They can work and make their own money," Dillon said defensively.

"No," Sam said. "Some of them work all year long and don't make as much money as we can in a day. They're trying, but their children are still dying, and they are still starving."

"Well . . ."

"If we're able, we should help them," Sam finished. "I don't think it's right that some of us have lots and some have nothing. Do you?"

Dillon shook his head. "No, I guess you're right. It could just as easily be us who are in need."

😊 **What is wrong with wanting to earn a lot of money? What kinds of attitudes does having money create in us? Is it harder to give money up when you have a lot or when you have a little? (Think carefully; that's a trick question!)**

😊 **Give an offering to a local charity.**

Paid For

But now you belong to Jesus Christ, and though you once were far away from God, now you have been brought very near to him because of what Jesus Christ has done for you with his blood. Ephesians 2:13, TLB.

There were several things Will couldn't do as well as his companions that made him feel as though he wasn't part of their group. Maybe you know how Will felt.

Will watched and he practiced. He wanted to learn how to set a trap the right way. And since he wasn't a very good shot, he also wanted to learn how to shoot better. Determined to prove himself, Will set out one day on a hunting trip, hoping that if he was successful his companions would stop calling him a greenhorn.

While Will was out hunting, he heard rustling behind him. He turned around to see a grizzly bear only a few steps away. He was so close that he could smell its awful breath. That was too close! He dropped his pack and ran, with the bear charging close behind.

When Will reached a tree, he tossed away his rifle and climbed as fast as he could. Since the bear couldn't climb after Will, it decided to wait him out.

Will stayed in his perch all night. When morning came, he saw that the bear had gone. Warily he climbed down and gathered up his rifle and pack, then headed back to camp, where he told his story.

I think I would have been embarrassed to admit that I had been treed by a bear all night. But Will told his story anyway, and his companions decided that he wasn't a greenhorn anymore if he had been chased by a grizzly.

We don't have to shoot straight or even be chased by a bear to be accepted by God. According to Paul in the above verse, Jesus paid for us with His blood so that we may have eternal life.

Why was Will accepted only after he had been chased by a bear? Do we have to prove ourselves to God before we are accepted by Him?

Do you know some people who are trying hard to be accepted? Find a way to help them feel accepted today.

Hot! Hot!

In love he predestined us to be adopted as his sons through Jesus Christ, in accordance with his pleasure and will—to the praise of his glorious grace, which he has freely given us in the One he loves. Ephesians 1:5, 6, NIV.

L ike Will, who thought that the only way he could be accepted was to learn to do everything as well as everyone else, I once thought that I would be more accepted if I ate an onion.

One Sabbath evening after worship, one of the games we played at Pathfinder camporee was a relay. Each Pathfinder was to reach into a bag, pull out a vegetable, and eat it. The winning team would be the one that emptied its bag first.

Unfortunately, I was the last Pathfinder on my team to reach into the bag. I don't know if we were winning or not, but I was determined to eat as quickly as possible whatever I pulled out of the bag!

My first bite wasn't so bad. In fact, it was sort of sweet. I definitely knew that I had taken a bite out of a big, yellow onion, but I resolved to finish the contest. I decided that I would try to win, no matter what. Most of all, I was determined not to quit—not in front of all my friends. So I continued to eat one bite after another, even after I began to feel the burning in my mouth.

I never did finish the onion. The burning got to be too much for me. My mouth was on fire, and my eyes had turned into a waterfall. I had to quit.

I think I know how Will felt when he got back to camp after being chased by the bear. He probably felt a little ridiculous, just as I felt after trying to eat an onion all at once. But there is something about Jesus that is very, very important to me. I hope it is to you, too. Listen: Jesus loves you and me. He accepts us just as we are. Do we have to prove anything to Jesus first to be accepted by Him? No!

🙂 **Why is it important for people to feel they are accepted? How does Jesus help people feel accepted?**

🙂 **Plan a strategy with some of your friends to show someone who feels left out that you care about them.**

Proud Parent

You are our father. Our ancestors Abraham and Jacob do not acknowledge us, but you, Lord, are our father, the one who has always rescued us. Isaiah 63:16, TEV.

Have you ever seen a baby learning how to walk? I suppose I've seen it on television, but it never meant the same thing as when my own son learned how to walk. We were at an auction. He was holding my hand, and his uncle David was a few feet away, trying to coax him to walk toward him.

Josh took one little step and then speeded up, forgetting to hold my hand. He was walking! He went a little way and then fell *kerplop* onto the grass. And what did I do? I picked him up, dusted him off, and helped him try again.

You would have thought I was some kind of bad mother if I had hauled him up by one arm, smacked his bottom, and said, "Stupid kid! That's not how it's done. Now try again!" You'd probably call the police and report me for abusing my child!

But you know what? Isn't that how we imagine God is toward us when we fail? He is our heavenly Father, and yet when we blow it, we expect Him to be sitting up there in heaven waiting for us to mess up so He can zap us with lightning. Can't you just hear Him saying "How many times are you going to make the same mistake? I've told you and told you. Now shape up and do it right"?

God loves us much more than I love my son. I know my son will make mistakes as he's growing up. That's what kids do. And God knows we will make mistakes as we are growing up to be mature Christians. That's what baby Christians do.

God loves you. When you make a mistake, He holds out His hand and helps you up. The next time you fall, take His hand.

🙂 **Why do we expect God to treat us worse than earthly parents treat their children? How do you picture God? Is He anything like your parents?**

🙂 **Make a list of all the characteristics you believe God has. Then find a Bible text to support each one.**

Taking a Stand

Do not be overcome by evil, but overcome evil with good. Romans 12:21, NIV.

ick could hear a group of guys from his class talking. When he got closer, the words became clearer, and he decided not to join them. Suddenly Jeff hollered for him to come over and join them.

Rick shook his head. "No, thanks." That was all he was going to say, but then something more came out of his mouth. "I heard what you guys were talking about. I guess I want people to know that I respect them. It makes me uncomfortable to degrade others the way you are doing."

Rick wasn't prepared for what happened later at lunch. Well, besides eating alone because all his would-be friends were hovering around Jeff, that is. *Why did I have to go and spout off that I didn't like the way they were degrading girls?* he wondered to himself. *Now everyone thinks I'm a freak!* Then someone tapped him on the shoulder.

"Do you mind if I sit here?" Janet asked.

Rick choked. "Well, uh, no, I guess not," he stammered.

"I heard what you said to Jeff this morning."

"You heard?" he asked uncomfortably.

Janet leaned forward. "Actually, one of the guys hanging out with Jeff is the brother of one of my friend's friends."

Rick's brain was still trying to make the connection when Janet started talking again.

"Anyway, he was really impressed by what you told Jeff," she said. "And I am too. Jeff and other guys who think the way he does make me feel uncomfortable. It's nice to know there are some real cool guys like you who aren't afraid to stand up for what they believe. I'm sure that took courage."

Rick blushed. "Well, uh, maybe a little."

Does how much you value other people affect what you say about them? How can you positively change the way you talk about other people?

The next time you are talking about someone else, think about what you are saying and thinking. Are you lifting them up, or are you degrading them?

Taking It One Step at a Time

At last the wall was completed to half its original height around the entire city—for the workers worked hard. Nehemiah 4:6, TLB.

I love the feeling of accomplishment. Do you like the same "I've finished it" feeling? Do you know the feeling you get when you have finished a long written report for school? How does it feel to complete a difficult test? Or maybe you like how your room looks when it is sparkling clean. But it takes a lot of work before you have that feeling. It takes time to complete the task.

What if you are at the beginning of a big project or task? Is it possible to imagine the task completed?

When I was in high school I worked with my father during the summer as a carpenter. Many times we drove up to an empty lot where there were only weeds and bare ground. It was hard to imagine that before long a finished house would be sitting there.

The first step was to dig a hole for the foundation. Then we set forms and poured the footings and foundation walls. A few days later the floor was down, and we would be framing the walls. A week later we set trusses and stapled plywood on the roof. Then came the sheathing, siding, shingles, trim, wiring, plumbing, insulation, sheetrock, and eventually, the cabinets. As you know, many more steps than I have mentioned go into building a house. Some of the houses even had a yard and sprinklers before we left. But in the end, in the very spot that used to be a field of weeds stood a new house. The big project had been completed.

If a project looks too big and overwhelming, whether it's building a house or writing a school report, don't concentrate on how big it is. Tackle it one small step at a time. Give yourself plenty of time, and do each small step well. Before you know it, the project will be finished. And it will be good.

🙂 **When was the last time you forged ahead to complete a huge, impossible-looking task by completing one small step at a time?**

🙂 **If you have a task to do that seems overwhelming, break it down into small steps.**

Dinosaur Disaster, Part 1

Look up at the sky! Who created the stars you see? The one who leads them out like an army, he knows how many there are and calls each one by name! His power is so great—not one of them is ever missing. Isaiah 40:26, TEV.

I probably shouldn't say this, but I really didn't want to go to Uncle Greg and Aunt Shonna's in the first place. Oh, it's not that I didn't like them. They're pretty cool, but they're so isolated that if they ordered pizza, the delivery person would have to pack a suitcase.

It's just that, well, there was going to be this dinosaur exhibit at our local mall that was supposed to put *Jurassic Park* to shame. Of course, it had to be there the two weeks I would be away. Just my luck.

Mom was going to a writers' conference, and Dad decided that that would be a great time to put in that addition. Wouldn't you know it, I'm allergic to sawdust. And so faster than you could say triceratops I was on a train to Uncle Greg and Aunt Shonna's.

"Dana!" Aunt Shonna gushed when I got there. "You've grown up so much! Look at you." She grabbed my suitcase right out of my hands. "Go for a walk—you must be sick of sitting. But Dana, the blue herons are nesting right now, so be sure to leave them alone, OK? They're really shy."

"Oh, yeah, sure," I said. I had no clue what a blue heron looked like. If you asked me, they spent too much time worrying about birds around that place. Every time I visited, Uncle Greg was busy checking nests and counting eggs and building bird boxes. What was the big deal?

Then I looked up, and there it was, flying slowly, laboriously. A pterodactyl—one of the flying members of the dinosaur family. It was easy to identify by the vicious-looking head with its beady eyes. It looked huge.

- What do you know about dinosaurs? Who do you think made dinosaurs? Why do you think they are extinct?

- Build a model of a dinosaur with toothpicks and clay. If your friends make dinosaurs too, you can have an exhibit.

Dinosaur Disaster, Part 2

God is the one who made the mountains and created the winds. He makes his thoughts known to man; he changes day into night. He walks on the heights of the earth. This is his name: The Lord God Almighty! Amos 4:13, TEV.

Chills chased up and down my spine. This was impossible! Had I stepped back in time somehow? I ran to keep up with the flying pterodactyl. Flopping quickly onto my belly, I watched it land on a pond just down the hill, partially disguised in the long grasses that grew there. While I was watching, another one flew in and landed. I rolled over onto my back and stared into the sky, dazed, while my heart skidded around in my chest.

I couldn't believe it! Uncle Greg and Aunt Shonna had built their own Jurassic Park. They had figured out some way to hatch dinosaurs, just like in the movie. That's probably what Uncle Greg was doing all the time when he said he was "checking the nests"! It was all clear now.

If they had been able to hatch pterodactyls, there was no telling what other species they had on their property. I wanted a closer look at that dinosaur. Who knew when I'd have a better chance? I crept forward on my belly, trying to keep as low as I could. It almost looked as though they might have a nest. Maybe even babies.

I don't know what happened, but one moment I was crawling along and the next moment I was underwater. I came up sputtering. Fortunately, it was shallow. Unfortunately, I had made such a racket that the two pterodactyls were flying into the sunset.

But they had left their nest behind.

Mud sucked at my shoes as I waded toward it. It contained two large eggs. Without stopping to think, I grabbed one of the eggs and wrapped it in my shirt. That should keep it warm.

How much of what people believe about dinosaurs do you think is true? Why do you think God allows scientists to keep finding dinosaur bones?

Look up pterodactyls in the encyclopedia. What modern-day bird do they look like? (Hint: check out a bird book!)

335

Dinosaur Disaster, Part 3

Everything that God has created is good; nothing is to be rejected, but everything is to be received with a prayer of thanks. 1 Timothy 4:4, TEV.

Dana, what do you have?" Uncle Greg looked pale.

"I know what you're doing!" I cried triumphantly as I carefully unwrapped the egg. "This is a pterodactyl egg."

"Oh, Dana!" Aunt Shonna wailed, dashing down the steps to where I stood. "I thought I told you to keep away from the blue herons' nests!" She gazed with dismay at the egg I held in my hands. Uncle Greg gently took the egg.

"Where is he going?" I asked quietly, watching his receding back.

"To put the egg in the incubator until we can return it," Aunt Shonna replied. "Dana, how could you? I told you specifically to keep away from the herons. They're so sensitive."

I hung my head in shame. "I thought they were pterodactyls," I muttered miserably.

"Pterodac—you mean, dinosaurs?" Aunt Shonna gasped. "Dana, you know that movies like *Jurassic Park* aren't real. There used to be dinosaurs, sure, but for some reason God decided that dinosaurs should be extinct. They existed once, but don't anymore."

"I'm really sorry I disobeyed you, Aunt Shonna," I gulped. "I just got so excited thinking about pterodactyls that I lost my head. Will you forgive me?"

Aunt Shonna gave me a bear hug. "Of course we forgive you."

Uncle Greg opened the back door and came into the kitchen. He smiled slowly. "It's OK. They've accepted the egg. Tomorrow, young man, we're going to take a little hike around this property. I'll show you all the birds and anything else you're interested in."

"Except dinosaurs," I grinned.

"Especially dinosaurs," Uncle Greg chuckled.

🙂 **Can human beings "create" anything, give anything life? Why not? Do you think that if humans could create beings and give life that they would be responsible with that gift? Why or why not?**

🙂 **Draw a picture of a pterodactyl and a picture of a blue heron. How are they similar?**

Jesus Knows How I Feel

I came forth from the Father and have come into the world. Again, I leave the world and go to the Father. John 16:28, NKJV.

When I was a kid, my mother watched a boy named Max, who was a little older than I was. One day when we were all playing with his cowboy and Indian action figures, he decided we should pretend my man was wounded. That was fine, at first. I didn't plan for my cowboy to be wounded for very long. But since they were his toys, I thought I should play along for a while. But "a while" turned out to be a long time. Whenever I wanted my cowboy to get well, Max said that he had to stay in bed.

"You can't move him," Max said. "He's still wounded."

So I left my cowboy lying on a make-believe bed in a make-believe cabin, while Max and my brother played. And when Max's mother came to pick him up, I was still waiting to play.

I've always remembered the feeling of being purposely left out. Because I know that feeling, I try to be sure I never leave anyone out.

Imagine, feelings and all, a Man who lived 2,000 years ago. He associated with outcasts and nobodies. He stood up for anyone who was being taken advantage of or criticized. He encouraged those who were tired. "Important" people would rather have ignored Him altogether. But they couldn't. Jesus was making a huge impression with common, everyday people.

Why should Jesus take time for so many people in unimportant positions? Because He is a God who knows each one of us from the inside out. He knows our feelings—after all, He feels the same feelings we do. When you feel left out, Jesus knows just how you feel. I imagine that He was left out quite a bit when He was growing up. He was certainly treated unfairly *after* He was a grown-up. He came to this earth in order to experience what we have to experience. I love having a God who knows what I feel like inside.

🙂 **When have you ever felt left out? Have you ever imagined how someone else felt who was being left out?**

🙂 **In your next activity, include anyone who wants to be involved.**

Buffy

Each of you should look not only to your own interests, but also to the interests of others. Philippians 2:4, NIV.

Grandma never intended to get another dog. But the little cocker spaniel needed a friend in the worst way. It didn't appear as though it had ever had a friend in its short life. When my grandmother spotted her, Buffy was lying beside the road. She had a mass of cockleburs buried so tightly in her fur that she had to be completely shaved. She had sores on her body, her paws were bleeding, and she was severely dehydrated and malnourished. Buffy was barely alive when Grandma rushed her to the veterinarian. The vet discovered that Buffy also had cockleburs caught in her throat. Who knows how long she had been unable to eat?

Someone had apparently just dumped Buffy along the road. She looked like a dog who had attempted to go home, but had made a wrong turn into a patch of cockleburs. There, she simply gave up. What was there to go home to, anyway? More abuse?

Buffy stayed with the veterinarian for two weeks before she was able to go to her new home. But when she did get to go with Grandma, she had the best kind of life. Grandma always treated Buffy with kindness.

I hope you love animals as much as my grandmother does. I hope you always remember how much God loves animals. They were not put on this earth to be mistreated and abused. They are here, first of all, because God loves and enjoys them, the same way He wishes us to love and enjoy them. He was pleased with what He had created during Creation week. As I pet our dog Scotty, or scratch Tender's ears, or listen to Shasta purr, I'm glad God gave us animals to love. I intend to care for them as God would want me to.

🙂 **How do you feel when you see someone abuse an animal? Can people see your kindness in the way you treat your pets?**

🙂 **If you see someone mistreating an animal, tell your parents about it. They can inform the local humane society.**

Funny Side Up

He sets the time for sorrow and the time for joy, the time for mourning and the time for dancing. Ecclesiastes 3:4, TEV.

According to Christian comedian Ken Davis, the secret to seeing the funny side of things is to ask "What if . . . ?"

"If when you drop a piece of bread it always lands with the buttered side down, and if when you drop a cat it always lands on its feet, then what if you drop a cat with a piece of buttered bread tied to its back?"

Ken has no trouble seeing the funny side of things. For instance, one day he learned an important lesson from the business end of a skunk. He says, "I found out that you have no business looking into the business end of a skunk. He must have been a religious skunk, though, because he said 'Let's spray' before he let me have it. I also found out that people respect your space when you have been sprayed by the black-and-white odor king. I went to church the same day and had a *peuw* all to myself. Know what I mean?"

He also finds humor in everyday situations. Such as gym class.

"My worst day in gym class was the day they conducted hand-eye coordination tests. I had the coordination of a carp and made a total fool of myself by missing the football every time they threw it to me. The best day was April 15, 1962. They canceled gym class that day."

I think God laughs. Ken does too. "God laughs when He sees His people experiencing true joy. I hope I make Him laugh a lot."

What about you? Do you make God laugh a lot?

- **Why do you think it's important for us to laugh? Do you think God wants us to be somber Christians? Which kind of Christian would you be more drawn to—a cheerful one, or a solemn one?**

- **Find five good jokes. Share one with a friend each day this week.**

What if So-and-so Did?

Wise people store up knowledge, but the mouth of the foolish is near destruction. Proverbs 10:14, NKJV.

In September of 1923 a squadron of 14 destroyers returning from maneuvers was steaming toward its home port of San Diego. Captain Watson, the commander in charge, ordered the squadron to form three columns and maintain a distance of 150 feet between the stern and bow of each ship. They were to also maintain a speed of 20 knots.

As darkness fell, a light fog settled in along the coast. Radar was not yet available in 1923, and Captain Watson and Captain Hunter (the commanding officer of the lead ship *Delphi*) distrusted the radio directional finder (RDF) system. They elected not to use it and plotted their course by dead reckoning.

Later another bearing was taken using the RDF. It indicated the squadron was closer to shore than either Watson or Hunter believed it was. The cautious navigator took another bearing a few minutes later, which again differed with Watson's and Hunter's dead reckoning. However, Watson ignored the navigator's suggestion for caution.

A few minutes later, assuming they would be heading into the Santa Barbara channel, Watson and Hunter ordered the squadron to change course, still holding its 20-knot speed. Moments later the *Delphi* suddenly rammed itself upon the rocks, followed at two-minute intervals by the *S. P. Lee, Nicholas, Woodbury, Young, Chauncey,* and *Fuller.* All seven ships crashed into the rocky coastline.

Not all the squadron's ships were lost. A few of the captains were wise enough to think on their own. They realized before it was too late that their leader was on a course toward disaster.

Many people allow others to make their choices for them, even bad choices, because they haven't enough courage to choose for themselves.

🙂 **When have you let your peers make your choices for you? How do you deal with peer pressure?**

🙂 **Find a promise in the Bible to remember when you are confronted with peer pressure.**

The Christmas Bible, Part 1

Let the word of Christ dwell in you richly as you teach and admonish one another with all wisdom. Colossians 3:16, NIV.

The cold damp air blowing in off the Hudson River wrapped around Anna Mittzenschnabel, and she grasped her grandfather's hand more tightly. Grandfather cast a worried frown at the threadbare winter coat she wore, and took longer strides. The coat had been handed down through the 10 older Mittzenschnabel children, and Mama told Anna she was fortunate to be able to wear it. She said this with a sigh, though, as she held the little coat up to the light.

But today she hardly noticed the cold air. Her tiny body was tense with anticipation and excitement. They were on their way to buy Anna her very own Bible.

"If you could have anything you wanted for Christmas, my little *lieben,* what would you want?" Grandfather had asked her.

Anna's smile was dreamy. "I have always wanted my own Bible," she said.

"But you have a Bible," said Enrich.

"No," Anna contradicted him. "I have your old Bible. I have never had my own anything. I would like my own Bible."

The old man chuckled. "A Bible, eh? Not so very much to ask, I think."

"Oh, but Grandfather, Bibles are very expensive. Mama said so," Anna replied. Her blue eyes were very serious.

"Then we will try not to think of what it costs, *ja?*" Grandfather said. "I know a man who sells only Bibles. He has big Bibles, small Bibles, fat Bibles, and thin Bibles. Do you think maybe he would have a Bible you would like?"

Anna's eyes widened in delight. *"Ja,* Grandfather. I am sure he would."

Why is it important to treat our Bibles with respect? Which is your favorite version of the Bible?

The next time you have some money saved up, instead of buying something you don't really need, choose a nice copy of the Bible in the version you like best.

341

The Christmas Bible, Part 2

Man does not live on bread alone but on every word that comes from the mouth of the Lord. Deuteronomy 8:3, NIV.

Grandfather pushed open the door of the little shop; the bells tinkled merrily. Anna looked around in wide-eyed wonder, inhaling the smells of leather and new ink.

"Monsieur Krueger, how very nice to see you once again!" exclaimed the shopkeeper, pumping Grandfather's hand vigorously and babbling on in a peculiar accent.

He was French, Grandfather had told her. Anna had never seen a Frenchman before. He had dark skin and hair. His eyes were not brown, yet they were not black, either. A large nose, jutting out prominently from between his eyes, suddenly pointed straight at her. "And whom do we have here, eh? This lovely young lady is too beautiful to be your granddaughter. She must be a princess."

Anna giggled self-consciously as he picked up her little mittened hand and kissed it.

Grandfather laughed. "Anna would like a Bible for Christmas. The very nicest you have, Lucien."

Lucien's smile was so wide it nearly split his face. "But of course." And leading them over to a corner, he swept his hand toward a whole row of massive, leather-bound books. "These are the best. The very best leather and paper. You would like one of these?"

Anna looked at the books. They were so big. "Do you have any like these—only smaller?" she asked hopefully.

"I have just the thing." He soon returned with a small Bible and handed it to Anna.

She pressed her face against the soft, rose-colored leather. She took off her mitten and touched the crisp printing on the almost-transparent pages. "It is beautiful," she breathed.

🙂 **How many versions of the Bible can you name? Why are there so many different versions?**

🙂 **Look up today's verse in as many versions of the Bible as you have in your house.**

342

The Christmas Bible, Part 3

Every word of God is flawless; he is a shield to those who take refuge in him. Proverbs 30:5, NIV.

Are there . . . other . . . Bibles, not so expensive as this?" she asked, stumbling over her words.

Lucien laughed. "There is every kind of Bible here, cherie."

"No, please," Anna begged. "I would like, instead, 11 less expensive Bibles."

Grandfather looked down at her in astonishment. "What would you do with 11 Bibles, *lieben?*" he asked.

"I would like to give the other children a new Bible also," she pleaded. "None of us has ever had a new Bible. So we should each have one together."

"Are you sure that is what you want, *lieben?*" Grandfather asked gently.

Her eyes shone brightly as Lucien placed the precious Bible back on the shelf and took down instead 11 cheaper Bibles. The covers were thick paper, like a schoolbook, stamped to look like leather. But there were 11 of them. *One for each of us,* she thought happily.

As she held tightly to Grandfather's hand on the way back home, she thought that no one could be as happy as she was at that moment.

Then Grandfather dug in the bag of Bibles and pulled the beautiful rose-colored Bible from the bag and handed it to her.

"Merry Christmas, *lieben,*" he said softly.

"Oh, Grandfather!" Anna exclaimed. *"Danke, danke!"* she cried, throwing her arms around him.

Grandfather patted her head. "Well, now, each of the other children is getting a new Bible too, so there is no reason you cannot have this one."

Hugging the Bible close to her, Anna took his gloved hand in her own mittened one. "It is the nicest gift you could have given me, Grandfather," she said, smiling up at him happily.

If you were Anna, what would you have done? Are we always rewarded for being selfless? Does that matter?

Make or buy a cover for your Bible to protect it.

Who's on the Line?

But you have not so learned Christ. Ephesians 4:20, NKJV.

The person who answered the phone didn't sound like Philip, so I announced my name. I thought it must be Philip's friend. When he learned who I was, we instantly launched into a friendly conversation.

"Doing anything special tonight?" I asked.

"Dave and Marty are coming over," the voice on the other end replied.

I didn't exactly know who Dave and Marty were. I was almost completely sure I had never met them before. But to keep from sounding foolish, I sidestepped Dave and Marty and asked about Robert, someone I did know.

"Who?"

"You know, your brother—"

"I don't have a brother," he said.

I think that was about the time a startling revelation came over both us. I *wasn't* talking to Philip's friend. Whomever I *was* talking to suddenly realized he wasn't talking to a friend of his whose name also happened to be Eric. Two rather embarrassed strangers sheepishly hung up the phone.

It's easy to pick up the phone and make a call to family members and friends. When we hear a familiar voice on the other end of the line, we instantly feel comfort. It's as if they are right there with us, and that's important. It is the same kind of relationship Jesus wants with us. He wants us to know Him well enough to make a call whenever we need Him, and talk to Him about whatever we want. Don't you agree that Jesus would rather we knew Him as our friend instead of as a stranger somewhere on the other end of the line?

Why is it important to take time to get to know people? Why is it important to get to know Jesus?

The next time you have an opportunity to get to know a new kid at school, in church, or in your neighborhood, go for it. See what makes them who they are. Become their friend.

Love Alert!

Honor your father and your mother, so that you may live long in the land the Lord your God is giving you. Exodus 20:12, NIV.

My son, Corey, and I have a lot of fun together. Sometimes kids and parents don't always see eye-to-eye. No big surprise. And you can probably already imagine, without me having to telling you, that Corey and I have had some disagreements from time to time. That's normal.

One of the most important things I want Corey to know is that he can trust me unconditionally to do what I think is best for him. Since I'm human I run a good risk of not always making the right choices myself. But I do have many more years of experience than Corey does. All I can do is tell him what I know and hope he listens to what I have to say.

In the same way, God asks us to trust Him. He doesn't rule with an iron fist. He doesn't demand that we read about the mistakes people in the Bible made and never make the same mistakes ourselves. Even when we do make mistakes, He is always ready to forgive us. I do think, though, that one of the important reasons God gave us the Bible (besides to show His love and plans for us) was to help us learn from the mistakes other people made.

I have never drunk alcohol, but I know what excessive drinking does to people. I also know people who have died because someone drank before driving. I know that drugs kill. I know that smoking causes cancer. I know that AIDS is most easily transmitted through promiscuous sex and unsterile hypodermic needles. I don't have to try any of those vices myself to know they are bad for me, because I can learn from the mistakes of others.

All I can do for Corey is tell him what I know, just as the adults in your life do for you. When parents give you advice, think of it as a love alert, because that's just what it is. I know. I've got parents too. And I still listen, because I know that what I'm hearing is a love alert.

😊 **When was the last time you heard a love alert?**

😊 **Make a "I choose not to" list. Write down what you know to be wrong.**

The Lord's Great Love

Because of the Lord's great love we are not consumed, for his compassions never fail. Lamentations 3:22, NIV.

Was Jesus a tough person? or was He a pushover? He didn't push people into arguments or start fights with them if they didn't agree with Him. He certainly had some hotheaded disciples, who were ready for a good rumble. After all, Peter was swinging a sword when the chief priests and the Temple guard came for Jesus.

During the Gulf War the allied forces were so sophisticated and powerful that they triumphed against Iraq's forces in less than 100 hours. The multinational force put on an overwhelming show of power and pounded the enemy into submission. But that's not how God operates.

Jesus, the One with the most power ever, chose not to use force. Before He was taken into custody that fateful night in the garden, He said to Peter, "Do you think I cannot call on my Father, and he will at once put at my disposal more than twelve legions of angels?" (Matthew 26:53, NIV). The people of Jesus' day understood a legion to be up to 6,000 soldiers. Imagine 72,000 angels showing up all at once! But Jesus couldn't call in the troops. Not if He wanted to fulfill the plan He and God had to save us. Jesus could have been tough, but instead He chose to die on the cross for our sins.

Many people want to follow only leaders who have wealth, popularity, and power. They respect only money and power. Yet Jesus, the greatest leader of all, doesn't want us to obey Him because of His power. He wants us to love and respect Him because of His fairness and His love. When we choose to know and love Jesus, we choose an all-powerful friend, just like the disciples had when Jesus was on earth.

🙂 **Why do you love and obey Jesus? Why is it important to know Jesus?**

🙂 **The next time someone provokes you in such a way that you want to retaliate with harsh words, choose, instead of violence, to imitate Jesus.**

346

You Deserve It

Those who know your name will trust in you, for you, Lord, have never forsaken those who seek you. Psalm 9:10, NIV.

Be happy, joyful, and full of thanksgiving this week. Give yourself a hand. You deserve it. You are a son or daughter of God. Being a Christian is like having Christmas every day simply because God is on your side. As you begin school this week, think about some of the reasons you have to be happy.

- I know God. Many people don't know God. Imagine what it must be like not to know Him.
- I have hope. You know this world will pass away. You have the hope of eternal life because of your relationship with God. Imagine what it must be like to have no hope.
- I am God's creation. You know that you were made after God's own image. Imagine what it must be like to believe in evolution.
- I can contribute something special to make the world a better place. With the talents God gave you, you have the opportunity to have a positive influence in people's lives. Imagine what it must be like to live only for one's self.
- I am getting an education. You have the opportunity to learn. Imagine what it must be like not to have an education.
- I praise God for being with me. You have a heavenly Father who is with you 24 hours a day. Imagine always feeling hopeless and alone.
- God loves me. God loves you so much that He *gave* His only Son to die for you. Imagine feeling worthless.

Consider all that you have with God. Are you ready to begin a new week with a positive attitude?

What would life be like if you didn't know God? How does it make you feel to have all those positives going for you? What can you accomplish this week? How can you help someone else know God?

If one of your classmates is depressed, share with him or her what there is to be thankful for.

347

Blanket for Jesus, Part 1

He went there to register with Mary, who was pledged to be married to him and was expecting a child. While they were there, the time came for the baby to be born. Luke 2:5, 6, NIV.

Mary hurried to get the children dressed and ready to leave. The two older girls, Laura and Cindy, would go to school. Little Becky would go with her while she cleaned houses in the neighborhood. Mary just wished the children didn't have to walk so far in the cold.

Becky ran up, breathless, a ragged doll in her arms. "I'm ready, Mama, but we forgot to dress Charlie."

Mary glanced at the clock and then at Becky's smiling face. Quickly she dressed the doll, wrapped him in the blanket, and handed him back. Then the little family headed out into the cold winter morning.

Ever since her husband had left them there had been no money for anything that wasn't a necessity. Christmas was always especially hard. It was as if the whole world celebrated Christmas and they were left out.

She dropped the two older girls off at school, then made her way to the Littles' house, which she cleaned every Monday. The Littles had been getting ready for Christmas, and the house was decorated beautifully.

Becky made her way to the chair where she would spend the morning pointing out particularly beautiful things to Charlie and trying to guess what was in the packages beneath the tree. Mary tried to ignore the beautiful decorations. When Laura and Cindy came in for lunch, they didn't look either. It hurt too much.

Even Becky knew something was different about the Littles' house. "Why are there so many presents? Is it someone's birthday?"

🙂 **What is the most important thing for us to remember at Christmastime? How do you feel about the commercial part of Christmas—the Santa stuff, the TV specials, the focus on getting presents?**

🙂 **Make your own crèche (nativity set) out of craft supplies. Put it up in your room.**

348

Blanket for Jesus, Part 2

And she gave birth to her firstborn, a son. She wrapped him in cloths and placed him in a manger, because there was no room for them in the inn. Luke 2:7, NIV.

Yes, Becky, it is Someone's birthday." She told the girls all about why we celebrate Christmas.

Becky hugged Charlie close. "Poor Baby. It must have been cold in the stable. I wish I could have seen it, though."

"You can see it," Mary said. "Come on. We're going for a walk." She led the girls down the street to a church, where a large crèche was displayed on the lawn. The girls stared wide-eyed at the simple scene for a long time. Becky didn't want to leave.

All the following week Becky held Charlie in her arms, telling him the story again and again. She begged her sisters to take her to see the story "for true" each day, but they dragged her away long before she was through looking.

Mary tried not to let it show, but it broke her heart to see Laura and Cindy hurt because they couldn't participate. Only Becky seemed not to notice the Christmas preparations going on all around her.

When Christmas morning came, Mary was horrified to find that Becky was gone! Looking around carefully, she noticed Charlie sitting in a chair, face to the window, his blanket gone. Suddenly she knew. She ran down the street to the church. There was Becky, tucking Charlie's blanket around the baby Jesus figure.

"I didn't want Him to think we'd forgotten Him on His birthday," the little girl explained when she saw her mother.

Mary scooped Becky up in her arms. "I did forget, honey. Dear Lord, I'm so sorry I forgot."

Tenderly Mary carried Becky home. They had only a houseplant to decorate, and only a few "practical" presents, but they did have the true spirit of Christmas.

- If you could be any one of the participants in the Christmas story, who would you be?

- Spend some time thinking about what it must have been like when Jesus was born.

"Jump!"

My son, keep your father's commands and do not forsake your mother's teaching. Proverbs 6:20, NIV.

I trusted my father completely and unconditionally. I trusted him when I was young, and I trust him even more now. In the same way, I trust God more now than I did 20 years ago, or even last week. Trust can come only when you know the person in whom you place your trust. Let me tell you a story.

I was trying to get into the saddle on Dad's horse to take a ride. But Charro was being particularly unruly. She danced around every time I got one foot into the stirrup, making me hop on my right foot until I could get set to swing up. Finally, as I swung my right leg up, Charro took off. I barely got seated when she turned under a swing set in our backyard. I leaned all the way back, clearing the bar by inches. However, in the process my foot got caught in one of the swings.

In half a second the chain tightened, launching the swing set into a crashing somersault. Charro thought she was about to be swallowed by a creature with metal legs. She kicked in her turbo boost, and we shot past another piece of play equipment, a 12-foot metal tower. The swing set snagged the tower and yanked that over, too. Now Charro was completely out of control. I was determined to try and stay in the saddle, no matter where Charro wound up.

Then I heard Dad. Knowing Charro was terrified and fearing the situation would get much worse, he yelled at me to jump off. Without a moment's hesitation I jumped! If I'd bailed out a second later, I would have tangled with a fence. There was no time for me to question Dad's orders. I did exactly what he said because I trusted him. And I was awfully thankful that I did.

🙂 **When have you obeyed your parents without questioning why and were thankful you did? Do you know God well enough to trust Him as much?**

🙂 **Try this "trust" test with your parents: Fall backward with your body stiff as a board and have Mom or Dad catch you.**

Climbing Back On

I tell you the truth, if you have faith as small as a mustard seed, you can say to this mountain, "Move from here to there" and it will move. Nothing will be impossible for you. Matthew 17:20, NIV.

The times I got dumped off—or even jumped off—a horse, Dad had sympathy, compassion, and above all, a very wise piece of advice. After the shock and pain had worn off, he would say, "Eric, it's time to get back in the saddle."

At the time those were not the words I wanted to hear. I would look at him for a few long moments, all the time thinking, *I don't ever want to get back on a horse again.* Especially the one that I had just been ejected from. But I always did, even after the catastrophe with the swing set. Mom had just fixed up my skinned knees and scraped-up side when Dad came into the room.

"Are you ready to get back on?"

"What?" I asked incredulously.

"If you don't get back on Charro now, you possibly never will."

Dad's words had the ring of truth in them, because at that moment I didn't think I ever wanted to ride again. Ever! Nevertheless, I set my jaw, walked out, and got back in the saddle.

Since those days I have seen some beautiful country from the back of a horse that I would never have seen otherwise. If I hadn't swallowed my fear and climbed back into the saddle, I wouldn't be riding a horse today. And I would feel pretty rotten about it, too.

Think of fear as a mountain to be crossed or a fence to be jumped. If your fears are a fence, do they keep diverting you from doing things you would really like to do? If your fears are a mountain, are you missing seeing the beautiful valley on the other side? Overcoming one's fear gives you more strength to overcome the next fear, and the next, and the next.

😊 **What are some of your fears? What are some of the great things you could be doing if fear wasn't stopping you?**

😊 **Don't let fear conquer you. Conquer your fear by trying again.**

It's Not Too Late

But as for you, be strong and do not give up, for your work will be rewarded. 2 Chronicles 15:7, NIV.

o you ever feel so uncoordinated that playing any sport well seems absolutely impossible? On top of that, does it seem as if you are always one of the last people picked to play a team sport? If you've ever felt like giving up, listen to this.

Many people have the idea that if people don't show athletic ability when they are very young, they will never play sports well enough to be a pro. There was one boy, though, who apparently wasn't listening to that theory. He was too busy not giving up to listen to what everyone else was saying.

First of all, Bob tried playing football his freshman year in high school, but the opposing team ran all over him. Next he tried out for the basketball team. He didn't score a point in three games. He tried to get on the baseball team, but was the first one who was cut. Bob wasn't about to give up, however. During his sophomore year he tried again to make the basketball team. The coach told him to forget about playing.

Bob's father put up a basketball hoop and encouraged him to keep practicing. Little by little Bob's shooting began to improve. By the time he was a senior, his long hours of practice paid off when he received several college scholarship offers. Later while working at a Wisconsin summer camp he met Ray Meyer, who coached him into becoming a great shooter.

Bob Pettit played 11 seasons as a pro, scoring 20,880 points before he retired in 1965. Instead of giving up, he went on to become one of the all-time greatest players in the game of basketball.

Has anyone ever told you that you were not good enough to do something you really wanted to do? How did you feel? What did you do about it?

Take time to encourage someone who doesn't play your favorite sport as well as you do. Can you give them some helpful pointers?

The Yellow Rose

If I gave everything I have to poor people, . . . but didn't love others, it would be of no value whatever. 1 Corinthians 13:3, TLB.

Author Linda Porter Carlyle tells a revealing story about the tremendous power of kindness that's locked inside one simple yellow rose. While preparing to meet a friend for lunch one day, Linda decided to take along a bouquet of fragrant roses she had picked from her backyard.

Later, as she drove to her friend's house, she encountered a road construction site. The blond woman who was directing traffic motioned for Linda to slow to a stop. "It'll be just a few minutes before you can go on through," she told Linda.

Sensing the woman was having a bad day, Linda smiled warmly. "That's quite all right," she said. "I'm in no hurry."

Suddenly, although they were complete strangers, the woman began to tell Linda about some troubles she was having at home. She mentioned that the wind and rain seemed to be beating her spirits even lower. Linda listened with a sympathetic ear.

When it was time for traffic to move again, she remembered the roses and, taking one bright-yellow rose from the bouquet, handed it to the woman. "I want you to have this," she said.

The next day she made a special trip to the construction site, hoping to talk to the woman again. But she wasn't working. Determined to make sure everything was all right, Linda went back again the next day. This time the woman *was* there, and she immediately recognized Linda.

"Thank you for the flower," she said, obviously more cheerful than she had been two days before. "Right when life seemed so rotten it meant so much to me for you to give me that yellow rose."

Of course, there was no awesome power of kindness inside the rose itself. It was inside Linda, just as it is inside each one of us. All we have to do is transfer it to others through a kind word, a compliment, a warm smile—or maybe even a simple yellow rose.

🙂 **How did you use the power of kindness today?**

🙂 **Plan to take warm drinks to workers at a road construction site. See what kind of reaction you get.**

Academic Advisers

Plans fail for lack of counsel, but with many advisers they succeed. Proverbs 15:22, NIV.

I 've tried to figure it out, but I just don't get it!" Zeb jabbered all the way from the door of the clubhouse to his chair.

"What's wrong?" Dillon asked. "You usually have everything figured out."

"It's my English class. What's with all those adverbs, adjectives, nouns, verbs, fragments, and compound sentences? I don't understand. And why can't verbs just get along?"

Dillon suddenly stopped working. "What do you mean, 'Why can't verbs just get along?'"

Sam giggled. "I think Zeb is talking about subject and verb agreement. You know, like which of these is right: 'Each of us *are* able to make learning interesting and easy' or 'Each of us *is* able to make learning interesting and easy'?"

"OK, I get it," Dillon said, although he still looked unsure.

Zeb was still confused. "You lost me, Sam."

"Which of the two sentences *is* correct?"

Zeb scratched his head. "Why does it matter?"

"That's a good point, Zeb," Sam said. "If you aren't sure why you are going to the effort of learning something, then you probably won't feel like trying to understand it."

"Exactly!" Zeb exclaimed. "OK, Sam. How do I find out why I need to know about things and how to make them interesting?"

Sam smiled. "If you're still having trouble understanding, let your teacher and parents know. I know my parents really want me to ask them when I have problems understanding. And Dillon and I will also help, if you want us to."

☺ **Why is it hard to learn when what you are studying isn't interesting to you?**

☺ **If you are having trouble understanding a school subject or why you need to learn it, talk to a teacher or your parents for help.**

Remarkable Comeback

I know whom I have believed, and am convinced that he is able to guard what I have entrusted to him for that day. 2 Timothy 1:12, NIV.

George was so far in debt that it looked as though he would soon be tossed into debtor's prison. Though he was an accomplished musician who had mastered the violin, clavichord, and oboe, as well as being a brilliant organist, what would either make or break him was whether or not audiences would pack the concert halls to listen to his compositions. And there certainly had not been enough support for his work, for he was near financial ruin. Terribly discouraged, he planned to retire at the age of 56.

Then he received a commission to compose a work for a charity benefit. On August 22 he started composing the work that would soon absorb him to the point that he rarely left his room and scarcely took time even to eat. At times George was so filled with emotion that he sobbed while he wrote.

Amazingly, within 23 days he had composed a completed manuscript of 260 pages. Sir Newman Flower says of George's work: "Considering the immensity of the work, and the short time involved, it will remain, perhaps forever, the greatest feat in the history of music composition." The name of the work? *Messiah.*

George Frideric Handel's *Messiah* opened on April 13, 1742, and raised enough money to free more than 100 men from debtor's prison. Because of the many charity performances of *Messiah,* Handel would go from nearly being cast into debtor's prison himself to creating a work that would benefit more people through charity than any other musical production in the world.

After the completion of *Messiah,* Handel's life turned around dramatically. Where it had once been a struggle even to survive, his popularity soared, and he began to prosper financially.

🙂 **Have you ever felt that God had forgotten about you? Why do you keep trusting Him? Why do you think Handel never lost faith in God?**

🙂 **Listen to Handel's *Messiah* this Christmas.**

Big Gifts Come in All Packages, Part 1

A gift opens the way for the giver and ushers him into the presence of the great. Proverbs 18:16, NIV.

My sister, Erin, watched me suspiciously as I wrapped bright Christmas paper around the "Chillin' Mega Blaster" CD player. "Is it really necessary to wrap a present you're giving yourself?"

I snorted. "It's not for me; it's for Jennie," I explained patiently.

"Let me get this straight," Erin said. "You worked all summer mowing lawns so you could get that silly CD player, and now you're giving it to Jennie?"

Erin may be my big sister, but sometimes she can be dense. "That's the beauty of it. Jennie got the same amount of money I did, so she's getting me the same thing!"

Erin rolled her eyes. "You're getting each other the same gift for Christmas? Why don't you save yourself the trouble of wrapping it and each keep your own CD player?"

"Duh," I said, pointing my finger at my head and twirling it in the age-old sign for insanity. "Because this way it's more special. Every time I listen to a CD, I won't be thinking of sweating over Mr. Patterson's lawn—I'll think of Jennie."

Christmas Eve, after I had opened lots of presents from my grandparents (all CDs—the only thing I had asked for), I took Jennie's CD player over to her house to give to her. The package was huge, and I struggled through the deep snow with it. When I knocked on Jennie's door, I had to balance it on my knee.

"Sarah, come in," she squealed.

I set the CD player on the table and looked around eagerly for mine. But all I saw was one small package on the table with my name on it.

🙂 **What is the real meaning of Christmas? Why do we give gifts at Christmas? How would you feel if your family decided this year that they would not exchange gifts?**

🙂 **Find a small box and wrap it up with really nice wrapping paper and a bow. Put it on your dresser to remind yourself that big gifts come in all packages.**

Big Gifts Come in All Packages, Part 2

Every good and perfect gift is from above, coming down from the Father of the heavenly lights, who does not change like shifting shadows. James 1:17, NIV.

Here's your present," Jennie said shyly, handing it to me. Confused, I took the small box and ripped the wrapping off. Inside was a tiny pewter frame that held a photo of the two of us. Jennie's mom had taken the picture last summer after we'd put in a hard day mowing lawns.

Jennie was watching me closely. "I decided to do something a little different," she explained. "I hope you don't mind." Then she dragged over a huge plastic bag.

I grinned. So *that's* where she was hiding the CD player! I reached into the bag eagerly, but all I came up with was handsful of teddy bears.

Jennie giggled. "I made them. Aren't they sweet?"

I couldn't figure it out. "You made me a bag of teddy bears?"

"Sort of. My mom helped me. They're for you to give away at the orphanage. I already told your mom. She said it was OK for you to come with us."

I blinked at her stupidly. "Soooo . . . you used the money you made from mowing lawns to buy material and make teddy bears to give me so that I could give them to the orphans?"

Jennie nodded. "Are you glad?"

Glad? *Glad?* Would teddy bears play a CD?

I sat in the darkened back seat on the way to the orphanage, trying desperately not to cry. I had a stack of CDs—and no CD player. Christmas was ruined.

🙂 **Have you ever been disappointed with a gift you received? How would you feel if you didn't receive any presents at all this Christmas? Would you feel as though Christmas was ruined?**

🙂 **Try this experiment. As you look at your Christmas gifts this year, choose one that you will give away. Then open your presents. How do you feel about giving the present away now that you know what it is? Can you do it?**

357

Big Gifts Come in All Packages, Part 3

For the wages of sin is death, but the gift of God is eternal life in Christ Jesus our Lord. Romans 6:23, NIV.

When I set the bag of teddy bears down in the middle of the floor at the orphanage and began pulling out teddy bears, I was immediately the center of attention. Children gathered all around me. I felt a tug on my sleeve. A little girl looked up at me with wide eyes.

"Are you Thanta Clauth?" she lisped in a whisper.

I laughed in spite of myself. "No, but would you like a teddy bear?"

"Yeth, pleathe!" She pulled the teddy bear into her arms and hugged him fiercely. "Whath your name?"

"Sarah," I replied.

"Then I'm going to name him Tharah," she said, smiling so big that I could see her front teeth were missing.

As soon as I had given all the teddy bears away, I sat off to one side and watched the kids playing with them. One little girl had made her teddy bear a diaper out of wrapping paper. I started laughing. I couldn't help it. Pretty soon Jennie was laughing too.

"Do you like your present?" Jennie asked.

I looked around at all the happy children. CD players would come and go, but the feeling I had gotten from handing out all those teddy bears could never be replaced. All of a sudden I realized it didn't matter anymore about the CD player.

"Yes, I like my present. Thank you."

Besides, Jennie had a CD player, and I had loads of CDs. What a beautiful friendship!

- **Does the size of the package determine the value of the gift? Name some big gifts that come in small packages.**

- **Make presents for your local orphanage, the pediatric wing of the hospital, or a nursing home. Call ahead of time to find out how many presents you will need. Ask some friends to help you, then schedule a caroling date when all of you will go and deliver the gifts.**

Happy Are They

Happy are the people whose God is the Lord! Psalm 144:15, NKJV.

My friend Paul Ricchiuti has worked for many years on *Primary Treasure* and *Our Little Friend* magazines and has written many stories and books about Christian leaders. Paul likes to have fun. He believes that Christians have more fun than anybody, because Jesus Himself loves fun.

One day I asked Paul if Ellen White liked to laugh and have fun as much as he does. He told me this story:

Just before Ellen settled at her Elmshaven home, the ship she was traveling on from Australia anchored in Samoa. Boats came to ferry passengers to the beach. As the boats could not go all the way ashore, several islanders carried the travelers the last few yards to shore. Two of the islanders made a chair with their crossed arms for Ellen to ride on, and she climbed aboard, clinging to their shoulders to keep from falling off.

After Ellen had been safely deposited on the beach, she sat upon a rock to watch the remaining procession of passengers going ashore. While she watched, the plight of her daughter-in-law began to amuse her. Apparently the younger Mrs. White was making a most desperate attempt to keep her dress dry while she was being carried to shore by one of the islanders. At the same time she kept losing her grip on the man's shoulders as he sloshed toward shore with her squealing child tucked under his free arm. To make matters even more comical, she was determined to shade herself, the baby, *and* the native with her parasol.

The sight got to be too much for poor Ellen. Suddenly she burst out with such uncontrolled laughter that she knocked herself backward over the rock, and for a short time all anyone could see of Ellen White was two feet sticking straight up in the air.

- How important is fun and laughter? Do you think Jesus laughed often when He was on earth? How can you have fun today?

- Make at least five people laugh today. Plan a fun activity this week with your family.

The Biggest Birth Announcement

Suddenly a great company of the heavenly host appeared with the angel, praising God and saying, "Glory to God in the highest, and on earth peace to men on whom his favor rests." Luke 2:13, 14, NIV.

When a baby is born, it's a very exciting time. The parents are excited. The siblings are excited. The grandparents are excited. Aunts, uncles, and friends are excited. New life does that to people. They want to tell everyone about the wonderful thing that's happened, the wonderful little person who has just been born.

That's why one of the first things new parents do is send out a birth announcement. It looks something like this one we sent out when our son was born:

The handiwork of God—a new hand in ours.
Name: Joshua Anthony Walker
Arrived: June 19, 1993
Weight: 8 pounds
Parents: Rob and Celeste Walker

But the baby who got the biggest birth announcement in history was Jesus. When He was born, God sent a whole choir of heavenly angels to sing to the whole countryside. Imagine!

Parents are proud of their new child and want everyone to know about their new baby. God was proud of Jesus. He wanted everyone to know that Jesus had been born. Like most births, it was a long-anticipated event. Most parents have to wait for nine long months before their baby is born. And it takes that long to get ready, to have all the little clothes ready, to take childbirth classes, and to prepare the baby's room.

For many years the Jews expected Jesus to come, but most of them still weren't ready. The day on which we celebrate the birth of Jesus is right around the corner. Are you ready?

😊 **Why do you think parents send out birth announcements? How do you think God felt the day Jesus was born?**

😊 **This year make your own birth announcements and send them out like Christmas cards to the kids in your class or to friends around your neighborhood.**

The Wisest Investment

So let us come boldly to the very throne of God and stay there to receive his mercy and to find grace to help us in our times of need. Hebrews 4:16, TLB.

Right now is the best time to think about investing in your future. Whenever you take the time to learn something new, you are making an investment. Each time you set a goal for yourself, you have to invest your time and sometimes even money to achieve it. But there is a different kind of investment too. A spiritual investment—the wisest investment of all.

Conrad Hilton knew how to make a hotel chain work and prosper. His dream was to own the Waldorf-Astoria one day. He envisioned the day he could tell his mother that he owned that great hotel. His mother, however, knew there was something far more important than making a fortune.

While Conrad was pouring so much time and energy into running a hotel, his mother often told him, "Don't talk about all the important people you have to see, Connie. You get along over to church and see God first. Prayer is the best investment you'll ever make. Don't you forget it."

Conrad Hilton remembered those words. When the Depression hit, he owned 1,800 rooms, but there were no customers. He lost some of his hotels. Then when things couldn't seem to get any worse, his brother died.

Eventually Conrad bought the Waldorf-Astoria, just as he had said he would. And every day he continued to pray and go to church. He didn't stop believing that visiting with the Lord was the best investment a person could make.

- Do you think praying to Jesus and studying about Him is the best investment you can make? Why? Does anyone you know make a habit of staying close to Jesus through prayer and study?

- If you haven't already made praying a habit before you begin your new day, invest time each morning this week in getting closer to Jesus.

The Christmas Dress, Part 1

The poor you will always have with you, and you can help them any time you want. Mark 14:7, NIV.

I came across a picture in the newspaper of a smiling Bulgarian couple and their 6-year-old daughter. The article painted a dreary picture. The daughter had been born with a rare disease that made the left side of her face smaller than the right. Since Boston Children's Hospital was the only hospital in the world equipped to help the little girl, the family had moved to Boston.

Although they had been successful people in Bulgaria, the couple wasn't able to find work in Boston. They were living in a broken-down house in a neighborhood they considered too dangerous to let the little girl play in.

I've never been in a strange country, desperate for friendship, uncertain about my family's future, but I can imagine how frightening it must be. Quickly I typed up a note, asking if they needed anything, and what the little girl would like for Christmas.

I gave them the address of my church so they could write back. Just when I was beginning to wonder if they had ever received my letter, I received a reply—the Sabbath before Christmas.

They were happy I had written. Nothing had changed since the article had been written. Both parents were still unemployed. If it wasn't too much trouble, they said, their little girl wished for a "frilly little lady's dress" for Christmas.

That's how I came to find myself jammed into an almost bare department store the Sunday before Christmas. I looked around in dismay. There was absolutely nothing resembling a "frilly little lady's dress" on the racks. In fact, there was almost nothing *on* the racks. I had no time, no money, and no choices.

🙂 **Do you know anyone who could use some help this Christmas? What is the real meaning of Christmas?**

🙂 **Volunteer to help at a soup kitchen. Buy gifts for a needy child through a community-sponsored program. Help your church deliver food baskets to needy families.**

The Christmas Dress, Part 2

But when you give a banquet, invite the poor, the crippled, the lame, the blind, and you will be blessed. Although they cannot repay you, you will be repaid at the resurrection of the righteous. Luke 14:13, 14, NIV.

L ord," I breathed, "You've just got to help me find something. There's nothing here." I wandered around, repeating that prayer over and over. Finally I picked out a jean skirt and a sweater. But I wasn't happy with them. And I kept feeling I should go around the corner to Montgomery Ward.

"But Lord," I argued under my breath as I hustled through the mall, "You know they're going to be expensive, and I don't have much money."

Minutes later I stood in the middle of their girls' department, grinning from ear to ear. They had beautiful dresses! On sale!

"You knew that, Lord, didn't You?"

Now I had the dress. But I still had to mail it. Mail slows down to a sluggish crawl near a holiday. "It's never going to get there, Lord," I worried. "It's only got two days, and one of them is Christmas Eve." Then I quit worrying. "Well, You found the dress. I know You'll make sure she gets it by Christmas."

As I was jogging on Christmas morning, I prayed again that the package would arrive on time and brighten that family's holiday. I tried to imagine them opening it . . . the surprise . . . the excitement. I tried to believe it was happening at that very moment. I tried to trust God to have done it.

I have never received mail on Christmas Day. (I think the post office takes that day off.) Imagine my surprise two months later to learn that my package arrived *on Christmas Day!* I don't know how. I'll probably never know how. But that doesn't really matter.

It was enough to know that the dress fit perfectly, although I didn't know what size to get. It was enough that the gift brought happiness and surprise on the day we celebrate the Source of happiness and surprise. What a great gift from the Giver of all gifts.

 **Have you ever gotten a surprise Christmas gift? What made it so special?**

Plan to give someone a surprise Christmas gift this year.

Trading Places

Today in the town of David a Savior has been born to you; he is Christ the Lord. This will be a sign to you: You will find a baby wrapped in strips of cloth and lying in a manger. Luke 2:11, 12, NIV.

Every year for the past 26 years Albert Rosen, who is a Jew, has traded places with someone on Christmas Eve. Albert is a retired salesperson. Every Christmas Eve he looks for a Christian who has to work on Christmas Eve and takes that person's place so he or she can spend the holiday with family. He picks the person at random and doesn't accept payment for his work.

His last job was filling in for a doorkeeper at the Milwaukee Hilton Hotel. He had to greet customers, help with luggage, hail taxis, and give any assistance needed. His other Christmas Eve jobs have included being a hospital clerk, a disc jockey, a television news reporter, and a police clerk.

Wouldn't it be great if someone would take your place at school for one day? Or take your place at the dinner table the night your mom makes her famous "Brussels Sprouts Almondine"? How about switching places with you when you have to clean your room? That'd be great, wouldn't it?

On Christmas Eve there is another Person who trades places with someone. Jesus, whose birth we celebrate on Christmas, came to earth to take *our* place. He took our place on earth so that we could take His place in heaven. This Christmas, when you're singing about the Baby lying in a manger, remember just why He's lying there. It makes all the difference in the world.

- Why do you suppose Albert Rosen trades places with someone every Christmas Eve? Why do you think he doesn't accept payment for his work?

- Why don't you try trading places with someone? Take over a friend's newspaper route for one day, or mow lawns for someone. Remember, don't accept any pay. Gratitude is all the payment you'll need.

The Spirit of Christmas

If you have any encouragement from being united with Christ, if any comfort from his love, if any fellowship with the Spirit, if any tenderness and compassion, then make my joy complete by being like-minded, having the same love, being one in spirit and purpose. Do nothing out of selfish ambition or vain conceit, but in humility consider others better than yourselves. Philippians 2:1-3, NIV.

The snow is softly falling. Carols drift in the cold night air from a group of people singing, strolling down the sidewalk. Their cheeks are pink with cold, but they don't seem to notice it. All around, people are bustling here and there.

Nice picture, isn't it? Christmas means different things to different people. Some may have a fir tree and snow. Others decorate a cactus with lights and have to imagine snow if they want it. But the one thing that holds true for Christmas anywhere is the sense of peace and goodwill that permeates the season.

One man, whose name is a secret, leaves a trail of happy tears each year. He looks for those whose needs are the greatest and hands them hundreds of dollars. He waits for their reaction, then vanishes before they get over their shock enough to thank him. He considers this his own Christmas present.

"It's probably against the law to have this much fun, to see their faces when you show up!" he says.

Wouldn't it be wonderful if that kind of Christmas spirit could be around 365 days a year? It should be. Christmas is a celebration of Jesus' birth, but Jesus didn't help people only on Christmas. He served them every day of the year. And we can too. Make a decision to keep the spirit of the season in your heart, not only today, but every day this coming year.

🙂 **What makes Christmas a special time of year? What kinds of things can you do to carry the spirit of Christmas through the rest of the year?**

🙂 **Practice a random act of kindness. Find some unsuspecting person, sneak up on him or her, and do a good deed. Then run for it!**

Going the Wrong Way

I am sending you to open their eyes and turn them from darkness to light, and from the power of Satan to God, so that they may receive forgiveness of sins and a place among those who are sanctified by faith in me. Acts 26:17, 18, NIV.

Douglas Corrigan had just set a speed record flying from California to New York. He wanted to go on and fly across the Atlantic Ocean, but authorities denied him permission, citing the rickety condition of his aircraft. So Corrigan took off from Floyd Bennett Field early on a foggy morning to fly back to California. Shortly after lifting off, he misread his compass, and by the time he emerged from the fog 24 hours later, he was flying over Ireland.

Wrong-way Corrigan, for that is what people began calling him, reminds me a lot of myself. It seems that I make a lot of turns in the wrong direction—away from Jesus instead of toward Him. Maybe you feel the same way sometimes. Maybe you feel as though you've sinned so many times that Jesus can't possibly love you or want to save you. Well, let me tell you something: that is exactly what Satan wants you to believe.

Jesus really wanted each one of us to know that He made it possible to be saved, if we just accept Him. So He took a man who was definitely going the wrong way and turned him around to teach that very lesson.

If you think Jesus can't save you, think about what He did on the road to Damascus with a man named Paul. Paul had been out chasing Christians wherever he could sniff them out. He was a good detective, possibly the best. When he heard there were many Christians in Damascus, he got permission from the high priest to go after them.

Paul was definitely going the wrong direction. Maybe he was in the same type of fog we all get into when Satan tries to keep us apart from Jesus. But Jesus turned him around.

😊 **Are there things you believe Jesus can't forgive you for?**

😊 **Read *Steps to Christ* to see how you are saved through the grace of Christ.**

We Are Called to Belong to Jesus

And you also are among those who are called to belong to Jesus Christ. Romans 1:6, NIV.

*P*aul did an about-face from being the most persistent enemy of the new Christian church to becoming Jesus' greatest evangelist and most loyal champion. According to history, Paul didn't appear to have the physical makings of a great leader. Although he proved to be very persistent and good at his job when he was persecuting Christian believers, he was a rather short man in stature. He probably stood slightly less than five feet tall and was going prematurely bald when he was 30 years old.

Paul was a person who was very serious about what he believed. His downfall early in life was that he believed in the law more than in the One who gave the law. Jesus knew that Paul would be His greatest champion for the new Christian church. He just had to discover that Jesus was his Saviour, and that there was nothing he could do by himself to be saved.

When Paul watched Stephen being stoned, he saw that the young Christian had something he didn't have. Stephen died at peace because he knew Jesus. Paul must have wondered about that. He might have asked himself, *Do I have that much faith?*

Have you ever wondered why people who are following Jesus are so happy? I think Paul wondered the same thing. It may have been irritating to him that the Christians he was persecuting were so happy. You see, even though Paul had always been very good at following all the rules he had learned as a Pharisee, he was still not a happy man. He didn't know Jesus.

When Paul met Jesus on the road to Damascus, he was ready to devote his life to leading people to Jesus. He was called to belong to Jesus, and he answered the call. Jesus calls us to belong to Him too.

☺ **Why do you tell people about Jesus? Why are you happy knowing Jesus? Why do you think Paul became Jesus' greatest champion?**

☺ **In your worship group discuss ways you can be champions for Jesus.**

367

Increase Your Potential

Wisdom is the principal thing; therefore get wisdom. And in all your getting, get understanding. Proverbs 4:7, NKJV.

Every Monday during the school year you have read why studying is important and how to make it easier. Hopefully you have been inspired to make some positive changes toward schoolwork. After all, the more you increase your education, the more you increase your potential. As you fill up your mind with new concepts and ideas, the easier it will be to think creatively, as well as critically.

Many of the world's most popular discoveries happen when people think of a new way to solve existing problems. For instance, in 1974 math teacher Erno Rubik invented the Rubik's Cube to help his students develop their math skills. Five years later the Hungarian sold the rights to Ideal Toy Corporation and became a millionaire.

Of course, one's goal when inventing isn't necessarily to become a millionaire. It may just be a way to make a living, as Alfred Butts started out thinking. Alfred was an out-of-work architect who was hoping to support his family when he invented the board game that would later be known as Scrabble. Eventually Scrabble became the second best-selling game in history.

The Slinky happened more or less by accident when Richard James, a marine engineer, was trying to develop a spring that would compensate for the effects of a boat's movement on navigational instruments. The spring uncoiled like a snake when he knocked it off a shelf, and he quickly realized he had a unique toy.

As you continue going to school, I hope you always realize how great a privilege it is to get an education. I hope you will find ways to make learning fun, as well as challenging. Above all, remember God, who gives us the ability and the opportunity to learn.

What are some of your ideas for inventions? Would it be easy to develop your ideas without an education?

Make a list of your ideas. Try writing a plan for turning your best idea into a reality.

My Jesus

For the Son of Man came to seek and to save what was lost. Luke 19:10, NIV.

Don't you wish more had been written about Jesus' growing-up years? I do. After all, He came to this earth as a human being to be part of us, not just physically, but emotionally as well. He suffered with the same problems we all do, probably even being teased when He stuck up for others.

I imagine there were kids who mistreated a crippled boy across the street, or the blind girl down the road, and Jesus jumped to the rescue. In those times people thought sick and disabled people were being punished for their sins or the sins of their parents. But I imagine young Jesus continued to associate with that crippled boy, and the two of them probably enjoyed hanging out with the blind girl down the street. I like that picture of Jesus. I think Jesus probably gave the blind girl a description of the trees and birds she would never forget. Maybe He helped His crippled friend go places he might never have gotten to go without a friend's help.

I'm sure Jesus felt their sadness at being outcasts. And perhaps He said to Himself *When I'm older and begin My work here on earth, I'm coming back here to heal My friends. They won't be crippled and blind forever.* Jesus was born—and died—on this sinful planet because He loves each of us with much more love than we can understand.

The story about a 7-year-old girl who had been bitten by a black bear cub reminds me of that love. Fearing rabies, the authorities wanted to have the cub killed and examined. But when the girl realized that the cub would have to die in order to be examined, she offered to take the seven required rabies shots in order to save its life. Each shot had to be given with a five-inch needle.

Jesus knows how we feel and what we think. He knows everything about us, and He loves us immeasurably, whether we are the ones being teased—or if we're the bullies. You see, He died for us.

- How do you think Jesus treated people as He was growing up?

- Share your image of Jesus with your family. Ask a friend what their image of Jesus is like.

369

The Better Side of a Major Mistake

Create in me a pure heart, O God, and renew a steadfast
spirit within me. Psalm 51:10, NIV.

Jim had made a promise—then broke it. As a young man he joined a trapping expedition. The company of men left Fort Kiowa in September of 1823, very aware of the constant danger of being attacked by Indians. One day their leader, Andrew Henry, ordered a couple men to hunt for food ahead of the party.

One of the men who went ahead was Hugh Glass. Before long Hugh got into trouble with a grizzly. His screams brought his companions running, but the grizzly had already badly mauled him. It was amazing he was still alive.

Fearing an attack from Indians that might wipe them all out, Andrew Henry elected to take the company on to the fort. He asked for volunteers to stay with Hugh until he either died or could travel. He even offered to pay six months' wages.

Jim was one of two men who stayed with Hugh. It is hard to say why Jim then abandoned the injured man five days later. Maybe his companion talked him into it. Maybe he was just young and scared. Whatever his reasons, he deserted Hugh.

Hugh Glass *was* alive, however. Courageously he crawled and limped his way back to civilization. Eventually he found Jim. Though some might have thought he had every right to seek revenge, Hugh forgave the young man and let him go.

Fortunately, we know many more good things about Jim Bridger than the mistake he made when he was young. In the years after he was forgiven, he went on to became a well-respected guide and scout.

- Can you think of a time when you bailed out on someone during a difficult situation? How do you rebuild their trust?

- There is a positive side to making a mistake, and that is knowing enough to avoid it next time. Ask Jesus to help you learn from your mistakes.

Thinking Versus Quitting

The intelligent man is always open to new ideas. In fact, he looks for them. Proverbs 18:15, TLB.

Jobs were pretty hard to come by, but that didn't discourage Freddie. He told his dad that a person who thinks hard can solve problems. And one who thinks positively can always get a job. So Freddie went in search of a job. The applicants were to show up at 8:00 the next morning. Even though Freddie got there 15 minutes early, 20 boys were already in line.

He didn't give up, knowing that if he thought hard enough, he could come up with a plan. Sure enough, Freddie got an idea. He approached the secretary with a note. The secretary read the note, then smiled. Then she gave the note to the boss. Freddie's solution had been simple and, apparently, very clever.

Then there was the man who failed in business in 1831. In 1832 he was defeated for the legislature. A year later he failed in business a second time. He suffered a nervous breakdown in 1836. And two years later he was defeated for speaker of the house. In 1840 he was defeated for elector. And in 1843 he was defeated for Congress. He ran for the Senate in 1855 and was defeated. He was defeated for vice president in 1856. He ran again for the Senate two years later and was defeated a second time. From 1831 to 1858 he met with nearly a dozen major failures.

Then in 1860 he was elected president of the United States. He never quit. His name was Abraham Lincoln. And Freddie's note? It simply said, "Dear Sir: I am the twenty-first kid in line. Don't do anything until you see me." He thought the problem through and discovered an answer. And he got the job.

🙂 **What do you do when you are faced with a problem? Do you think it through?**

🙂 **The next time you have a problem, don't get depressed and/or ignore it. Give yourself a chance to think it through.**

SCRIPTURE INDEX

373

374

4:29 . . . . Feb. 1
4:32 . . . . Jan. 8
5:2 . . . . Oct. 25
6:18 . . . . . . Aug. 25

PHILIPPIANS
2:1-3 . . . . . . Dec. 25
2:4 . . . . Nov. 28
4:4 . . . . Nov. 13
4:5 . . . . Oct. 14
4:8 . . . . June 26
4:12, 13 . . . . Feb. 27
4:13 . . . . Mar. 5

COLOSSIANS
1:9 . . . . Aug. 12
1:29 . . . . Apr. 17
3:2 . . . . July 11
3:16 . . . . Dec. 1
3:17 . . . . Apr. 24
4:6 . . . . July 28

1 THESSALONIANS
3:5 . . . . Oct. 16
5:16, 17 . . . . . Jan. 2
5:21 . . . . . . Aug. 28

2 THESSALONIANS
1:4 . . . . Sept. 29

1 TIMOTHY
4:4 . . . . . . Nov. 26
4:12 . . . . . . May 16
6:9 . . . . . . Nov. 18
6:18 . . . . . . Jan. 13

2 TIMOTHY
1:12 . . . . . . Dec. 15
2:26 . . . . Nov. 4

TITUS
2:7, 8 . . . . . Sept. 27

HEBREWS
2:17, 18 . . . . July 18
3:6 . . . . . . Sept. 25
4:16 . . . . . . Dec. 21
12:1 . . . . . . Oct. 28
12:2 . . . . Apr. 4
12:12, 13 . . . June 7
12:14 . . . . . June 29
13:3 . . . . Nov. 5
13:5 . . . . . Aug. 18
13:15 . . . . . Mar. 17
13:16 . . . . . Mar. 18
13:16 . . . . . . Oct. 4

JAMES
1:2-4 . . . . . July 15
1:5 . . . . May 25

1:17 . . . . . . Dec. 17
2:14-17 . . . . June 22
3:7, 8 . . . . June 19
3:17 . . . . . . Apr. 23
4:7 . . . . July 3
5:16 . . . . . Aug. 26

1 PETER
2:9 . . . . Feb. 11
2:15 . . . . . . Mar. 1
3:15 . . . . . . Apr. 21
5:8 . . . . . . Mar. 13
5:8 . . . . Apr. 1

2 PETER
1:7 . . . . . . Mar. 10
1:8 . . . . . . Mar. 11

1 JOHN
2:10 . . . . . June 23
2:24 . . . . . . Apr. 26
3:10 . . . . . June 24
3:11 . . . . . . July 2
4:18 . . . . . . Sept. 7

REVELATION
1:3 . . . . . . Nov. 14
3:20 . . . . . . July 30
14:12 . . . . . Apr. 25
21:16, 17 . . July 26
22:11 . . . . . May 19

376